DIE WEHRMACHT IM KAMPF

LENINGRAD

The Advance of Panzer Group 4, 1941

WALTER CHALES DE BEAULIEU

Translated by
LINDEN LYONS

Series editor:
MATTHIAS STROHN

CASEMATE
Philadelphia & Oxford

This book is dedicated to the memory of the highly respected Colonel-General Erich Hoepner by his chief of staff.

AN AUSA BOOK
Association of the United States Army
2425 Wilson Boulevard, Arlington, Virginia, 22201, USA

Published in the United States of America and Great Britain in 2020 by
CASEMATE PUBLISHERS
1950 Lawrence Road, Havertown, PA 19083, USA
and
The Old Music Hall, 106–108 Cowley Road, Oxford OX4 1JE, UK

Originally published as Die Wehrmacht im Kampf 29: Chales de Beaulieu, *Der Vorstoss der Panzergruppe 4 auf Leningrad* (Kurt Vowinckel Verlag Heidelberg, 1961)

Hardback Edition: ISBN 978-1-61200-875-2
Digital Edition: ISBN 978-1-61200-876-9

A CIP record for this book is available from the British Library

Printed and bound in the United States by Sheridan

Typeset by Versatile PreMedia Service (P) Ltd

For a complete list of Casemate titles, please contact:

CASEMATE PUBLISHERS (US)
Telephone (610) 853-9131
Fax (610) 853-9146
Email: casemate@casematepublishers.com
www.casematepublishers.com

CASEMATE PUBLISHERS (UK)
Telephone (01865) 241249
Email: casemate-uk@casematepublishers.co.uk
www.casematepublishers.co.uk

Cover image: The police division issuing orders on the Eastern Front, August 1941 (Bundesarchiv Bild 121-1179)

Contents

Foreword

The war on the Eastern Front between 1941 and 1945 was the bloodiest theatre of war of the bloodiest war in history. And yet, the knowledge of this cataclysmic struggle between two evil regimes is often confined to a handful of events, campaigns and battles. Everybody has heard of Stalingrad, Kursk and the battle for Moscow. Other events are often overlooked. Operation *Barbarossa*, the initial German invasion of the Soviet Union in 1941, is one of the near-forgotten 'episodes' in this war. Perhaps the reason for this is that, from a distance, the advance seemed to be perfectly planned and executed by the Germans. Like a knife through hot butter the Germans pushed through the Soviet lines and gained vast stretches of Soviet territory, before the exhausted German troops, suffering from the cold Russian winter, were finally stopped at the gates of Moscow and Leningrad. So the story goes. However, the reality was different, and, despite the seemingly easy German victories over numerically vastly superior Soviet forces, the Germans encountered problems from an early stage.

This book tells the story of Panzer Group 4, which formed part of Army Group North and whose task it was to reach Leningrad, the second city of the Soviet Union. The author of this book, Walter Chales de Beaulieu, was born in Saalfeld in 1898. He joined the Prussian artillery as an ensign in 1915 and served on the Eastern Front between December 1915 and December 1916. His unit was stationed in the area of Dünaburg, in modern-day Latvia. He was thus familiar with the area through which the German Army Group North advanced in the summer of 1941. From 1916 to 1918 he fought on the Western Front and continued to serve in the army after Germany's surrender. In the inter-war period, he was trained as a general staff officer. This was in breach of the Versailles Treaty, but it showed his great military skills and determination. When the Germans invaded the Soviet Union in June 1941, Chales de Beaulieu, holding the rank of full Colonel, served as Chief of Staff of Panzer Group 4. Later, he commanded the 168th and 23rd Infantry Divisions on the Eastern Front, the latter again in the area that Army Group North had conquered in 1941. On 12 September 1944, Chales de Beaulieu was transferred to the *Führerreserve* (the 'reserve of leaders') and was finally discharged from the army on 31 January 1945. The main reason for this was that Chales de Beaulieu was no longer seen as politically reliable by the Nazi regime considering that he had served as Chief of Staff to the commanding officer of Panzer Group 4, Generaloberst Erich Hoepner. Hoepner had been dishonourably discharged from the Wehrmacht in 1942 and had been one of protagonists of the failed putsch to kill Hitler on 20 July 1944.

Despite his fate in the Third Reich, it is interesting to note that Chales de Beaulieu did not solely blame Hitler for the failure of *Barbarossa* and the difficulties that Panzer Group 4 encountered during the advance into the Soviet Union. Chales de Beaulieu published his book in German in 1961 and this was the time when numerous apologetic studies, autobiographies and the like were published by former German generals. The usual theme of these publications was that the Wehrmacht had fought honourably and that Hitler was solely to blame for the defeat of Germany. The operational masterminds of the German general staff had been defeated not by the enemy, but by the strategic dilettantism of Hitler. Chales de Beaulieu's book stands out from this general – and incorrect – theme. With the clear and analytical view of a general staff officer, he describes the challenges and problems that the Wehrmacht had to face against the Soviet Union right from the beginning: a poor road network, supply issues and a general lack of troops to first conquer and then control the Soviet territory. He also points out that the Soviet military leadership was poor, but that the Soviet soldiers fought bravely. In 1961, the Cold War could have turned hot very easily and this would have resulted in a clash of NATO and Warsaw Pact troops. In a nearly textbook fashion, Chales de Beaulieu presents his operational lessons from the war in the East – lessons that would be useful in a conventional clash of Titans in the 1960s. He stresses the importance of the element of surprise, command and control, supply, and the necessity for a joint Army and Air Force conduct of battles and operations. These points are as relevant today as they were in 1961 or 1941. Therefore, this book does not only offer an unusually frank assessment of the German situation in 1941, but it also offers an insight into the character and also the unchanging nature of war.

Dr Matthias Strohn, M.St., FRHistS
Head of Historical Analysis,
Centre for Historical Analysis and Conflict Research, Camberley

Senior Lecturer,
Royal Military Academy Sandhurst

Reader in Modern War Studies,
University of Buckingham

Introduction

The events described in this book are portrayed in the way they were seen and experienced by the command element of Panzer Group 4. The description is based on original records and documents (war diary, orders, reports, situation reports, etc.). This goes also for the description of the views and assessments of the leadership of the panzer group. No changes or additions have been made whatsoever. The author was the chief of staff of the panzer group during the events described. Any explanations or opinions regarding the events can be recognised as such, and they take into account the (still minimal) research that has been undertaken since the war. Concluding remarks on the entire operation in the northern sector of the Eastern Front are made in the last two chapters.

The focus of this book is the fighting undertaken by the panzer arm. The descriptions should place the reader in their shoes, as far as is possible within the limited scope of a book, so that he can experience the atmosphere of the situation and the unfolding of events and so that he can thus understand the decision-making process in an ever-changing environment full of obstacles. It should be pointed out here that the events resulting from a decision do not always correspond to what might have been planned. This is mainly because the enemy would take his own measures governed by his own will. The terrain and weather could offer a number of surprises, and other factors like time, place, and supply could play a role in how the situation developed. It was therefore not often that easy for the commander of a panzer formation to gain an idea of all decisive influences, to dismiss the insignificant, to order everything that was necessary according to his will, and to hold out with the utmost resolution.

Chales de Beaulieu,
Hamburg, December 1960

Place Names

German usage	*English usage*
Alexandrowka	Alexandrovka
Alekßandrowskoje	Alexandrovskaya
Animisowo	Animisovo
Batjetzkaja	Batetskaya
Beisogala	Baisogala
Bialystock	Bialystok
Biegunizy	Begunitsy
Bol.Samostje	Bolshaya Samostye
Borowitschi	Borovichi
Cholm	Kholm
Ciblas	Cibla
Diwenskaja	Divenskaya
Djetskoje Selo	Detskoe Selo
Drikaschki	Drikashki
e Dubissa	Dubysa
e Düna	Western Dvina
Fedjorowski-Poßad	Fodorovskoye-Posad
Gankowa	Gankova
Gdow	Gdov
Gubanizy	Gubanitsy
Ilmensee	Lake Ilmen
Ishora	Izhora
Iswos	Izvoz
Iwanowskaja	Ivanovskoye
Jablonitzy	Yablonitsy

Jamkino	Yamkino
Jamtesowo	Yamtesovo
Jaschtschera	Yashchera
Jonawa	Jonava
Joswainiai	Josvainiai
Jurka	Yurka
Karsawa	Karsava
Kingissepp	Kingisepp
Kowno	Kovno
Krasnogwardeisk	Krasnogvardeysk
Krasnoj	Krasnoi
Krasnoje Selo	Krasnoye Selo
Kreslau	Kraslava
Kuptschino	Kupchino
Kurowizy	Kurovitsy
Lemberg	Lvov
Ljady	Lyady
Ljuban	Lyuban
Lopez	Lopets
Ludsen	Ludza
Lydavenai	Lyduvenai
Malnawa	Malnava
Mal. Utorgosch	Malaya Utorgosh
Marjino	Maryino
Marschino	Marshino
Meshno	Mezhno
e Mituwa	Mituva
Moloskowitzy	Moloskovitsy
e Mschaga	Mshaga
e Newa	Neva
Newel	Nevel
Nikolajewka	Nikolayevka
Nikolajewo	Nikolayevo
Nikolskoje	Nikolskoye
r Njemen	Neman
Nowgorod	Novgorod

Noworshew	Novorzhev
Nowo Siverskaja	Novosiverskaya
Nowoßjelje	Novoselye
Opolje	Opolye
Opotschka	Opochka
Orjedjesch	Oredezh
Orlinßkoje-See	Lake Orlinskoye
Oßmino	Osmino
Ostrow	Ostrov
Peipussee	Lake Peipus
Pishma	Pizhma
Pleskau	Pskov
Pljussa	Plyussa
Polozk	Polotsk
Ponjewisch	Poniewiez
Porchow	Porkhov
Porietschje	Porechye
Prokowsina	Prokovsina
Pudostja	Pudostya
Pulkowa	Pulkovo
Pustoschka	Pustoshka
Reznassee	Lake Rezna
Rjelbitzy	Ryelbitsy
Romanowa	Romanova
Ropscha	Ropsha
Rosenow	Rosenovo
Rossienie	Raseiniai
Samra-See	Lake Samro
Sapolje	Zapolye
Sarutchje	Zaruchye
Schadow	Seduva
Schanino	Shanino
Schaulen	Saule
Schestiperowa	Shestiperova
Schlüsselburg	Shlisselburg
Sebesh	Sebezh

Shiltzy	Zheltsy
Sholtzy	Soltsy
Sirkowizy	Syrkovitsy
Skrudalieno	Skrudaliena
Slutzk	Slutsk
Solotuchina	Solotukhina
Spaßkoje	Spaskoye
Staraja Russa	Staraya Russa
Starokworitzy	Starokvoritsy
Stary Mjedwed	Stary Myedved
Strugi Krasnyje	Strugi Krasnye
Sussanino	Susanino
Szitnja	Sitnya
Taizy	Taytsy
Tichwin	Tikhvin
Tischina	Tishina
Tolmatschewo	Tolmachyovo
Toßno	Tosno
Tscherjemjenskoje-See	Lake Cheremenets
Tscherskaja-Gorbowa	Cherskaya-Gorbova
Tschudowo	Chudovo
Uritzk	Uritsk
Ussadischtsche	Usadishche
Utorgosch	Utorgosh
Waldai-Höhen	Valdai Hills
Walday	Valday
Wasselkowa	Vasselkova
e Welikaja	Velikaya
Weliki Luki / Welukije Luki	Velikiye Luki
Welish	Velizh
Wilna	Vilnius
Witebsk	Vitebsk
r Wolchow	Volkhov
Wolossowo	Volosovo
Woskressenskoje	Voskresenskoye
Wyssozkoje	Vysotskoye
Zaiginis	Zaiginys

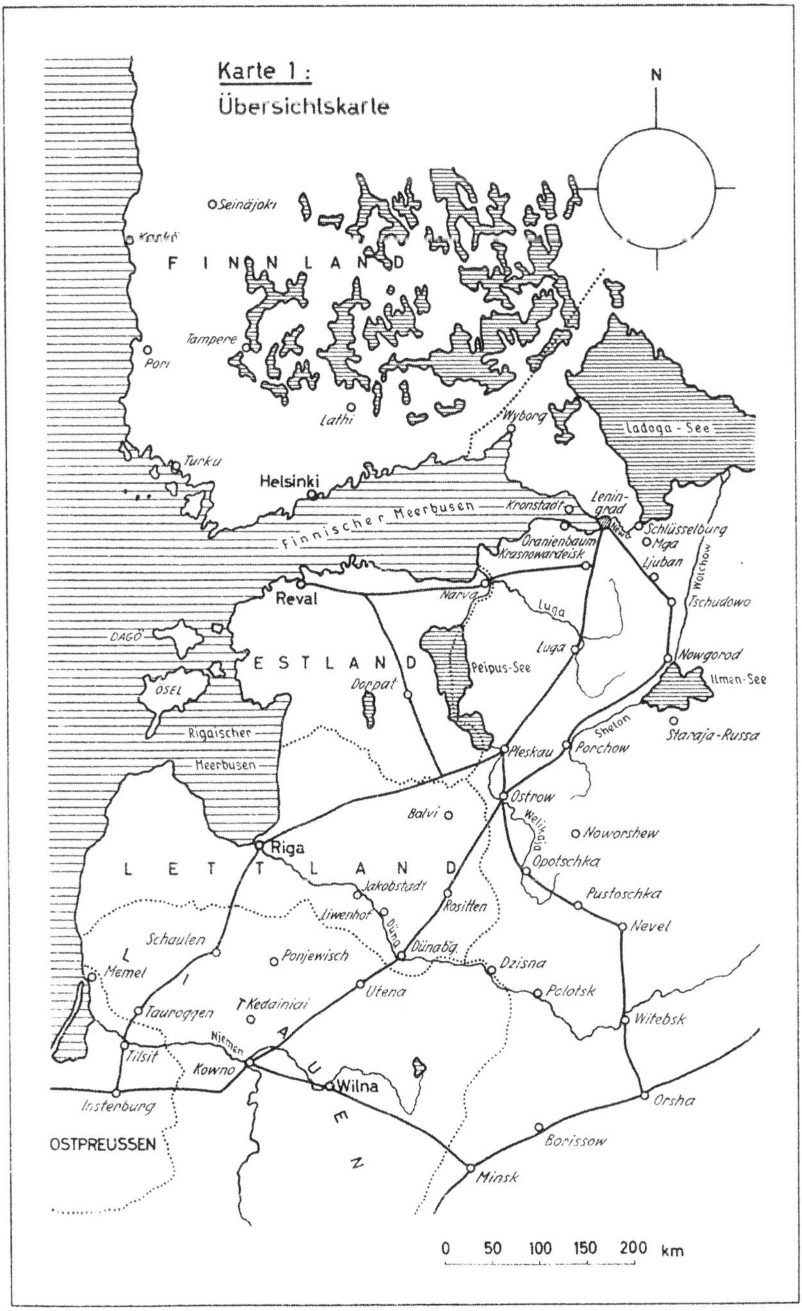

Map 1: The Baltic region

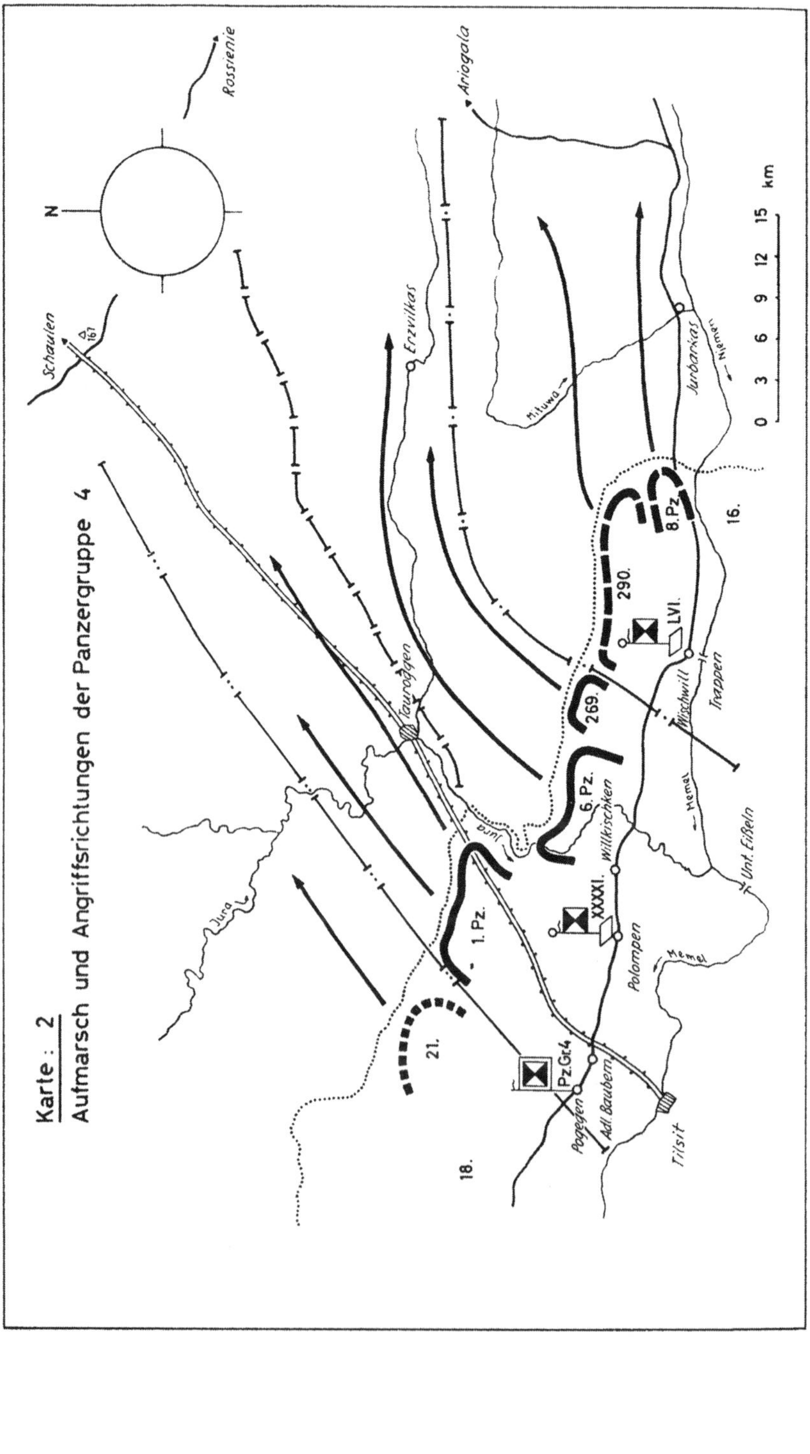

Map 2: Deployment and lines of advance of Panzer Group 4

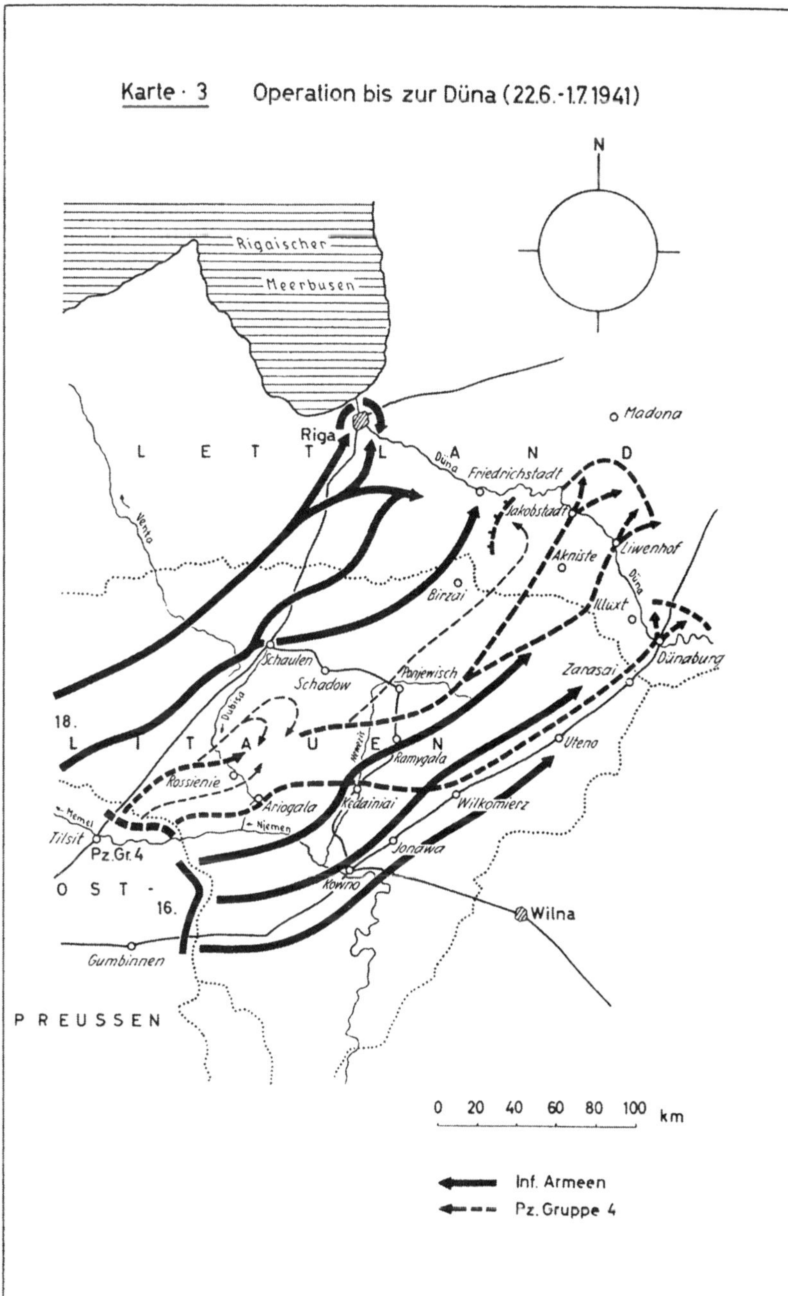

Map 3: Operations up the Western Dvina, 22 June–1 July 1941

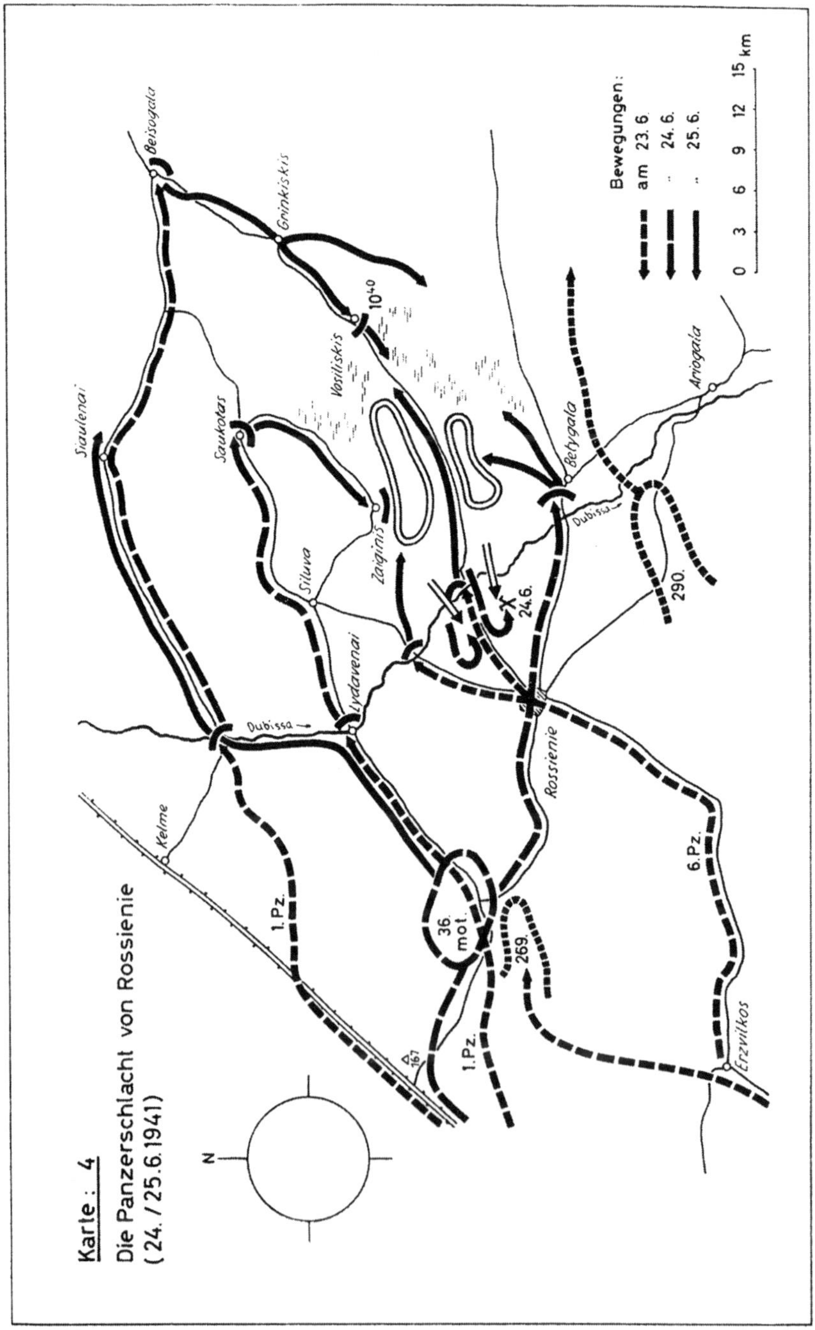

Map 4: The tank battle of Raseiniai, 24–25 June 1941

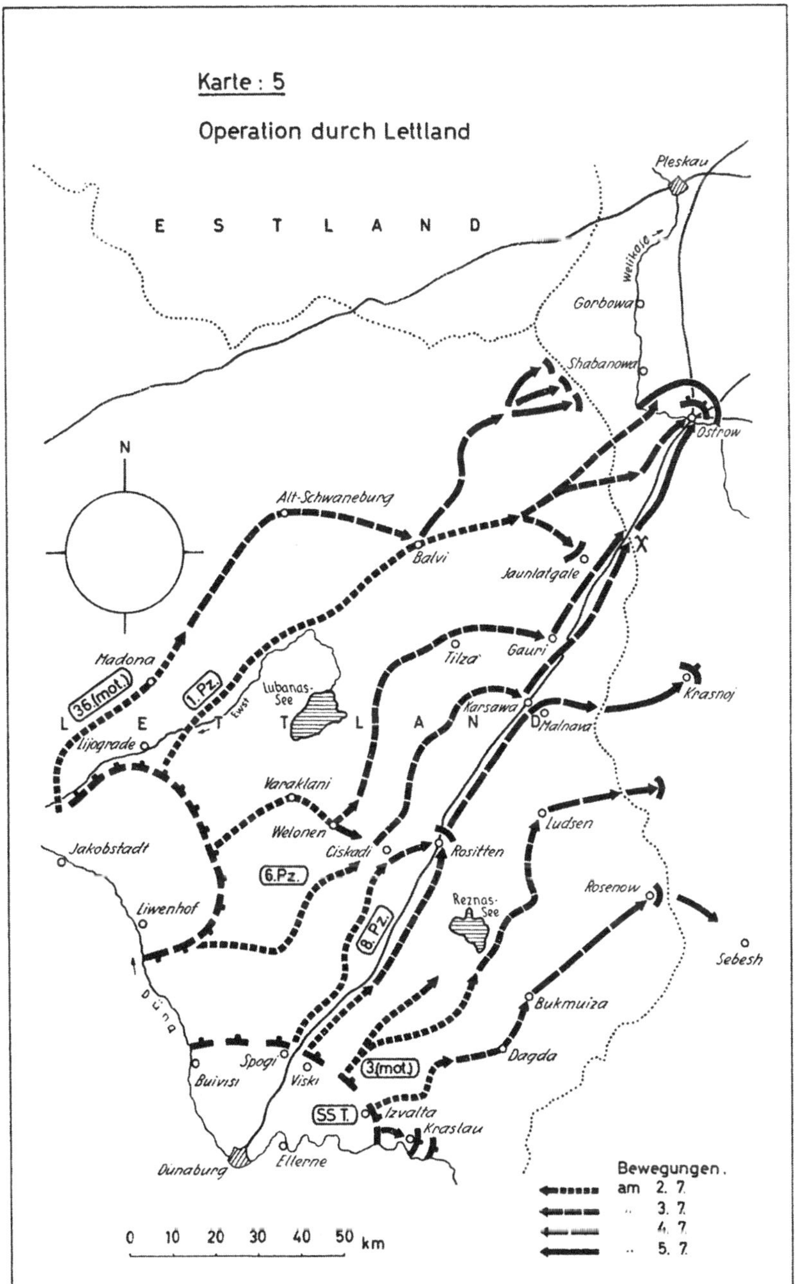

Map 5: Operations through Latvia, 25 July 1941

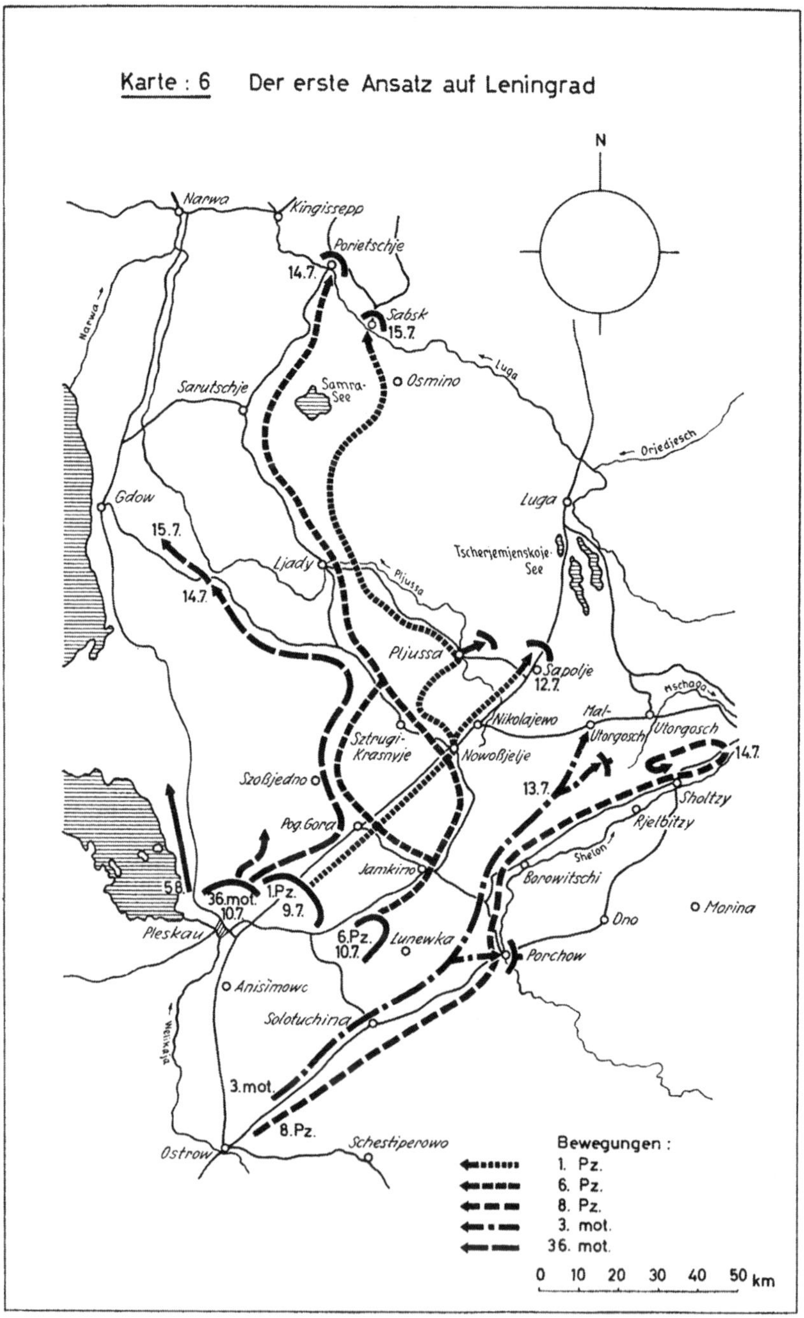

Map 6: The first push towards Leningrad, July 1941

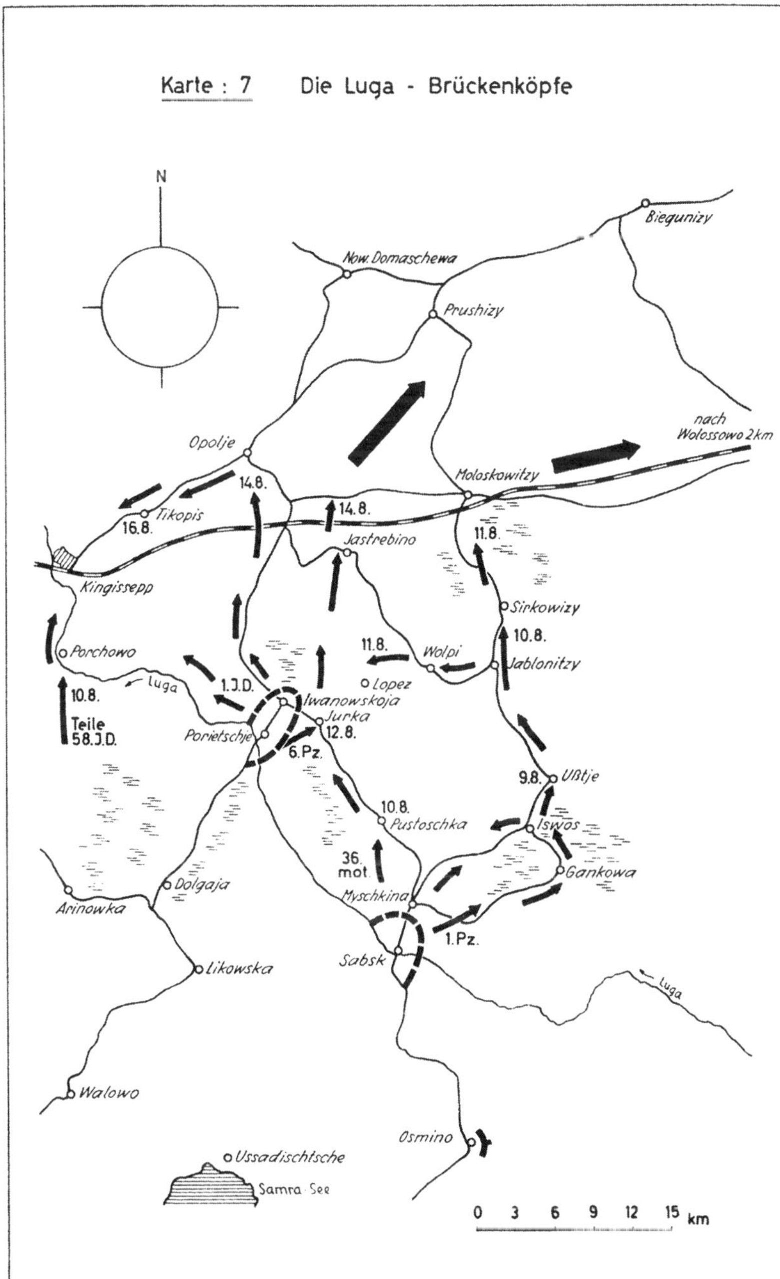

Map 7: The Luga bridgeheads, August 1941

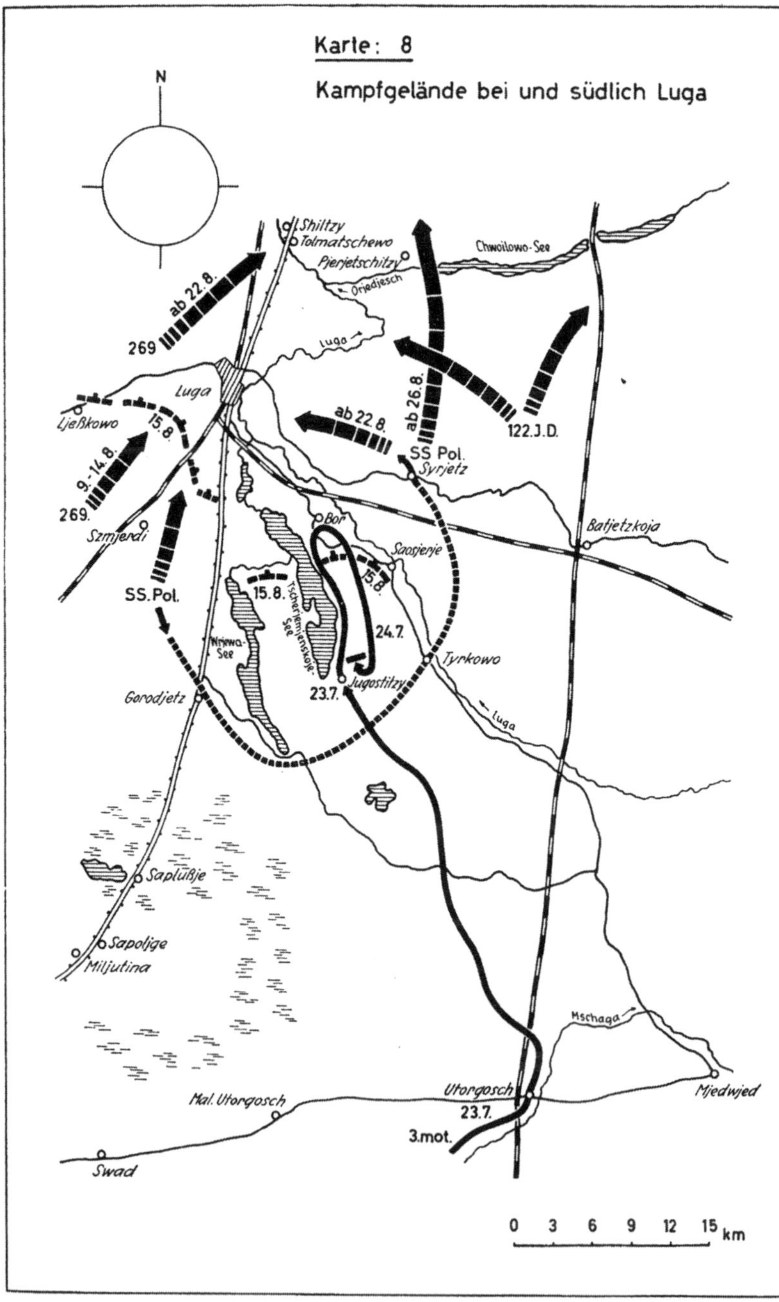

Map 8: The combat terrain near and to the south of Luga, July–August 1941

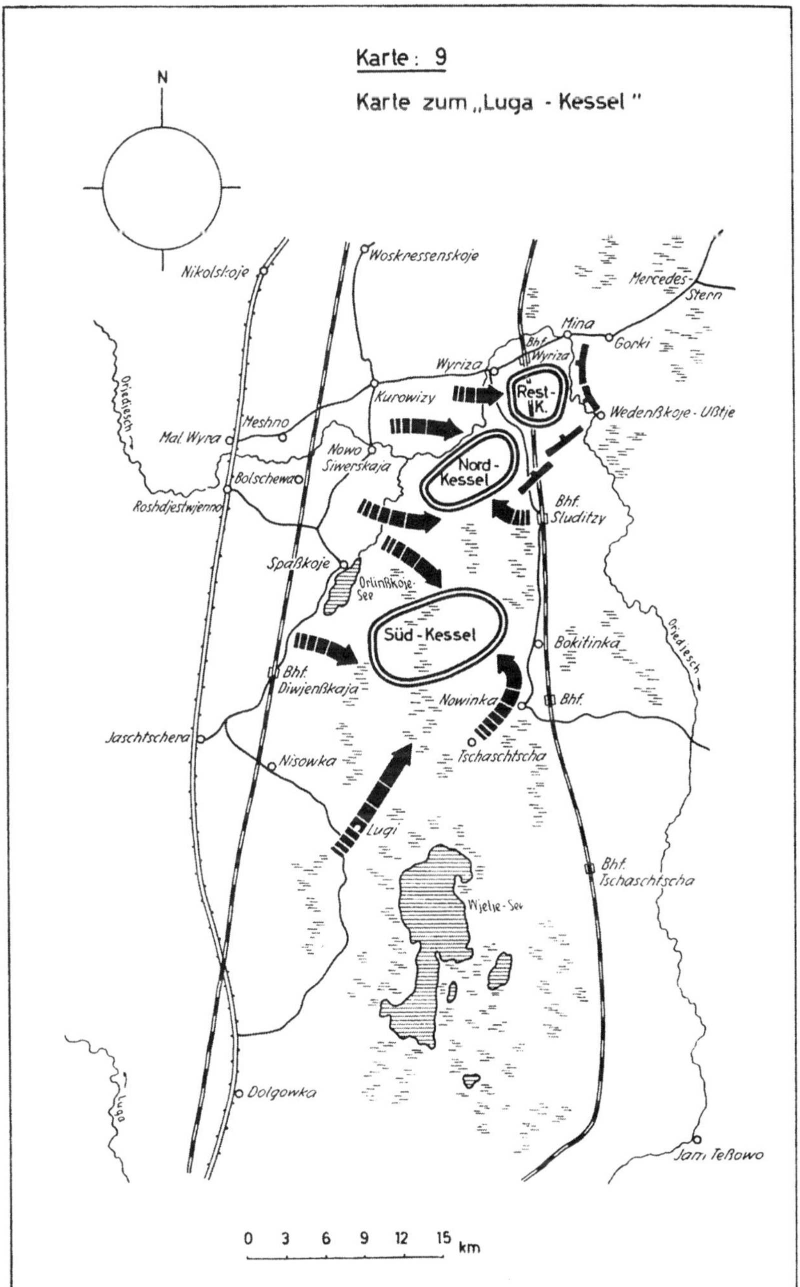

Map 9: The Luga pocket

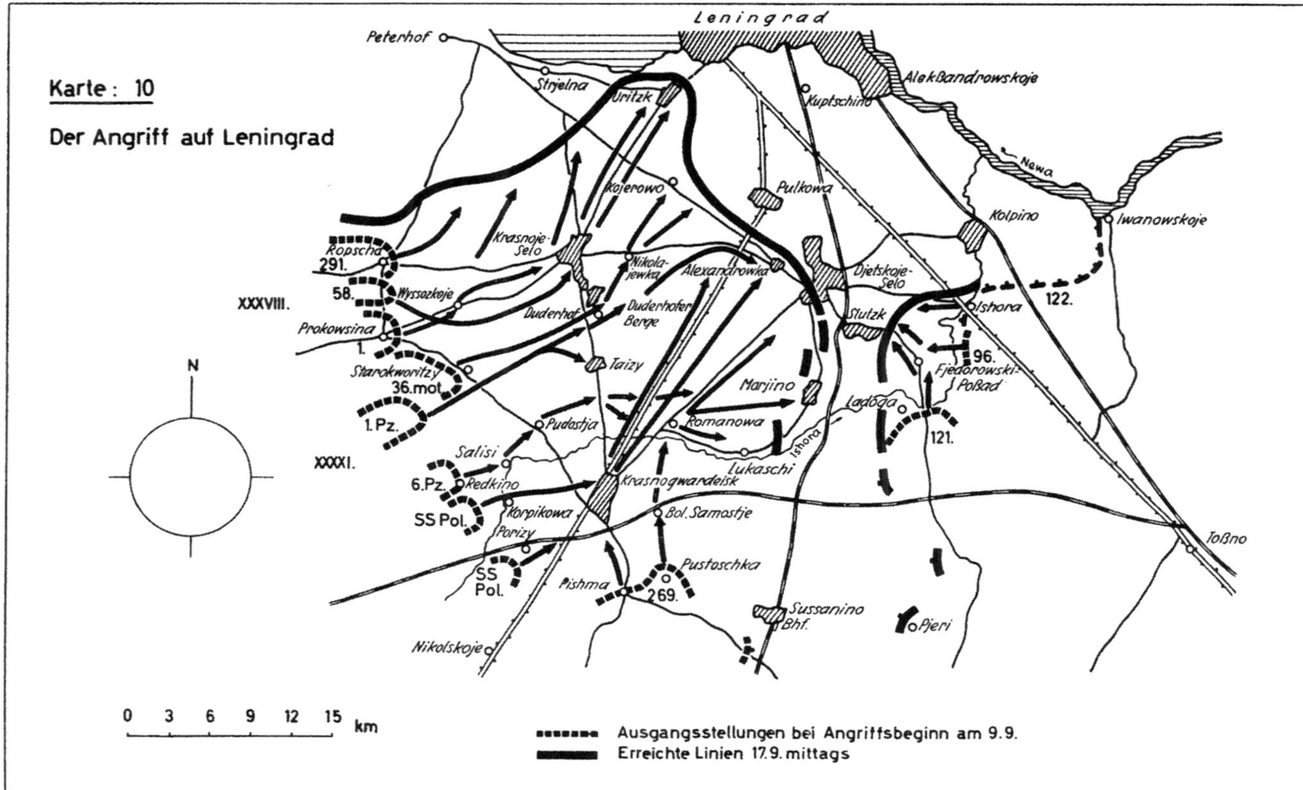

Map 10: The attack on Leningrad, 9–17 September 1941

CHAPTER I

Preparation and deployment

The objective for Army Group North (Map 1)

According to the Barbarossa Plan that had been drawn up by the High Command of the German Army (OKH) on 31 March 1941, the operational objective of the Russian campaign was 'to tear open the front of the Russian army, the bulk of which is in western Russia, and to advance deep into enemy territory with strong, mobile units, isolating and destroying the enemy's formations in the process'. The northernmost of the three army groups assigned to this operation was Army Group North. Its commander in chief was Field-Marshal Wilhelm Ritter von Leeb and its chief of staff was Lieutenant-General Kurt Brennecke, and it was given the following task: 'to annihilate enemy forces in the Baltic region and, in conjunction with the Finnish Army, to finally eliminate any resistance in northern Russia so as to guarantee freedom of movement for further operations'.

While the main emphasis of the entire operation would initially lie with Army Group Centre, it was considered possible that some forces might be diverted from the centre to the weaker north, although there was no precise indication as to when or where this would take place. It would simply depend upon the development of the situation.

Army Group North was allocated 20 infantry divisions, three panzer divisions, and three motorised infantry divisions. These were organised into two infantry armies (the Sixteenth and the Eighteenth Armies) and one panzer group (Panzer Group 4). Colonel-General Erich Hoepner was the commander of Panzer Group 4, and I, Colonel Walter Chales de Beaulieu, was its chief of staff.

Leningrad was the operational objective of Army Group North. This city was approximately 800 kilometres away to the northeast. The enemy had placed most of his forces between the border and the Ostrov–Pskov area. According to an estimate of ours at the end of April 1941, these forces comprised 18–20 infantry divisions (of which three were motorised divisions), two cavalry divisions, and eight or nine mechanised brigades. It was by no means certain that we would be able to encircle and eliminate strong Russian forces in the border areas (i.e. to the west of the obstacle that was the Western Dvina River!) in the way that could be expected in the central and southern sectors (with enemy concentrations in Bialystok and Lvov). It was therefore crucial that we rapidly approach and cross the Western Dvina, for we would need to penetrate the Russian defensive front before it had properly organised itself behind this large water obstacle. We would have to overcome any enemy units in the border areas as quickly as possible and race the 300 kilometres to the river. Any delay would remove the element of surprise. Mobile units would be required (i.e. fully motorised units, panzer divisions, motorised infantry divisions, and several special units). Field-Marshal von Leeb thus decided:

(a) that mobile forces would be combined under the command of Panzer Group 4 (even though the Sixteenth and Eighteenth Armies had sought to keep such forces to facilitate their crossing, respectively, of the Neman near Kovno and of the Western Dvina near Riga),
(b) that the main effort of the advance by Army Group North would be placed where the Western Dvina could be reached most rapidly (i.e. in the central sector of the army group) and that it was here where Panzer Group 4 would be deployed,
(c) that Panzer Group 4 would be directly subordinate to Army Group North, thereby allowing the army group to assign objectives to the panzer group (something the other army groups could not do, for the other panzer groups were subordinate to infantry armies),
(d) that Panzer Group 4, though it would be somewhat cramped, would be positioned north of the Memel (Neman) in the East Prussian border area so that it would not have to cross the river under enemy fire, and

(e) that both infantry armies (the Sixteenth on the right and the Eighteenth on the left) would have to push forward most energetically on their inner wings so as to take advantage of the prospective territorial gain of Panzer Group 4 and to provide flank protection for the armoured troops.

The planned operation of Army Group North thus resembled a wedge whose point would be driven through Dünaburg towards Leningrad. Since this spearhead would be faster and more mobile than the rest of the army group, it was essential that it achieve rapid success. The initially wide and robust wedge would become thin and elongated, but, by driving deep, it would possess great operational possibilities. It could stay on course for Leningrad or it could swing to the left to eliminate enemy forces in Latvia and Estonia. To ensure the spearhead stayed sharp, the wedge formation would have to be maintained and enemy pressure against the flanks, primarily from the south, would have to be neutralised. The unit to our right (the Ninth Army of Army Group Centre) would have to participate in the preparation of an army group boundary that would extend northeast and gradually curve further north.

Army Group North was assigned the following deployment and battle orders for Barbarossa:

> The objective of the operation is the annihilation of enemy forces in the Baltic states and the seizure of the Baltic ports, and thereupon the conquest of Leningrad and Kronstadt. On B-Day at Y-Hour, Army Group North will break through enemy lines along the border and, with Panzer Group 4 in front, cross the Western Dvina between Dünaburg and Rembate (halfway between Jakobstadt and Riga). After crossing the river, the army group, still led by Panzer Group 4, shall advance rapidly to the northeast. The bulk of the army group will drive around the southern side of Lake Peipus. This will prevent enemy troops in the Baltic states from fleeing eastward and will create the preconditions for pushing on towards Leningrad. In order to achieve this overall objective, it is imperative that every opportunity to forge ahead be exploited, thus denying the enemy time to construct a defensive front further east.

The task for Panzer Group 4 was:

> to break through the enemy border zone between the Neman and the Tilsit–Riga road and, before long, the Dubysa sector between the mouth of the river and Saule. Panzer Group 4 shall then thrust to the Western Dvina and establish

> bridgeheads between Dünaburg and Jakobstadt. The point of main effort, so far as the situation allows, will be in the area of Dünaburg. Orders for further operations will then be issued by the army group.

The outlook and measures of Panzer Group 4

To carry out its task, Panzer Group 4 had at its disposal the XXXXI and LVI Panzer Corps. This included the mobile forces of three panzer divisions (1st, 6th, and 8th) and three motorised infantry divisions (3rd, 36th, and SS-Totenkopf).[1] There were also two infantry divisions (269th and 290th), whose task was to secure the assembly position, to overcome enemy resistance in the border area, to comb through forest terrain, and, later, to clear out any enemy elements that remained behind the mobile units. Hoepner had requested an infantry corps headquarters for the difficult coordination of the slow-moving infantry with the motorised advance, but this could not be made available by the army group.

The initial stages of the offensive would be greatly shaped by our assessment of probable enemy activity, of the terrain, and of the possibilities for assembly and movement.

Given the overall assessment, *enemy resistance* along the frontier, if he were taken by surprise, could probably be assumed to be weak despite his numerous entrenchments and field fortifications. Most of these defensive works were around and to the east of Tauroggen. According to all available intelligence, a surprise attack was quite possible. The thickly wooded eastern part of the attack sector afforded valuable cover. If we could strike deeply into enemy territory and cross the Dubysa on the first day of the offensive, the enemy would barely have a chance to form a new front before the Western Dvina. He would only be able to establish a handful of small defensive sectors and pockets of resistance. Nevertheless, we could expect that the deeply echeloned enemy groups might launch counterthrusts against the flanks of our armoured formations. We would meet this prospective development with the echelonment of our own

1 See Appendix 1 for the order of battle of Panzer Group 4. It contains the allocation of both army and Luftwaffe units. See Appendices 2a and 2b for the organisation of divisions.

formations, although this would contribute to the difficulties involved in deploying our troops.

The first major obstacle offered by the *terrain* behind the border was the Dubysa. It was possible that the enemy would cling here tenaciously. Approximately 55 kilometres east of the frontier, the river flowed from Saule to the Neman. With its partly carved valley, it would be challenging to cross. As far as our military intelligence service was aware, there were no defensive constructions on the east bank. If we were to conduct a quick operation, we would need to overcome this obstacle without delay. Even with our well-trained and well-equipped troops, the Dubysa sector constituted a major question mark in all of the considerations of the headquarters of the panzer group. Should we be brought to a standstill at the river, our hopes for a swift victory would be dashed. All levels of command were therefore instilled with a sense of the importance of quick, independent action. Beyond the Dubysa and up to the Western Dvina, the terrain of attack was broken and the road network in poor condition, but it also made more difficult for the enemy his defence and offered our own tanks the opportunity to carry out surprise attacks.

For the *conduct of the attack*, we had to overrun Russian resistance in the border area, particularly on our left flank, as quickly as possible. Any mopping up was a matter for the infantry divisions, as our mobile units would need to drive towards and over the Dubysa. To prepare for a rapid advance, we had to adapt ourselves to the narrow assembly area north of the Memel. The eastern part of this cramped region allowed the assembly of just one infantry division and one mobile division. Our mobile units would be most constrained as they moved through the area. To maintain secrecy, the bulk of the three panzer divisions would not be permitted north of the Memel until the last moment (i.e. the night of 21/22 June). Only smaller elements had been able to cross the river the night before. The three motorised infantry divisions had to remain south of the river until the night of the attack. The only road bridge over the Memel was in Tilsit, so two military bridges were prepared upstream, although they were only in place from the night of 20/21 June. Our forces were therefore deployed in considerable depth, which was disadvantageous for our units in the eastern part of the assembly area. Whilst their line of advance would be towards Dünaburg, the heaviest fighting could be expected on the left flank of the attack sector. Also to be taken into account was the supply of the three panzer divisions, which was to be given priority over building up reserves. Our antiaircraft weapons would be concentrated around the three bridgeheads over the Memel,[2] especially near Tilsit, for our forces would be bottlenecked when crossing the river and would need protection from any Russian air strikes.

So it transpired that Panzer Group 4 stood ready to attack with the LVI Panzer Corps on its right wing and the XXXXI Panzer Corps on its left (see Map 2). Assembled in the eastern sector were the 8th Panzer Division on the right and the 290th Infantry Division on the left. The former would advance towards Ariogala (on the Dubysa) via Jurbarkas, whilst the latter would advance through woodlands. The 3rd Motorised Infantry Division waited to the south of the Memel and was at the disposal of the LVI Panzer Corps. In the area of the XXXXI Panzer Corps, both the 269th Infantry Division and the 6th Panzer Division were faced with a number of dense forests. On and to the west of the Tilsit–Tauroggen road was the 1st Panzer Division. It would attack through more open terrain and would be strongly backed by our artillery. The 36th Motorised Infantry Division would also be available to the XXXXI Panzer Corps. Our left-hand neighbour would be the 21st Infantry Division of the Eighteenth Army.

The shape of the frontier would make the *conduct of the attack* of the panzer group quite difficult. We would at first have to strike northwards before swinging towards the northeast. Only the 8th Panzer Division would be able to head east from the outset. The challenge here, though, was that this narrow armoured thrust would soon need to be augmented with another mobile division; the front would become ever wider, and the 8th Panzer Division would need some sort of protection on its southern flank. The advance of both divisions, as well as that of the SS-Totenkopf Division, would have to proceed along the road through Jurbarkas. On the other hand, the front of the right-hand corps could not be allowed to become too wide, otherwise its lunge towards Dünaburg might lose momentum. After crossing the Dubysa, the objective of the corps was

2 See Appendix 1.

to advance through Kedainiai and to seize the Kovno–Dünaburg road at Wilkomierz. The roads up to this point were in rather poor condition, but from here the corps would be able to charge forward towards Dünaburg. Whilst the LVI Panzer Corps would have to distribute itself narrowly and in depth, the XXXXI Panzer Corps would need to advance with a wide front over the border and towards the Western Dvina so as to be able to shatter the enemy defence at several points along the frontier. The corps could then choose a suitable location for the point of main effort and cross the river as quickly as possible. The road network in the sector of the XXXXI Panzer Corps was quite bad, so it would be permitted to advance up to Saule along the road, in the sector of the Eighteenth Army, that led to Riga. However, the commander of the panzer group only regarded this as a stopgap solution. Any local skirmishes would consume time, and the capture of Saule was unimportant for our overall objective. A reserve division (the 36th Motorised Infantry Division) was absolutely necessary for the corps, for, upon circling to the northeast, the left flank of the corps would become exposed to enemy tanks approaching from Riga. Aside from flank protection on the left, the XXXXI Panzer Corps would need a third mobile division to be able to widen the front as it neared the Western Dvina. Otherwise, the commander of the panzer group had already, in his orders for the conduct of the attack, expressly stated that he would, 'according to the development of the situation, assign to the most rapidly advancing corps the main thrust against Dünaburg'.

With each panzer corps urgently requiring three mobile divisions to carry out their tasks, the creation of a *reserve for the panzer group* could not practically be realised. There were only six mobile divisions available. It was inconceivable that a large armoured formation could wage war without reserves, especially in conditions that would be changing all the time. With such an ambitious objective, one that was more than 300 kilometres away, we would need deeply echeloned reserves, which, at the very least, would draw upon one third of our forces. Hoepner had sought a third mobile corps for the panzer group from the outset, but this could not be granted due to the fact that all of the German forces were overstretched. He thus put the third mobile division of the LVI Panzer Corps, the SS-Totenkopf Division, into panzer group reserve, since it could not cross the Memel immediately anyway. He did this despite his certainty that three mobile divisions would be the minimum requirement for a successful thrust by the LVI Panzer Corps towards Dünaburg. The panzer group had no real reserve to speak of. There were simply insufficient forces available. Hoepner wanted to keep open the possibility of quickly reinforcing the left-hand corps should the thrust by the LVI Panzer Corps fail. However, if Dünaburg was captured without delay, the 36th Motorised Infantry Division might be placed into panzer group reserve. This was the only solution for the panzer group given that it did not have three pennies to rub together! Neither of the two infantry divisions could be regarded as a substitute for mobile reserves.

There was one final problem that had to be dealt with in the preparations for the offensive. *Supplies for our troops had to be safeguarded*, especially if our supply lines were suddenly extended by a rapid advance on the Western Dvina. We had no experience of conducting operations over such vast terrain, and the road network in Lithuania was poorly developed and in terrible condition. Each corps would have a supply road committed to it. The right-hand corps would certainly be better placed once it reached the main road leading to Dünaburg, but the road network before that point was shocking. It was worse for the left-hand corps, since its supply convoy would be compelled to traverse narrow country roads and sandy paths, particularly over the last 100 kilometres to the Western Dvina. The trucks navigating these roads would be relying heavily on the weather remaining dry. Any disruption of supply would hamper the entire operation. It was likely that both corps would need to halt at the Kedainiai–Seduva line in order to refuel. That naturally meant that there would already be some delay! So as to avoid or minimise such delay, both corps were advised to send advanced detachments beyond the refueling line. These small but combat-powerful groups would therefore be the first to receive fuel. Some units, in the event of insufficient supply, might have to temporarily remain behind. We ought to be able to reach the Western Dvina in one uninterrupted thrust if the situation developed favourably and if supplies flowed smoothly. Nonetheless, it was clear that the Western Dvina was the furthest point that could be reached by supply columns from East Prussia. Any advance beyond the river would require the construction of a new supply base. Little would be changed by having our weak supply troops closer to the front, but we hoped that the spoils of a quick advance would yield enough fuel and food to substantially increase our range. We also had to hope that the stop that would probably be necessary at the Western Dvina would allow sufficient time for goods and equipment to reach the front. Given the many ways in which the supply situation could develop, the German leadership was taking a huge risk by already chalking up a victory on the basis of factors that were by no means certain (spoils, smoothly flowing transport, and good traffic conditions). The critical distance for our supply would be reached at the Western Dvina at the very latest! The continuation of the operation would be decisively influenced by our ability to lengthen our supply lines.

So all preparations were made and it seemed as if everything had been thought of. The command staff of the panzer group met at their headquarters to the north of Tilsit eight days before the beginning of the offensive and assumed command of their sector of the front, albeit with only a few elements of the panzer divisions to the north of the Memel. Up until this time, the 269th and 290th Infantry Divisions of the Eighteenth Army had been responsible for the security of the border area. In the early hours of 22 June (B-Day), those of our troops along the border moved into position, our tanks rolled over the three Memel bridges, and, to the south of the river, our reserves moved forward. Everything proceeded according to schedule. Nobody seemed to stir on the Russian side. Would the enemy be taken by surprise? Or was he lying in wait, fully prepared to defend himself? Moments as crucial as this one cause a great deal of suspense, and the uncertainty only heightened the tension. Would everything be ready in time? But we were reasonably confident, and all the more so when at 2:50 am both corps headquarters reported that our troops were in position. Even the three panzer divisions were at their starting points! The offensive, as intended, could commence at 3:05 am.

CHAPTER 2

Rush to the Western Dvina

Border combat on 22 June 1941 (Maps 2 and 3)

As dawn broke on 22 June, it was apparent that a beautiful day was in store. The commander of the panzer group had set off to visit the XXXXI Panzer Corps before daybreak, as it was in the vicinity of Tauroggen that the heaviest fighting could be expected. Once he had formed an impression of the situation there, Hoepner went to the LVI Panzer Corps. This formation was to charge towards Dünaburg, and its success or failure that day would be entirely dependent on the degree of surprise attained.

At 3:05 am, from the command post of the panzer group, we could hear in the distance the dull rumble of the fire of approximately 120 artillery pieces of all calibres against their assigned targets in the area of Tauroggen. A clear summer's day had begun, and it was into the tranquillity of the countryside that the events of the war unfolded. The first reports arrived quickly. We had taken prisoner almost all enemy troops along the border. From 4 am, the initial results were conveyed via radio and telephone. On the right, both divisions of the LVI Panzer Corps pressed forward on a wide front against the enemy's weak forces. On the left, near and to the east of Tauroggen, the XXXXI Panzer Corps encountered stiff resistance. Fierce fighting was underway in the woodlands through which the 269th Infantry Division and the 6th Panzer Division had to navigate. Even so, enemy resistance here seemed to be poorly organised. We made our first situation report to the army group at 4:40 am, but it was at 6 am that we received the first truly significant piece of news: Jurbarkas was taken with its bridge over the Mituva River intact. Further north, the forward elements of the 290th Infantry Division had already crossed the Mituva. Towards noon, we had completely overcome the weak Russian defence along the border and had penetrated beyond Jurbarkas. According to the information we received from the army group, the enemy had been similarly weak before the armies that neighboured the panzer group. What remained unclear was where the enemy would next position his forces. In the course of the afternoon, the 8th Panzer Division took a number of undamaged bridges over the lower reaches of the Dubysa, downhill from Ariogala. By the evening, the 290th Infantry Division had advanced approximately 30 kilometres into hostile territory. The XXXXI Panzer Corps had made similar progress, although it had been engaged in particularly fierce combat, with the 269th Infantry Division and the 6th Panzer Division suffering heavy losses in the woodlands. Nevertheless, enemy resistance had been broken everywhere. The remaining stragglers in the woodlands caused problems for our supply, so our rear troops were required to mop them up. Aerial reconnaissance over the Kovno–Vilnius line and the Western Dvina detected no new enemy forces, but there was significant armoured and motorised activity approximately 40 kilometres to the southwest of Saule. The 616th Panzerjäger Battalion was therefore taken out of panzer group reserve and put under the control of the 1st Panzer Division in order to safeguard the northern flank in the area of the major road. We expected that a Russian motorised or mechanised brigade would be headed there the next day. However, it was not Hoepner's intention to divert strong forces to the north. He preferred to remain on the defensive there and to leave it to the approaching Eighteenth Army to wipe out the Russian brigade. Our own objectives lay to the east and northeast. By the end of the day, the panzer group had pushed as far as Ariogala, 70 kilometres deep into enemy territory. Our task for the next day would be to commence our thrust towards the Western Dvina.

Engage in armoured combat or push on towards Dünaburg?

From early in the morning on 23 June, the headquarters of the panzer group was preoccupied with the question as to what the enemy might do next, especially with his motorised and armoured forces.

The panzer group formation was still quite narrow. The 8th Panzer Division was its spearhead. The left-hand corps, meanwhile, lagged behind. Not only did this corps have to circle gradually to the east; it was compelled to do so against stiff resistance. Aerial reconnaissance in the morning revealed Russian motorised forces still situated southwest of Saule, although we had yet to discern precisely where they would be committed. We also identified fresh forces approaching our right wing. At 4 am, the road leading from the southeast was filled with motorised vehicles and tanks between Jonava and Kedainiai. It became clear in the next few hours that enemy movements from Kedainiai would only continue northwards and northwestwards rather than towards the west, where the 8th Panzer Division was to be found. Enemy tanks numbered between 200 and 300. They probably belonged to the 2nd Russian Tank Division, originally positioned in the area of Jonava and possibly reinforced with additional motorised units. By noon, the 8th Panzer Division had still not made contact with the enemy tanks. Their passivity was astonishing, but our aerial reconnaissance soon spotted them on their way to Raseiniai. We now anticipated that they would clash with the 6th Panzer Division. Just in case, the 8th Panzer Division had to be prepared to send a detachment northwards so as to relieve the 6th Panzer Division. However, when at 1:50 pm the LVI Panzer Corps reported the readiness of the 8th Panzer Division, now near Ariogala, for defence or for attack, the panzer group immediately emphasised to the corps that the eastward advance of the division was not to be held in check under any circumstances. It was our intention that Kedainiai be taken on this day. The town would then serve as a springboard for the continuation of the offensive. The 8th Panzer Division would simply maintain contact with the 6th Panzer Division so that it would be ready to render assistance should the need arise. The seizure of Kedainiai would offer the best relief for our northern neighbour and would at the same time disrupt the retreat of the enemy to the southeast.

In the area of the XXXXI Panzer Corps, the 6th Panzer Division had taken the small town of Raseiniai in the afternoon. The Russians launched a tank attack, supported by artillery and cavalry, against the town from the east and northeast, but we managed to repel them towards 5 pm. Parts of the 6th Panzer Division pursued the fleeing Russians, and by the late evening they had been able to establish a small bridgehead over the Dubysa. Further north, the two battle groups of the 1st Panzer Division had succeeded in creating bridgeheads over the river before nightfall – one near Lyduvenai and the other 10 kilometres to the north. The 36th Motorised Infantry Division had begun its advance along the major road through Tauroggen. It had been unable to do so earlier due to traffic congestion, but now it was in a position to provide flank protection to the north whilst standing ready for a further push to the northeast.

Things had gone smoothly on 23 June, especially for the 8th Panzer Division, which had taken Josvainiai, 10 kilometres west of Kedainiai, at 9:20 pm. The division had only encountered weak enemy resistance thus far, so the further advance towards Dünaburg seemed quite promising. Even so, on 24 June, the panzer group now awaited the reckoning with the Russian tank forces. Aerial reconnaissance had identified up to 350 tanks! This powerful enemy force had to be disposed of. It could not simply be bypassed. The commander of the panzer group was faced with the question as to whether the XXXXI Panzer Corps could deal with this task on its own, for the corps had already performed so skilfully against the enemy near Raseiniai, or whether all three panzer divisions should be employed so as to ensure a rapid success. There would be no further forces available for combat on 24 June; reinforcements would arrive only later that day. In this case, the thrust towards Dünaburg would have to be put on hold temporarily. Russian forces would thereby gain time, despite the fact that we had planned from the outset to overrun the enemy before he could react! If the 8th Panzer Division was permitted to undertake the seemingly ideal push further east via Kedainiai, the Russian tank formation, knowing that their route of retreat would be in danger, would respond by turning south. The 8th Panzer Division would then run the risk of being cut off. Could the division wait one day and still manage to advance to the east via Kedainiai tomorrow? Kedainiai and Rasciniai lay at least 60 kilometres away from one another! If, however, the Russian tanks embedded themselves along the Dubysa, our reinforcements would have a chance to arrive throughout the course of the day. The LVI Panzer Corps would then be free to advance further eastwards, especially as the 290th Infantry Division would be strong enough to secure the northern flank. Hoepner regarded our objective, Dünaburg, to be of such importance that the risk of being cut off had to be accepted. Both panzer corps were therefore to proceed with their advance on 24 June: the LVI would drive towards Wilkomierz, whilst the XXXXI was to encircle and annihilate the Russian tank formation. The latter corps would no longer be responsible for the security of the major road towards Saule; this would fall to the 616th Panzerjäger Battalion, now under the direct command of the panzer group.

The LVI Panzer Corps takes Dünaburg

The territorial gain of the LVI Panzer Corps on 23 June had been quite a bit less than that achieved the previous day. The 8th Panzer Division had become widely dispersed on 22 June due to the variable road conditions, but it had by now closed ranks so as to be able to sustain a further thrust to the east. Meanwhile, the forward elements of the 3rd Motorised Infantry Division had reached the east bank of the Dubysa. The division was now in a position to expand its front and partake in the fighting of 24 June. Furthermore, the 290th Infantry Division, near and to the northwest of Ariogala, guarded the northern flank of the corps against the Russian tank formation, but, at the crack of dawn on 24 June, the bulk of the division was to start advancing further east alongside the other two divisions of the corps. We were maintaining contact with our right-hand neighbour (the 30th Infantry Division of the X Corps of the Sixteenth Army) at the mouth of the Dubysa.

Kedainiai was taken by the 8th Panzer Division as early as 3:45 am. Undaunted by enemy forces to the north, the division advanced further and occupied Wilkomierz in the late afternoon. Facing only weak resistance, a forward group of the division drove approximately 15 kilometres along the road that had now been reached in the direction of Dünaburg. Significant progress had been made on this day. The distance to Dünaburg was now a mere 125 kilometres. The LVI Panzer Corps had some cause for concern that evening. The 8th Panzer Division was operating on a narrow front 100 kilometres in depth, and the 3rd Motorised Infantry Division, to the right of the 8th Panzer Division, was delayed due to poor road conditions.

The Russian tank forces had made their presence felt in the sector of the 290th Infantry Division on 24 June. A battle group of the division, striking north from Ariogala, had been thrown back several kilometres by the Russian tanks. Even so, the battle group had been successful in establishing contact with the 269th Infantry Division of the neighbouring corps on the west bank of the Dubysa. As will be described below, the XXXXI Panzer Corps had also experienced setbacks when engaged in tank combat on 24 June. The commander of the panzer group was nevertheless convinced that the panzer corps had to, and would be able to, cope with these Russian tanks, even though it seemed that they could not be budged. At no point during the day did our aerial reconnaissance spot additional enemy forces west of the Western Dvina. It was thus clear that we ought to be able to deal with the Russian tank formation in one single offensive action without wavering from our thrust towards Dünaburg. Any danger to the rear of the LVI Panzer Corps had to be swept away quickly. The SS-Totenkopf Division, in panzer group reserve, was therefore ordered to cross the Memel over the Trappen bridge in the afternoon and to proceed to a point halfway between Jurbarkas and Raseiniai.

The situation continued to develop favourably for the LVI Panzer Corps on 25 June. After some skirmishing along the Virinta, a stream 30 kilometres northeast of Wilkomierz, the 8th Panzer Division and the 3rd Motorised Infantry Division pushed further northeastwards. The former proceeded on and to the north of the main road; the latter, echeloned on the southern side on a front of 8–10 kilometres, headed towards Utena along secondary roads (although a few rear elements of the division did use the main road). Our reconnaissance of the terrain and of the enemy's positions was of increasingly great importance. We would have been unable to do without it! At 2.45 pm, the 8th Panzer Division took the small town of Utena. The enemy, equipped with tanks, resisted tenaciously on the main road, but the result was that a considerable quantity of his weaponry fell into our hands. We were more and more under the impression that the enemy possessed no additional forces to hurl against the corps and that he was simply seeking, despite our overwhelming air superiority, to delay our advance with any stopgap measures at his disposal. Only to the south was there cause for concern, for our aerial reconnaissance had identified groups of Russian forces, of varying strength, heading towards the main road that led to Dünaburg. Given the ever greater weakness of our own forces, we would be unable to build up a line of security to the south. Our southern sector was already more than 100 kilometres in length, for it stretched from Utena all the way back to Jonava. As a matter of fact, Jonava was only taken two days later (27 June) by parts of the Sixteenth Army. So as to achieve economy of manpower, Hoepner instructed the LVI Panzer Corps on the morning of 25 June 'to secure the Wilkomierz–Dünaburg road by preparing strongpoints only in Wilkomierz, Utena, and Zarasai'. While these strongpoints would defend those particular cities, they were also supposed to drive out any enemy forces that might try to bypass them. The road would thereby remain passable for our troops. The strongpoints would foreseeably be manned by the troops of the SS-Totenkopf Division and, from Utena, by those of the 290th Infantry Division. Although they were merely stopgaps, the strongpoints were able to prove their worth in the next few days. The Russian forces, weak as they were, evaded any serious combat.

The 8th Panzer Division, only 70 kilometres from Dünaburg after the capture of Utena, had been able to consolidate its success of 25 June by pushing further towards Dünaburg in the middle of the night. Full of suspense, the panzer corps and panzer group waited to see how the situation might develop the next day. We hoped to be able to realise the one thing that had spurred on our troops and commanders: the seizure of Dünaburg with both of its bridges in a single strike. The 8th Panzer Division did everything possible to prepare for its execution. Under cover of darkness, our panzer, panzer-grenadier, and panzer-pioneer troops approached Dünaburg along the major road. In front of them were two special battle groups. They had been chosen due to their special training to carry out the bold task of taking the two bridges over the Western Dvina (one was a road bridge and the other a railway bridge). Driving ahead on trucks, they were to infiltrate enemy lines, move onto the bridges, overpower the bridge garrisons, and prevent the bridges from being blown up.[3] Since both battle groups would be small (each was given two trucks), the following armoured units would need to be in a position to intervene quickly whilst being careful not to draw the attention of the enemy too early on. If the enemy had any cause to be wary, he would most certainly destroy both bridges. The city of Dünaburg lay on the right bank of the Western Dvina, i.e. on the opposite side of the river to that from which we were approaching. On our side of the river was Griwa, a locality which was quite suburban in character. Both battle groups, led by Lieutenant Hans-Wolfram Knaak, detached themselves from the panzer corps and entered Griwa on 26 June at 6:30 am. The four trucks proceeded unnoticed amidst enemy traffic and succeeded in nearing their objectives. Our men dismounted and secured the bridges despite tough resistance. Our armoured units arrived soon thereafter and wiped out the remaining enemy forces in the area. While the road bridge fell into our hands intact, the railway bridge, possibly amidst the combat, received minor damage when one of the explosive devices attached to it detonated. Unfortunately, Lieutenant Knaak had fallen whilst personally leading the raid against the road bridge. Our troops would otherwise be spared major bloodshed, for they need not struggle to cross the Western Dvina. Thereafter, Panzer Group 4 would need another swift success so that the advance on Leningrad could maintain its momentum. For the time being, though, the safety of the Dünaburg bridgehead, our jumping-off point for further operations, was of the utmost importance, for Russian countermeasures in the area could be expected.

The tank battle of Raseiniai (Map 4)

Despite the success of the 6th Panzer Division against the Russian tank force from Kedainiai on the evening of 23 June, the situation on the morning of 24 June appeared to be less favourable. In the face of a powerful Russian tank attack, we had been compelled to abandon the small Dubysa bridgehead early in the morning. On the other hand, the

3 Translator's note: The troops of the two battle groups consisted of fluent Russian speakers. They were dressed in Russian uniforms and would approach the bridges on captured Russian trucks.

advance of both battle groups of the 1st Panzer Division, further north, still continued unabated. The weak enemy forces here possessed no tanks and had to fall back to the east. Meanwhile, the 269th Infantry Division moved from its resting area (15 kilometres west of Raseiniai) towards Betygala via Raseiniai so as to be able to exert some sort of influence on the Dubysa by the afternoon. In the view of the XXXXI Panzer Corps and of the panzer group, the 290th Infantry Division (of the LVI Panzer Corps), already near and to the northwest of Ariogala, offered sufficient protection in the southern sector of the combat zone. The XXXXI Panzer Corps thus saw no cause to change its plans for the approaching 36th Motorised Infantry Division, which was earmarked for the expansion of the front on the left flank! Throughout the morning, it had become clear to the corps headquarters that the enemy was not satisfied with regaining the east bank of the Dubysa. His objective seemed to be Raseiniai, for his tanks were pressing towards the city from the northeast and the east. In response, the 6th Panzer Division had to go over to the defensive. As will be seen, a major crisis was to arise for our combat troops: the heaviest enemy tanks (Stalin I and Stalin II tanks) were to appear on the scene, and our antitank weapons would be ineffective against them. One of these monstrosities ploughed through our lines east of Raseiniai towards a heavy field howitzer (15 centimetres). The brave gun crew engaged in close combat with the enemy tank, opening fire whilst engaged. At 300 metres, the howitzer scored a direct hit. It was clearly observed and there was no doubt about it. The tank shook somewhat, but that was it. The projectile had been deflected. The tank continued its charge towards the howitzer and crushed it with its left caterpillar track. It would be understandable if experiences such as this during the battle of Raseiniai had taken our troops completely by surprise and dashed their hopes. Yet our men were not discouraged. They would close in on the monstrosities, blast off their caterpillar tracks, and do away with their crew. This had been the first appearance of these heavily armoured Russian combat vehicles. On the following afternoon, a commission from the army weapons agency came to thoroughly examine one of the disabled tanks, but our antitank weapons were unable to penetrate its exceptionally strong armour.

The fighting between Raseiniai and the Dubysa raged to and fro. We repelled a Russian tank attack immediately to the east of the city at 3 pm, but then an attack of our own, confronted with more enemy tanks, came to a halt west of the Dubysa at 3:30 pm. Aerial reconnaissance at 4 pm revealed even more tanks east of Raseiniai. Even so, the 6th Panzer Division gradually mastered the situation, driving the enemy from the west bank in the evening and even sending some units over the river towards the northeast. The Russian tank formation was on the back foot. In the meantime, the 1st Panzer Division had made good progress. By 3 pm, one of its battle groups had reached Baisogala (almost 15 kilometres south-southwest of Seduva); the other, with a southward-facing front, stood near Saukotas. The 269th Infantry Division reached the Dubysa in the evening, and by 9:30 pm it had established a bridgehead on the east bank of the river northwest of Betygala. On the heights to the west of Betygala, the division made contact with the left wing of the 290th Infantry Division.

It was now the plan of the XXXXI Panzer Corps to encircle the enemy tanks on 25 June. The north was already sealed off, but the east and south had to be taken care of. The 1st Panzer Division would assume responsibility for the east by ordering both of its battle groups to swivel to the southwest, one towards Zaiginys and the other towards Vosiliskis. The 269th Infantry Division was to head northeastwards from its bridgehead so as to complete the southern rim of the encirclement. A regimental group of the division would have to attack northwards. All of our actions were to be offensive in nature; we were not just going to block the enemy. Furthermore, the corps was to ready itself to resume the advance on the Western Dvina, with the 36th Motorised Infantry Division, on the northern wing, preparing to thrust towards Seduva.

After a quiet night, our early-morning reconnaissance on 25 June spotted Russian tanks driving along the Raseiniai–Seduva road towards the northeast. The enemy wanted to escape the ring of encirclement, but one of the battle groups of the 1st Panzer Division had already reached Vosiliskis, which was on this road, at 10:40 am. The other battle group of the division was able to prevent additional Russian tanks from breaking out near Zaiginys. The bulk of the Russian formation seemed to be further south and southeast, but it was hindered by the extensive marshland in this area. Any off-road movement was severely limited. The 269th Infantry Division was able to intercept the enemy's weak attempts to break out towards the south, whilst the 6th Panzer Division, on and to the north of the Raseiniai–Seduva road, pushed forward energetically and made good progress.

The impression at the headquarters of the XXXXI Panzer Corps on the evening of 25 June was that the next day's battle to annihilate the encircled enemy forces would be over very quickly. More than 100 tanks had already been captured! There was now only a six-kilometre gap between the 1st and 6th Panzer Divisions. The enemy's efforts had become disorganised. Sporadic assaults towards the north, east, and south were abandoned the moment we repelled them. Towards 6:30 am on 26 June, the two panzer divisions made contact on the road bordered on either side by marshland, about three kilometres southwest of Vosiliskis. The logically calculated and tenaciously fought tank battle east of Raseiniai was decided in favour of the XXXXI Panzer Corps. Not a single Russian motorised vehicle escaped. By noon, the headquarters of the XXXXI Panzer Corps was able to report the capture or destruction of 186 tanks (of which 29 were the superheavy Stalin tanks), 77 artillery pieces, 23 antitank guns, approximately 600 trucks and cars, as well as a variety of equipment and weaponry.

The XXXXI Panzer Corps reaches the Western Dvina

The morning of 26 June produced both results that had been sought by Panzer Group 4. One was the capture of Dünaburg thanks to 'the first successful thrust of the campaign from what had initially been an operationally defensive front'.[4] The other was the end of the battle of encirclement against the Russian tank formation east of Raseiniai. Yet the penetration of the Western Dvina front would only be meaningful

4 Remark of Colonel-General Erich Hoepner to the commander of the 8th Panzer Division, Lieutenant-General Erich Brandenberger, in Dünaburg, according to the war diary of the division.

if it could be achieved with considerable breadth, especially given that Russian countermeasures against the Dünaburg bridgehead could be expected over the next few days. Sending the XXXXI Panzer Corps there, despite the current strength of the enemy in the area, was not up for discussion. The corps would have to devote itself to swiftly overcoming the obstacle that was the Western Dvina. The present situation seemed to be favourable because, following the battle of annihilation against the Russian tanks, there were no strong groups of enemy forces to be found in the terrain leading up to the Western Dvina. According to an assessment of the situation on 26 June, the day on which the thrust towards the Western Dvina was well underway, it was expected that even most of the length of the river would only be weakly defended. Nonetheless, we would still have to cross the river, preferably with intact bridges at our disposal, for bridge construction was costly in time and materiel. The 1st Panzer Division would aim for the Jakobstadt bridge, whilst the 6th Panzer Division was to advance towards Illuxt and Liwenhof. Only river ferries were available in both towns.

The XXXXI Panzer Corps had resumed its advance on the Western Dvina even before the encirclement battle had reached its conclusion. Parts of the corps made good progress on 26 June. The 1st Panzer Division reached Krekenava, halfway between Kedainiai and Poniewiez, and, without pausing at nightfall, soon took Poniewiez. Further north, the 36th Motorised Infantry Division had arrived at the front throughout the course of the day, and it now pushed 25 kilometres further northeast via Seduva. The 6th Panzer Division was somewhat delayed by the bad roads in its departure area. The 269th Infantry Division was slightly behind the central sector of the corps.

Enemy resistance before the front of the XXXXI Panzer Corps remained fairly weak on 27 June. However, the roads in the area of the 6th Panzer Division continued to be quite bad. The division also had a shortage in the supply of fuel, so by the evening it was still approximately 100 kilometres from the Western Dvina. Better progress had been made by the 1st Panzer Division. Towards the evening, it had crossed the Lithuanian–Latvian border in the area south of Akniste and had reached a point 40 kilometres away from Jakobstadt. The leadership of the division prepared itself for the charge towards the Jakobstadt bridge that would take place the following morning, although it was probable that the enemy would have time to respond before the bridge could be captured.

Unfortunately, this was precisely what happened. As our troops approached early in the morning of 28 June, the enemy blew up the bridge that connected Jakobstadt and Kreuzburg (on the north bank of the river). We would need to construct a military bridge, and work commenced immediately. Since enemy resistance was still weak, we would be able to begin establishing a bridgehead, and two battalions of the division were on the other side of the river by the evening. More of our forces poured into the bridgehead on 29 June via ferry, and from 5:30 pm on 30 June via the completed military bridge. By the evening of 1 July, the bridgehead extended 30 kilometres deep into the territory on the eastern side of the river.

On the morning of 29 June, the northern group of the 6th Panzer Division reached the Western Dvina near Liwenhof, and at 2:30 pm it started to cross the river via ferry and to create a bridgehead on the other side. Steps were taken to build a military bridge here, and it was completed on the evening of 30 June. As was the case near Jakobstadt, enemy resistance was almost non-existent. It seemed that all Russian countermeasures were directed against the Dünaburg bridgehead. Only the enemy air force attempted to interfere with our river crossings. Yet his efforts were in vain, with many of his aircraft shot down. Throughout the day on 30 June, the southern battle group of the 6th Panzer Division relieved those elements of the 8th Panzer Division that were still near Illuxt, for they were urgently needed in the Dünaburg bridgehead. Enemy forces near Illuxt were soon hurled back over the Western Dvina, after which the southern group of the 6th Panzer Division moved itself into the Liwenhof bridgehead.

Our vehicles rolled en masse over both bridges on the night of 30 June/1 July, and by the end of the day the bridgehead of the XXXXI Panzer Corps was approximately 30 kilometres wide. In the afternoon, reinforced reconnaissance units of the 6th Panzer Division had thrust eastwards as far as Varaklani, which lay only 50 kilometres to the west of Rositten. Our combat troops were being resupplied as quickly as possible, for the panzer group intended to push ahead with the advance on 2 July. Enemy forces still appeared to be weak. Only to the northwest, between the Western Dvina and Madona (50 kilometres north of Jakobstadt), did the enemy probe the frontline. They were probably troops that had sought to evade the Eighteenth Army, but we soon drove them back. Nonetheless, the corps would have to secure its position, 40 kilometres west of Jakobstadt, on the southern side of the Western Dvina. This task would fall to the 36th Motorised Infantry Division, which meant that the division was now responsible for a 50-kilometre line of security. Fortunately, it did not need to stay put for long, as an advance detachment of the I Corps had infiltrated the southern part of Riga towards noon on 29 June.

The fighting at the Dünaburg bridgehead

In the late evening of 26 June, the headquarters of the panzer group assessed the situation of the LVI Panzer Corps as follows: the enemy had conducted a number of bombing raids against the small Dünaburg bridgehead, mainly against the bridges, in the afternoon, albeit without success. The 8th Panzer Division continued to reinforce itself on the north bank. A group of the 3rd Motorised Infantry Division, facing only weak enemy resistance, had reached Skrudaliena (12 kilometres southeast of Dünaburg) and was pushing further towards the Western Dvina. The south bank of the river behind the bridgehead was thereby secure. The bulk of the division would be drawn upon to strengthen the defence within the bridgehead itself. An advance detachment of the 290th Infantry Division had reached the Wilkomierz–Poniewiez road at a point approximately 20 kilometres to the north of Wilkomierz, but most of the division was still further behind. It had been affected by an order given that day by Army Group North for all units of Panzer Group 4 immediately to the northeast of Kedainiai to 'halt' between 4 am and 4 pm so that the entire X Corps could cross to the north.[5] The most disadvantageous impact was upon the SS-Totenkopf Division. It had been made available to the LVI Panzer Corps and had immediately set off,

5 The affected area included Kedainiai and Ramygala (see Map 3) and extended from this line approximately 20 kilometres to the east. The X Corps moved through this area from south to north.

but only the leading elements of the division had pushed through the dense traffic to Dünaburg before the halt took effect. The headquarters of the panzer group had objected strongly to the halt at that moment, for the Dünaburg bridgehead urgently needed to be reinforced, but the army group regarded the movement of the X Corps to be of greater importance for the entire operation.

The Dünaburg bridgehead was approximately 10 kilometres in depth by 27 June. The enemy carried out a number of successful bombing raids against the bridges, but his ground troops were unable to mount an assault against our lines. He even failed to make an impression against the eastern part of the bridgehead, despite his ever-increasing resistance. By the evening, the 8th Panzer Division (except for those elements near Illuxt) and most of the 3rd Motorised Infantry Division were in the bridgehead. It had not yet been possible for an advance detachment to be sent towards Rositten in accordance with an order that had been issued by the panzer group the day before at 3:35 pm to the effect that the bridgehead was to be extended 30 kilometres further to the north and east. Rather, the bridgehead would at first have to be secured against powerful Russian attacks.

The LVI Panzer Corps endeavoured to expand the bridgehead on 28 June so as to create the conditions for advancing further into Latvia. From the morning onwards, the 3rd Motorised Infantry Division (on the right) and the 8th Panzer Division (on the left) tried to push forward. The enemy put up little resistance against the 8th Panzer Division. Only on the main road did he defend fiercely, even launching a few armoured counterattacks. The 3rd Motorised Infantry Division, however, was compelled to overcome strong enemy resistance from the outset. Multiple counterattacks were launched by Russian tanks in the afternoon from the east and north. Only some of them could be intercepted to begin with, but it was not long, just as was the case on the main road, before numerous tanks were put out of action. We mastered the situation only by throwing into battle everything that was available. A reinforced battalion of the SS-Totenkopf Division engaged the enemy in the area of the 3rd Motorised Infantry Division. When more Russian tanks appeared in this area, the headquarters of the LVI Panzer Corps also sent in a panzer battalion of the 8th Panzer Division. The antitank battalions of the 290th Infantry Division and of the SS-Totenkopf Division were to be used to enhance our defensive power in the bridgehead, but they would barely arrive there before the evening. Unfortunately, the two assault gun batteries and heavy artillery promised by the Sixteenth Army were delayed. There was also a build-up of Russian tanks north of Kraslava (see Map 5). These tanks probably belonged to the reserve group from Pskov, and their intervention heavily occupied the minds of the staff not only at the headquarters of the panzer group but also at the headquarters of the army group. If they attacked at Dünaburg, they could perhaps be brought to a standstill and destroyed. If, however, they awaited our arrival in the area of Ostrov–Pskov, there would probably be heavy fighting, in poor conditions, along the old Russian border, for the enemy would have gained time to embed himself in his line of fortifications. The evidence gathered from captured Russian officers indicated that he would indeed most likely defend along the old border. Yet we still encountered an astonishing number of Russian tanks on this day. More than 74 tanks were disabled, and several antitank guns and artillery pieces were destroyed. Enemy losses were extraordinarily high, although our losses, especially those of the 3rd Motorised Infantry Division, were also rather heavy. On the evening of 28 June, despite the fact that not every Russian attack had been repelled, we had managed to extend the bridgehead so that it was about 15–18 kilometres in depth.

The fierce fighting in which the corps had been engaged eventually bore fruit on 29 June. Towards the evening, the bridgehead had achieved a depth of 30 kilometres. On the following day, the bulk of the three mobile divisions of the LVI Panzer Corps had entered the bridgehead. The 290th Infantry Division was now approaching quickly along the main road, on which it had previously been forbidden due to the priority that had been given to motorised traffic! The division was to reach Dünaburg on 1 July so that, if need be, it could relieve some of our mobile forces on the front. On the evening of 29 June, the reinforcements that had been promised by the Sixteenth Army arrived, and by the next day they were already engaged in combat. The primary goal for the LVI Panzer Corps on 1 July was to refuel and make preparations for the further advance to the east. It was certainly a stroke of luck that significant supplies of fuel had been taken in Dünaburg.

Retrospection

Whilst our officers and men must receive full credit for the rapid thrust towards and over the Western Dvina, there were nevertheless a number of circumstances outside our control which aided our success. Not least of these was the beautiful summer weather which ensured that the roads, in poor condition as they were, could serve the needs of our motorised units. Yet the limits of what could be achieved had been revealed. The first part of the operation had unfolded favourably, more or less as planned. We had *taken the enemy by surprise* and had fully exploited the situation through the concentration of our mobile forces. Our deep and rapid thrust disrupted the enemy to such a degree that he was unable to act decisively, even along the Western Dvina. The one significant formation that the enemy managed to put together, the reinforced 2nd Russian Tank Division, had the capacity to conduct operations precisely, but it was far too inflexible to be able to respond to the ever-changing situation. This made the measures we took easier to carry out. Even though we repeatedly encountered tough resistance, primarily along the roads and at the junctions, we were always able to eliminate the inferior Russian forces. It was thanks to the success of our surprise offensive that we were able to deal the enemy one devastating blow after another. Our advance had developed so much momentum that the enemy remained in a state of surprise as we crossed the Western Dvina.

The success of the surprise offensive had required *the concentration of all mobile forces*, and it had certainly been advantageous that they had been placed directly under the command of Army Group North. The subordination of the panzer group under an army would have bound it too closely to the interests of the infantry and would have thereby slowed it down dramatically. The army group had even considered this for a short time on 27 June should the panzer group advance on the north side of the Western Dvina in the direction of Riga. Prior to this, the Barbarossa Order had foreseen the possibility of such subordination had the panzer group, in whole or in part, been drawn upon to support the Sixteenth Army in its crossing of the Neman River at Kovno. A rapid advance to the Western Dvina would never have been undertaken by an infantry army!

Of considerable importance to our rapid success was the *air support from the Luftwaffe*. If the numerical superiority of the enemy had seemed overwhelming in the beginning, it was the Luftwaffe, with its outstanding equipment and training, that quickly gained for us the upper hand and helped our ground troops at the most decisive points. The First Air Fleet, operating in the area of Army Group North, supported the panzer group during the advance on and capture of Dünaburg, and it continued to do so when the Jakobstadt bridgehead had to be established and when Dünaburg had to be defended.

There are several lessons to be drawn from our combat sector regarding the *movement of operational units*, but we shall restrict ourselves here to the coordination of infantry and mobile units – a rather important matter at that time! In the area of Army Group North, a mobile formation had been placed between two infantry armies at the starting point. The idea behind this was that the mobile unit would storm ahead and that the infantry armies on either side would exploit the advance of the mobile unit for their own combat objectives whilst also providing security and support. The point of main effort would lie with the mobile unit which, though broadly maintaining a single line of advance towards its goal, would be capable of swinging left or right according to the situation. The panzer group was not assigned a particular zone of action. Instead, its rear operational area was divided between the two infantry armies. The reason for this was to free the panzer group from tasks subsidiary to pure combat. The headquarters of the panzer group, in contrast to the armies, had under its command only the most essential supply services. There were neither administrative bodies nor firmly established supply facilities. The panzer group was always reliant on the army in whose zone it was operating. We had not prior to this had any experience of conducting operations in such a manner. What effect did such an approach have in practice? The advance of the bulk of the mobile troops to the Western Dvina proceeded smoothly, taking approximately six days. Theoretically, the infantry should have been able to keep up, but, in practice, the SS-Totenkopf Division as well as two infantry divisions fell behind. With them was our entire supply, and the roads became more congested than had been expected. With the rear areas under the jurisdiction of the armies, the panzer group was not the master of the situation. The armies had their own wishes fulfilled more quickly, especially as they alone were responsible for supply. The quartermaster of the panzer group was compelled to deal with two senior quartermasters, one from each army. Delays in the movements of the panzer group were considerable when the X Corps crossed our path, although such a measure had been operationally necessary in the view of the army group. Despite the fact that the panzer group was the spearhead, and despite the precariousness of the situation, the army group thought it necessary to interfere with the rear elements of the panzer group. All of this was supposed to facilitate the smooth running of the operation! The friction and obstruction that ensued resulted from only *one* commander being allowed to issue instructions in any particular zone of action. It was already becoming apparent that a panzer group needed to have its own zone of action and that it should be able to temporarily take charge of any infantry units from the armies that wished to traverse the area to its rear. This was a solution that would only be applied gradually later on, so in the meantime the supply to the panzer group would continue to suffer.

The first phase of combat had already revealed *the importance of supply*. It was clear that supply greatly influenced the conduct of battle; indeed, previous campaigns had shown that it could decisively shape the way in which operations unfolded. Although supplies continued to flow towards the front, it was clear that a number of factors had arisen that had caused some delay. We could reasonably assume that such delays would continue into the future. The factors in question included traffic congestion, roads that were few in number and in bad condition, declining performance of our supply vehicles, vehicle breakdowns, and growing fuel consumption. So everything was going so well? It seemed that so many had fallen victim to false ideas of what could be achieved.

CHAPTER 3

Through Latvia to the Stalin Line

Conditions and orders for the advance (Map 5)

After the swift capture of Dünaburg, the army group, just like the panzer group, sought to resume the advance from the Western Dvina bridgeheads as quickly as possible. As soon as the XXXXI Panzer Corps had completed its crossing of the Western Dvina on 28 June, the question of the earliest possible time to renew the advance was discussed. The army group eventually decided upon 2 July, a date that had already been recommended by the panzer group on 29 June. The decision to wait a few days was not so much due to the ongoing fighting near Dünaburg as to the possibility of fully resupplying the troops. Most important was our fuel supply. The Ostrov–Opochka area was 250 kilometres away, but we calculated that in order to reach it our vehicles would require enough fuel for at least 450 kilometres. It would be difficult to sufficiently resupply the XXXXI Panzer Corps, for it had only just crossed the river, but even the resupply of the LVI Panzer Corps would be challenging owing to the strong Russian resistance near Dünaburg. Both corps would need to be completely ready; Hoepner had already decided that one corps on its own would lack penetrative power.

The task for Panzer Group 4 in the next phase of the campaign was outlined in a directive issued by Army Group North on the evening of 29 June:

> Panzer Group 4 shall prepare to advance via Opochka–Ostrov to the area northeast of Opochka. Should there still be enemy elements retreating from west to east on the southern side of Lake Peipus by the time this objective is reached, then this retreat is to be stopped.

How was this goal to be achieved? What would the enemy do? The panzer group was most concerned about the enemy forces in the vicinity of Pskov. We were certain that many of his troops stood between Pskov and Ostrov. This was confirmed by our air reconnaissance on 1 July, as was the fact that the enemy had at his disposal a number of armoured units. His conduct so far indicated that he would not drive forward to meet our attack. It was most likely that he would set up his defence along the old Russian frontier, making use of the fortified defence system there. The only Russian forces that the panzer group would therefore encounter in Latvia would be those that were already fighting there. We could count on these forces attempting some sort of delaying resistance. Heavy combat would then be awaiting us on the Latvian–Russian border. The panzer group would need to concentrate its forces against a single point so as to be able to pierce the defensive front. The probability of a surprise penetration of the frontier defence was quite low, although it was always possible to try to infiltrate this line with our mobile troops alongside the retreating enemy forces from Latvia. It was hoped that we could be finished with the enemy as quickly as possible. When the army group inquired as to whether the panzer group would need to await the arrival of infantry divisions to conduct such an infiltration, we responded in the negative. If we were to push forward quickly, it would have to be done with our own forces! Rapidity meant that there could be no delay. Good terrain would be important!

In fact, the terrain was quite favourable in our zone of operations right up to the Latvian–Russian border; further beyond, only the northern part was good (i.e. the Pskov–Ostrov area). Movement would be particularly difficult around and to the northeast of Opochka and would remain so right up to Leningrad. The penetration of the Stalin Line, a more or less fully developed line of security on the other side of the border, was very much a combat objective, but the extensive marshland beyond Opochka could lead to a number of pitfalls for our mobile troops. To place the point of main effort of the advance here would make no sense whatsoever, yet the possibility had evoked unease in the headquarters of the panzer group from the very beginning due to the tendency of the supreme command to make decisions from their maps. Hoepner was determined, as before, to maintain freedom of movement and to lead his forces in accordance with what was required or permitted by the situation and the terrain. He was not in the position to limit his attention to Ostrov–Pskov and neglect Opochka altogether, for Opochka, unfortunately, lay within the zone of operations of the panzer group.

The views of the panzer group and of the army group differed somewhat with regard to the best utilisation of mobile units. The panzer group considered the selection of suitable terrain to be of decisive importance in rapid movement and effective combat, but the army group was less concerned with the features of the terrain. With its thinking based on the traditional art of warfare, which was bound to the pace and possibilities of movement of the infantry, the army group placed greater value on space in conducting operations. The combat principles for mobile troops were still new and not yet common knowledge. This difference in opinion became quite clear in a meeting between the commander of the army group, Field-Marshal von Leeb, and the commander of the panzer group, Colonel-General Hoepner, on 1 July at the command post of the panzer group in Utena. Hoepner outlined his intended conduct of attack and once more requested that the panzer group be allocated its own zone of action. The field-marshal could not yet grant this request, and he proceeded to lay out his thoughts on the further advance of the armies, behind the panzer group, which was to begin on 4 July with the crossing of the Western Dvina. The objective of the Eighteenth Army would be Pskov; that of the Sixteenth Army to the east and southeast of the city. Von Leeb added:

> It can be the task of the panzer group to be the eastern spearhead. It will be able to launch a decisive attack whose reach will extend around Lake Ilmen.

This rather sketchy scenario took the command of the panzer group by surprise, for it would give up the idea of a rapid advance on Leningrad and would place the panzer group in impossible terrain (forest, marsh, and no roads!) with a difficult task whose worth was questionable. The field-marshal had in mind some sort of infantry phalanx with an enveloping armoured force on the flank. Yet this flank would be incapable of movement, lacking in supplies, and ineffective in combat! The commander of the panzer group immediately pointed out that any hopes of a quick capture of Leningrad would be dashed and that going around

Lake Ilmen would require far too much time. The assembly of the infantry for action would last approximately 14 days. The delay in the use of the infantry, argued Hoepner, need not prevent a rapid advance by the panzer group, but such an advance could only succeed if it were carried out between Lakes Ilmen and Peipus.

Attention has been drawn to the different views of the panzer group and of the army group due to their effect on subsequent events. The feasibility of the scenario outlined by the field-marshal shall not be examined here. There were a number of questions that would have arisen relating to forces, terrain, and supply, but these were not discussed at the time. The early, though perhaps not quite intended, abandonment by the army group of a swift victory against Leningrad was most unsatisfactory for the command of Panzer Group 4.

Onwards through Latvian territory

On 2 July, Panzer Group 4 renewed its advance. On the right, the LVI Panzer Corps would head in the general direction of Novorzhev; on the left, the XXXXI Panzer Corps would drive on Ostrov. The panzer group had shifted its command post from Utena to Viski, 30 kilometres northeast of Dünaburg. The attack would begin at 3 am for the LVI Panzer Corps and at 4:10 am for the XXXXI Panzer Corps. Both corps had been allowed to determine these times.

Dry, and at times quite warm, weather had prevailed thus far, but on the evening of 1 July it had begun to rain. It then rained all day long on 2 July. We therefore had to cope with the absence of air support during the commencement of the attack. Nevertheless, between 4 am and 6 am, our air reconnaissance was able to identify strong motorised enemy columns heading from Ostrov in the direction of Rositten. Had the enemy now made the decision to come and meet our advance, or was this just a detachment that was supposed to delay us? We remained uncertain about the conduct of the Pskov forces until the last moment; the situation would only become clear once we entered into combat.

Heavy fighting broke out on front of the LVI Panzer Corps. Enemy resistance was fierce on either side of the road leading to Rositten, and it was even more so before the eastern sector of the Dünaburg bridgehead.

Particularly difficult was the situation on the southern wing, with the SS-Totenkopf Division only taking Kraslava in the late afternoon. Progress was also slow for the 8th Panzer Division, yet it would have to take Rositten as quickly as possible for the operation to succeed. Given that the XXXXI Panzer Corps seemed to have encountered little resistance thus far, the panzer group ordered the 6th Panzer Division, which at 6 am stood immediately before Welonen with the intention of advancing further to the northeast, to send a detachment towards Rositten in support of the 8th Panzer Division. In the meantime, the 8th Panzer Division did manage an envelopment on the western side of the road. Towards the evening, elements of both divisions established contact near Ciskadi. The enemy had to yield here, and the 6th Panzer Division was also able to gain ground northwest of Rositten. Yet it was the 1st Panzer Division that made the greatest progress. The forward elements of the division had covered a distance of more than 100 kilometres by 3 pm. They drove through Balvi and then thrust a further 20 kilometres towards the northeast. The 36th Motorised Infantry Division, in left echelon formation, advanced through Madona.

Despite strong Russian resistance at the beginning of the day, the progress of the LVI Panzer Corps had been good. Meanwhile, the ground covered by the XXXXI Panzer Corps, especially by the 1st Panzer Division, had been unexpectedly tremendous: the spearhead of the division was only 50 kilometres away from Ostrov! A surprise success could still be achieved here, even though the spearhead was quite weak at that time. Our joy was somewhat limited by the heavy rainfalls, with traffic jams ensuing from the worsening road conditions. The commander of the panzer group felt compelled to point this out in his report to the army group. 'Delays in carrying out movements are inevitable,' he remarked. Bitter disappointment on the part of our leadership would be perfectly understandable if the rain were to suddenly cause the loss of operational mobility! The susceptibility of the Russian roads to ruin by the heavens could not be underestimated! But this did not happen yet. The weather cleared up on the evening of 2 July, and there was no rain on the following couple of days. It was warm, and even rather sultry.

The beautifully sunny day on 3 July saw the panzer group pressing forward on all fronts. There were a few spots where the enemy fought tenaciously. New formations kept appearing, but there was no organised defence. Enemy forces remained strong on the main road, but we were able to isolate them by enveloping them at several points from the west. The 8th Panzer Division was involved in particularly heavy fighting around Rositten, and by 5 pm the city had been taken. On the right, the 3rd Motorised Infantry Division had reached the small town of Ludza, 25 kilometres east-northeast of Rositten, by 9:30 pm. Furthest to the right, the SS-Totenkopf Division made better progress on this day with relatively little effort. The leading group of the division had advanced to the northeast as far as Bukmuiza, 35 kilometres south of Ludza. Enemy resistance had previously been strong here, but it was now broken. The 6th Panzer Division, following its diversion from the northern corps to the area of Rositten, had proceeded further to the north and had reached Karsava by the evening. The town, a vital junction, lay on the main road 35 kilometres northeast of Rositten. Another group of the division was located 18 kilometres further north. It had also approached the main road from the west and had closed in to within a few kilometres. The withdrawal of Russian forces along this road was no longer possible, especially as a battle group of the 1st Panzer Division, on its way to Ostrov from the southwest, had reached a point further north that was only 12 kilometres away from the road. The northern battle group of the division had even managed by the evening to take intact the bridge over the Velikaya near Tishina, 10 kilometres west of Ostrov, and to establish a small bridgehead there. Considering the weakness of the leading elements of our formations, with the muddy roads frequently splitting up our troops, the success of the northern wing of the panzer group on this day was tremendous. We had just crossed the old Russian border here, and the enemy was completely taken by surprise.

The result of 4 July was that the entire front of the panzer group reached the Latvian–Russian border, not to mention the fact that the northern wing was already pushing further beyond. The 1st Panzer Division had been able to infiltrate Ostrov in the evening and take intact the road bridge there over the Velikaya. The railway bridge over the river, approximately three kilometres west of the city, had already fallen into the hands of the division at 5 pm. Latvia was under German control, and the Russian border defence at Ostrov had been penetrated. It was our intention to gather together as many forces here as possible the next day, for the Pskov group would surely be bound to appear soon. Further south, the 6th Panzer Division had yet to achieve a breakthrough. It fought at the border, on both sides of the main road, against a fully developed defensive system that was not to be overcome without good preparation. The division continued to carry out minor assaults throughout the night, primarily exploiting the darkness to bring forward further forces, including heavy artillery. Only after eliminating more than 20 bunkers in a period of 15 hours did the division manage to break through. It was halfway between the border and Ostrov towards noon, and by the late afternoon it had established contact with the 1st Panzer Division. By the evening of 5 July, the Stalin Line had finally been penetrated.

A panzer corps must submit to the demands of the terrain

As soon as Opochka had been stipulated as an operational objective, the headquarters of the panzer group, just by glancing at the map, had immediately been struck by how unfriendly the terrain in the area would be. Only through very careful work were we able to trace three routes, one for each mobile division, heading towards and to either side of Opochka. They were narrow cross-country dirt roads that would lead through extensive marshland beyond the border. A continuous, paved road simply did not exist.

As the divisions of the LVI Panzer Corps reached the border area in the course of 4 July, they were greeted by a scene more terrible than expected. The narrow, twisting roads of the 3rd Motorised Infantry Division (headed towards Opochka) and those of the 8th Panzer Division (in the area of Krasnoi) were littered with abandoned enemy vehicles and artillery. Both divisions had to proceed on foot, clearing away the obstacles that slowed their progress. Yet it was primarily the terrain that slowed our pace to that of the infantry, provided any progress could be made at all through the marsh. The 'distress call' of the LVI Panzer Corps that reached the panzer group on the night of 4/5 July (see the situation report in Appendix 4) required that immediate measures be taken. Ostrov had just been captured on the northern wing, and this was largely because the terrain was far more favourable in the area of the XXXXI Panzer Corps. It is hardly surprising that the emphasis of our plan went in this direction, yet the Opochka area still had to be attended to somehow. It would not be a point of main effort for combat, but it would nevertheless be important from a security perspective. We would probably need to advance to the area around and to the northeast of Novorzhev, at least until the northern wing of the Sixteenth Army caught up. Unfortunately, it seemed as if that could take a while.

The commander of the panzer group set off for the headquarters of the LVI Panzer Corps early on the morning of 5 July. It was his intention to examine the possibilities for the further advance of the corps with its commander, General of the Infantry Erich von Manstein. The prospects of bringing more than one division through marshland in the foreseeable future were not good. The northern wing of the corps, which was headed towards Krasnoi, had the best chance of making some progress. As a result of the meeting, Panzer Group Order No. 9 assigned the corps the following task:

> The LVI Panzer Corps shall use all the means at its disposal to send a unit of divisional strength through Krasnoi to the area northwest of Novorzhev. The bulk of the corps is to stand ready in the vicinity of Ludza–Karsava so that it can set off in the direction of Ostrov early on the morning of 7 July. Those elements of the corps already in the Karsava area are to immediately head northeast along the Gauri–Drikashki road towards Marshino.[6] Objective: to assemble the corps to the east of Ostrov.

This meant that the operational conduct of the corps would change. It would relinquish control of what had so far been its southern attack sector. We had reached an agreement on 4 July with the chief of staff of the army group, Lieutenant-General Brennecke, that this sector would fall within the sphere of influence of the II Corps (of the Sixteenth Army) as soon as possible. Two mobile divisions of the LVI Panzer Corps could thereby remain on the western side of the marshland and proceed northeastwards

---

6 This road lay to the north of the 8th Panzer Division and had been reported by our air reconnaissance as one that could be used. It turned out to be quite unsuitable. All of our troops had to use the main road that led through Ostrov.

through Ostrov. Only one division would go through Krasnoi to the area east of Ostrov. All planned movements on 5 July were checked carefully by the headquarters of the panzer group as well as by that of the corps.

The execution of these movements placed considerable demands on the men and their commanders. The 8th Panzer Division had pushed the furthest, although it was this formation that was now earmarked for an advance through the marshland. Although there was little enemy resistance, the division had to struggle through to Krasnoi over country roads. Much clearance work was required, not to mention many kilometres of log carpets! The leading elements of the division, on foot, reached Krasnoi at 8 pm on 5 July, but the bulk of the division, remounted, could only get going again on 7 July. Meanwhile, the 3rd Motorised Infantry Division, soon to be relieved by parts of the 290th Infantry Division, was to withdraw from the front and march off in the direction of Ostrov. The 290th Infantry Division was still following behind in the central sector of the corps. It was divided into two groups: one had covered a distance of approximately 10 kilometres on the evening of 4 July to reach Bukmuiza; the other was further north in the vicinity of Lake Razna. The SS-Totenkopf Division, to be relieved, as necessary, by the remaining parts of the 290th Infantry Division, was the last mobile division of the LVI Panzer Corps that was, according to the agreed-upon plan, to complete the journey through Ludza, Karsava, and Ostrov. Those of us at the headquarters of the panzer group were thus most astounded when, on the evening of 5 July, we received the news from the corps that the SS-Totenkopf Division would instead be sent southeastwards from Rosenovo towards Sebezh, after which it would go through Opochka and advance towards the north. It was near Rosenovo that the corps had so far faced the strongest enemy resistance. Despite the fact that it had been our intention for the corps to proceed northwards through Ostrov, we now faced a situation in which a whole division would be committed to the southeast, far away from the line of attack of the panzer group. The terrain would be unfavourable and enemy resistance would be fierce.

The opinion at that time at the headquarters of the panzer group regarding the prospects of this unexpected employment of the SS-Totenkopf Division was laid out in a report of ours on 7 July 1941 (see Appendix 4). The panzer corps would surely find itself significantly delayed. It was questionable whether the SS-Totenkopf Division could drive as far as Opochka on its own. As it turned out, Opochka was only taken towards noon on 10 July with the help of the 30th Infantry Division (of the X Corps), which had just arrived from the west. As agreed with the headquarters of the Sixteenth Army, the SS-Totenkopf Division needed to remain in the Opochka area until it was relieved by other forces. This would only take place on 12 July at 2 pm. At that point in time, the LVI Panzer Corps was already fighting 170 kilometres further to the northeast, near Soltsy. The SS-Totenkopf Division was placed directly under the command of the panzer group so as to be available for flank protection if need be, for it seemed as if the arrival of the Sixteenth Army would be further delayed.[7] The division would consequently be unable to accompany the panzer corps in its movement to the northeast. Most unfortunately, the corps was then required to hand over the 290th Infantry Division, now also committed to Sebezh, to the Sixteenth Army. The corps would sorely miss this division later on.

Even by Russian standards, the LVI Panzer Corps had encountered terrain that, due to its impassability, had successfully secured the old Russian frontier in times past against enemy invasion. Our mobile troops could and should have been able to avoid this area. Unfortunately, the operational orders that had been issued could not be changed easily. The commander of the panzer group would have preferred to avoid this terrain from the outset, especially if there might be heavy fighting there. After the unsuitability of the terrain had been discovered through experience, the only possible decision, the only one that was correct, was to move the bulk of the LVI Panzer Corps behind the marshland towards the north. The distance involved was not as significant for the mobile troops as it would have been for the infantry. With maximum performance, the difference in time would have been about three to six hours. Going behind the marshland was safer and provided greater certainty than engaging the enemy in combat near Sebezh and Opochka. The combat prospects for the SS-Totenkopf Division, the only unit heading through Opochka

---

7 See the summary in Appendix 5 on how orders from the OKH influenced the conduct of battle of the Sixteenth Army.

before turning northwards, were not good. Success presupposed an already defeated and demoralised enemy, but we could not make such an assumption in the current situation. The fighting near Sebezh highlighted the unabated determination of the Russians. The commander of the LVI Panzer Corps had found it necessary to send the 290th Infantry Division there, as the SS-Totenkopf Division lacked the fighting capacity for rapid penetration. Although the 290th Infantry Division was now in position to relieve the SS-Totenkopf Division, it then had to remain there because the combat conditions demanded it. Moreover, the 290th Infantry Division was now too far away to rejoin the panzer corps. The result was that the corps suffered the misfortune of losing this division!

The outlook of the panzer group certainly differed somewhat to that of the panzer corps, but our report on the SS-Totenkopf Division clearly demonstrated how varied experiences of combat could still lead to a common understanding of the situation. An opportunity had presented itself which our troops had striven to exploit, in this case the possibility of the capture of Sebezh by the SS-Totenkopf Division. The division had felt certain that it could take the town quickly. The headquarters of the LVI Panzer Corps had become convinced by, and had succumbed to, this opportunity even though it was a significant diversion and the forces available for it were rather weak. The men and their commanders had placed all their hopes in this advance running smoothly. As expected, fierce enemy resistance slowed their progress, but their belief in their ability to succeed had not been crushed. Consequently, the corps headquarters became more and more dependent on hope alone. The division struggled to find a way to leap forward, and the panzer group, which had not been asked or informed about this diversion beforehand, urged it on 6 July to withdraw. Faced with the same demand on the evening of 7 July, the panzer corps portrayed the day's developments so favourably, it was as if it were now simply a case of pursuing a fleeing enemy. The advance towards Opochka via Sebezh therefore continued. Had the SS-Totenkopf Division gone around the western side of the marshland, as had been the original intention of the panzer group, the division could have been to the east of Ostrov three days earlier. Furthermore, the heavy losses near Sebezh and the even heavier losses near Opochka would have been avoided.

CHAPTER 4

The thrust towards the operational objective: Leningrad

The creation of a jump-off point for the operation (Map 6)

As reported by the panzer group to the army group on the evening of 4 July, 'the advance of the 1st Panzer Division had apparently taken the enemy by surprise'. The Russians had expected the advance from Rositten to proceed on or on either side of the major road, not on the smaller roads along which the division actually approached from the west. It was because of this that the division only encountered light resistance to begin with. The swift movement of mobile forces from an unexpected direction had brought success here. This also had an effect on the quantity of captured materiel. The division even seized a train with brand-new tanks.

It was quiet on the night of 5 July in the Ostrov area, but throughout the morning the Russians, with a degree of tank support, counterattacked the bridgehead at several points. These counterattacks increased in number and intensity later on. Particularly powerful were the afternoon attacks from the north. Numerous tanks appeared on the scene here, and Russian artillery fire took on dimensions that we had rarely encountered before. The enemy also threw cavalry into battle. It seemed as if the Pskov group was now sending in all of its forces. Yet the courageous defenders of the 1st Panzer Division managed not only to repel all attacks; they also disabled approximately 100 tanks and gained territory in a strike to the north. The enemy launched one assault after another, and each time he suffered bloody losses. The panzer group reported on the evening of 5 July that it had repelled all Russian assaults and that it had captured 154 tanks and armoured cars (amongst them six of the superheavy Stalin tanks), more than 100 guns of all types, more than 50 motor vehicles, and so on. This included the bulk of the enemy's armoured forces in the vicinity of Ostrov. His tanks literally covered the battlefield to the north of the town, indicating the ruthlessness with which he attempted to retake it. With tank and artillery support, he continued his counterattacks overnight, but made no progress. We were instead able to extend the depth of the bridgehead on the morning of 6 July to eight kilometres. The striking power of the enemy seemed to be broken, although the day would still bring about a number of skirmishes. By the end of the day, the bridgehead was ten kilometres in depth. The 6th Panzer Division had entered the bridgehead and had taken over its eastern sector.

During this fighting, the 36th Motorised Infantry Division protected the left flank of the corps against Russian forces that were constantly applying pressure there. In the next few days, the division was to take two bridges over the Velikaya between Ostrov and Pskov in a surprise strike, although the bulk of the division was to remain west of the river and approach Pskov from the southwest. The task of the 1st and 6th Panzer Divisions was to carry on with the destruction of the Pskov group by pushing northwards from Ostrov. Both the XXXXI Panzer Corps and the panzer group had gained the impression on 6 July that not only the striking power but also the defensive capability of the enemy was ebbing away. It appeared as if we might be able to push on, even without awaiting the arrival of the LVI Panzer Corps, whose divisions had been so significantly delayed by the terrain. The shattered enemy could not under any circumstances be permitted to rebuild his position around Pskov. The Pskov–Ostrov area would be required for the creation of an adequate jump-off point for the final assault on Leningrad.

Both panzer divisions of the XXXXI Panzer Corps therefore set off early on 7 July towards the north and the northeast. The corps had already been assured by the commander of the panzer group on 6 July that the forces of the 3rd Motorised Infantry Division would be entering the Ostrov bridgehead from 7 July. This division was to head east so as to prepare the LVI Panzer Corps for a subsequent advance in the direction of Porkhov. However, until the arrival of the LVI Panzer Corps, the division would be temporarily placed under the command of the XXXXI Panzer Corps. In the face of declining enemy resistance, the right battle group of the 6th Panzer Division reached the road fork in Solotukhina, halfway between Ostrov and Porkhov, in the evening. The left battle group had at the same time reached a position 25 kilometres further west. The 1st Panzer Division had advanced along the road to Pskov and was now less than 20 kilometres away from the city. Meanwhile, the 36th Motorised Infantry Division had been approaching the city from the southwest and had reached a point that was 40 kilometres away. In the east, the leading regiment of the 3rd Motorised Infantry Division arrived near Shestiperova, 30 kilometres east of Ostrov. The other regiment of the division was to follow the 6th Panzer Division from Ostrov towards the northeast on 8 July so that it could then take Porkhov.

On 8 July, the 36th Motorised Infantry Division entered Pskov from the west and occupied the city. Unfortunately, in the western part of the city, the enemy had time to blow up the 200-metre bridge over the Velikaya. On 9 July, the leading elements of the 1st Panzer Division stood approximately 20 kilometres to the east and northeast of Pskov. The 6th Panzer Division fought at a point on the railway line, halfway between Pskov and Porkhov, where the nature of the surrounding terrain was unknown. For the last couple of days, the division had faced tough resistance from the fresh forces of the Russian 3rd Tank Division. It was becoming clearer to our leadership just how significant our losses in personnel and materiel had been thus far. The demands on our combat troops had also been high, for they had already been in action for an uninterrupted two-and-a-half weeks. Our overall impression, though, was that the enemy only intended to delay the advance of the panzer group. Over the course of the last few days, our aerial reconnaissance had observed more enemy traffic heading east and northeast rather than towards the front. There was no indication of any well-prepared defence further back. Nevertheless, we were now entering an unclear, densely wooded, and marsh-filled zone that extended all the way to the outskirts of Leningrad.

Our plans for the conduct of operations

With the rapid and relatively easy success brought about by our convincing exploitation of the element of surprise, the army group now had to make an immediate decision regarding the further conduct of operations. The Stalin Line had been swiftly overcome, giving the enemy no time to organise his defences. Could such rapid progress continue as we neared Leningrad and its large reserve of forces? The terrain would be far less friendly from here on in. Would the panzer group be able to storm ahead on its own? We were about to lose contact with the armies on either side, so we could no longer count on sufficient flank protection. On our left, the Eighteenth Army would most likely head due north on the east side of Lake Peipus for the foreseeable future. On our right, the Sixteenth Army, as demanded by the OKH, had been increasingly engaged in the south.[8] Although its point of main effort was supposed to be on its left, the Sixteenth Army was now in a position where its central and northern sectors were quite weak. Yet it was the right flank of the panzer group that was the most endangered, and it would become more so the further to the north it pivoted, in the direction of Leningrad. The army group wanted to consult with the commander in chief of the army, Field-Marshal Walther von Brauchitsch, who was expected to arrive at the headquarters of the army group on 7 July. It was for this reason that, on the evening of 5 July, the army group requested from the panzer group its appraisal of the situation and an outline of its plans regarding Leningrad. We discussed the matter with the commander of the XXXXI Panzer Corps, General of the Panzer Troops Georg-Hans Reinhardt, before issuing our report to the army group on the evening of 6 July.[9]

In his report, Hoepner voiced his support for a rapid thrust as early as possible. The enemy had thus far demonstrated no orderliness in his movements. After his failure in the vicinity of Ostrov, he seemed to be falling back further to the east and northeast! The panzer group did not even expect any pressure from the enemy to the southeast. We had been

8 See report in Appendix 5.

9 See Appendix 6.

able to take advantage of the fact that the enemy had not yet organised a defence in depth, and our success could continue unabated for as long as he neglected to do so. In Hoepner's view, priority had to be given to rapid action. He even considered it worth renewing the advance without awaiting the complete reassembly of the LVI Panzer Corps. As he stated in his report:

> What is most important for the renewal of the advance of the panzer group in the direction of Leningrad is the assembly of the troops of the XXXXI Panzer Corps. This can be done by 8 July, so the panzer group will be able to begin its advance on 9 July. The XXXXI Panzer Corps shall proceed on and to the west, and initially also to the east, of the main road leading to Leningrad. The LVI Panzer Corps will drive further east towards Porkhov and Yamtesovo in the direction of Novgorod.

In our assessment, enemy resistance at the beginning would only amount to four mobile divisions, and it would not take long for the LVI Panzer Corps to catch up. Given the situation, the point of main effort, as far as one could be spoken of, would initially lie with the XXXXI Panzer Corps on the Pskov–Leningrad road.

On 7 July, towards 1:30 pm, the chief of staff of the army group, Lieutenant-General Kurt Brennecke, informed the panzer group by telephone that Brauchitsch, now at the headquarters of the army group, had declared himself to be in agreement with our plans. The resumption of the offensive from Pskov in the direction of Leningrad was earmarked for 10 July. This was confirmed in a telephone message from the army group at 6 pm. We could well take satisfaction from the fact that everyone had agreed with our view as to how best to continue the advance. The supreme command had even agreed with our assessment of the enemy, and on 8 July we received the official order from the army group for the continuation of the advance on Leningrad.[10] Indeed, this order seemed to be based on an exceptionally favourable evaluation of the prospective conduct of the enemy. Its assessment of what could be achieved and its corresponding assignment of objectives to the panzer

10 See Appendix 7.

group far exceeded what the headquarters of the panzer group regarded as feasible. Specifically, the panzer group was ordered:

> to encircle Leningrad between Lake Ladoga and the Gulf of Kronstadt as tightly as its forces could manage, to guard its own rear against enemy forces east of Lake Ilmen until the arrival of the Sixteenth Army, and to occupy the sector between Narva Bay and Lake Peipus so as to cut off the route of retreat of enemy forces in Estonia.

These seemingly small yet nonetheless demanding objectives would require our forces to cover a vast area. The panzer group could not possibly fulfil such demands. The distance we had yet to travel from Ostrov to reach Leningrad alone was considerable, being about 330 kilometres if going through Pskov and Luga and about 400 kilometres if via Porkhov and Novgorod. The flank that we were supposed to defend along the Volkhov between Lakes Ilmen and Ladoga extended over 200 kilometres, whilst the rear line between Novorzhev and Lake Ilmen would be another 200 kilometres! At best, the infantry units would only just be reaching Novorzhev at the time the mobile units would be ready to commence their raid on Leningrad. We believed that this would be in four days' time. The sector between Lake Peipus and Narva Bay had a width of 70 kilometres. And, on top of all of these secondary tasks, there would be the primary offensive front against Leningrad. Stretching from Chudovo to Narva, this front would be approximately 200 kilometres wide. With just six, already weakened, mobile divisions and one infantry division at our disposal, there was really very little we would be able to pour into this large area!

To detach elements of the panzer group all over the place – towards Novorzhev, the Volkhov, the Narva, and not to mention Leningrad – was out of the question. Our forces would become fragmented and ineffective. The one objective on which the panzer group could focus was the approach towards Leningrad, and it could only do so on roads or in friendly terrain. The two main lines of attack were through Novgorod–Chudovo and Pskov–Luga. This would mean one panzer corps per line of attack, but it was important that they maintain pace with one another. Mutual support between both panzer corps would be impossible if they were too far away from each other. Serious resistance by the enemy had not been taken into account by the army group. It was a mistake to assume that we could overcome Russian tenacity with ease, for we lacked the forces necessary to penetrate his defences. The reserves that we so urgently needed in this situation simply did not exist. We did not have a third panzer corps! It was already apparent that we could not undertake anything other than the advance on Leningrad. Due to shortage of materiel, the security of our right flank consisted of no more than aerial reconnaissance. Yet the army group was of the view that we could take the enemy by surprise. He was supposed to be crushed where he stood. We could not afford to be brought to a halt or to become engaged in static warfare. Russian forces were to be enveloped and eliminated; otherwise, they were to be bypassed. It was the intention of the commander of the panzer group to break through enemy resistance by concentrating the efforts of both corps at the most suitable point. From the outset, it was the main road to Leningrad that seemed to be the most suitable. It offered better opportunities for deployment and possessed less endangered flanks than the route via Novgorod, Chudovo, and the Volkhov River. This river divided the area from enemy terrain further east and would be a natural line of defence for the Russians. It flowed so closely alongside the road there that security forces in the vicinity would be unable to guarantee that the road remained open. Our vital supplies would thereby be endangered along this route.

At least our rear, or the troublesome right flank between Novorzhev and Lake Ilmen, would no longer remain uncovered. The SS-Totenkopf Division was soon to arrive in this sector. However, this division represented only a token reserve, as it would shortly be needed by the LVI Panzer Corps. The division arrived three days later and was initially placed into panzer group reserve. What we really had to await then was the movement of the northern wing of the Sixteenth Army from Opochka to Porkhov. According to the order of the army group, the primary task of the Sixteenth Army was 'the protection of the east flank and of the rear of Panzer Group 4'. Things were to turn out quite differently!

Despite many doubts and the risks involved, Hoepner was of the opinion that the only course for the panzer group to pursue was the one that had been aimed for since the beginning of the campaign – the rapid approach on Leningrad and, perhaps, the attainment of a surprise victory there. Hoepner might have had cause to be hopeful due to the success of his XVI Panzer Corps before Warsaw during the campaign in Poland in 1939. The corps had at that time reached the outskirts of the enemy capital only eight days after the beginning of the campaign. It had been a stunning achievement and had considerably boosted the morale of the troops. Yet the colonel-general now had to struggle hard on 9 July 1941 for his assessment of the situation to be accepted. He was quite concerned about the development of the enemy's position. This is clear from a supplementary directive he issued early on 10 July – the day for the renewal of the offensive! It was an addition to his Panzer Group Order No. 11 of 9 July that, in particular, clarified the enemy situation:

> Despite heavy resistance along the entire front of the panzer group, not to mention some isolated attacks, it is our view that we are facing the last combat-capable Russian units in the area to the east of Pskov and to the southwest of Leningrad. Some of these units have been partly destroyed. It now comes down to achieving a complete breakthrough and driving right up to the gates of Leningrad.

For carrying this out, the commander of the panzer group ordered his corps commanders to concentrate all efforts along the two main lines of advance and 'to charge ahead without regard to the surrounding terrain'. To reduce the breadth of its front, the LVI Panzer Corps was to withdraw the 8th Panzer Division from its current engagement between Krasnoi and Novorzhev and to send it through Ostrov and Porkhov along the main line of advance. Such a narrow and elongated front presented its own dangers, but, for now, this had to be accepted if the breakthrough was to have any chance of success. The die had been cast!

The panzer group begins its advance on Leningrad

Following Hoepner's directive to remain hot on the tail of the enemy and to deny him the chance to regather his forces, the divisions of Panzer Group 4 renewed their advance along the entire front on 10 July. The enemy defended himself with rearguard units. They were once more divisions that we had not previously encountered. Despite a few cases of heavy resistance, especially against the 6th Panzer Division, the panzer group gained the overall impression that the enemy was still falling back. This was verified by a number of aerial reconnaissance reports.

However, from 11 July, it was beginning to become clear that the thrust along the two roads could no longer be carried out with rapidity. We had entered the impenetrable forest terrain, and the XXXXI Panzer Corps had moreover become rather bogged down. It was terrain that favoured the enemy defence, and it was increasingly difficult to bring our superior firepower to bear.[11] What use was our strength if it was rendered ineffective? Placing a second panzer division on the main road to Leningrad would be worthless, for the 1st Panzer Division had as yet been unable to make any significant movement along this road. The division had taken Novoselye on the morning of 11 July, but further progress was slow. It was starting to look as if we might barely advance more than ten kilometres per day from now on. Russian forces retreated further east, with the strongest resistance at that time being against the LVI Panzer Corps. The enemy was far weaker in the area of the 36th Motorised Infantry Division, which was between the main road to Leningrad and the lower reaches of the Luga River. His forces in this area only seemed to be situated on the east bank of Lake Peipus, with the greatest concentration in the vicinity of Gdov.

Not wanting the advance to grind to a halt, the headquarters of the XXXXI Panzer Corps and that of the panzer group deliberated as to whether a change of plan was in order. We could not afford to sacrifice speed, for we were still 180 kilometres away from Leningrad! Awaiting the arrival of the infantry was out of the question, as this would mean at least a 14-day loss of time. I therefore studied our maps thoroughly and, at noon on 11 July, shortly after his return from a visit to the front, I drew Hoepner's attention to the good terrain which lay between Narva and Leningrad on the south bank of the Gulf of Finland and which appeared to offer decent, if not excellent, possibilities for our panzer forces in combat. But how were we to get there given the poor road conditions on the way? The commander of the XXXXI Panzer Corps had also been considering this question, and recommended at some point during a meeting at the command post of the panzer group in the late afternoon of 11 July that an attempt be made to gain territory on the northern side of the lower

11 See the description of the terrain in Appendix 8.

Luga. He did not expect any enemy forces to be found between here and the Luga, and he thought that we would probably also make it through the 20-kilometre forest zone on the northern side of the river, since the enemy would fail to anticipate such a line of thrust. We would then be in open terrain and could overcome even reasonably strong Russian forces in a final drive on Leningrad. What remained uncertain was how best to cover the distance between here and the lower Luga. A solid road was lacking. We would have to scout out the best route. Reinhardt requested immediate freedom of action in order to carry this out.

It was a difficult decision for the commander of the panzer group whether or not to order such a change in our operational plans. We were certain that the old direction no longer promised rapid results, but a couple of considerations counted against the new one. A good road network seemed to be lacking. This would cause our mobile combat troops difficulties, and it would be worse for our heavy supply vehicles, especially if the good weather we had experienced thus far gave way to rainfall! Furthermore, we would be reducing the striking power of our right wing, thereby abandoning the envelopment manoeuvre for which our supreme command, based on their misjudgement of the terrain, still hoped. If the XXXXI Panzer Corps were to head north over the lower Luga, our other panzer corps would have to shift its position accordingly. It would at least need to move onto the main road to Leningrad, but, if at all possible, it could even go behind the XXXXI Panzer Corps. Since the panzer group would have to concentrate its forces in order to strike forward effectively, an advance in the direction of Novgorod would have to be given up. Nonetheless, the commander of the panzer group decided upon the thrust over the lower Luga and granted the commander of the XXXXI Panzer Corps the freedom of action he had requested. All necessary preparations were to be made by the corps immediately. So as to be able to support his decision when he reported it to the army group, Hoepner asked Reinhardt to present to him a written assessment the following morning.[12] He could then show this to the chief of staff of the army group, who had been invited to visit the command post of

12 See the report of the commander of the XXXXI Panzer Corps in Appendix 8.

the panzer group on 12 July. The decision to proceed over the lower Luga had been made.

The XXXXI Panzer Corps turns to the north

At the meeting on 12 July, Hoepner explained to Brennecke the reasons that had led him to change the task to be undertaken by the XXXXI Panzer Corps. The infantry armies had thus far been following in the wake of the panzer group, which was, so to speak, the vanguard of the army group. Given the developments of the last couple of days, should the proposed change be pursued, or would the status quo simply remain in effect? Would we just have to stop and await the arrival of the infantry? That would mean a loss of time for us and a corresponding gain of time for the enemy. As a result of our detailed discussion with Reinhardt the previous day, we were convinced that we were still in a position from which we could break through the enemy front and, without the infantry, thrust as far as Leningrad. This was of course dependent on favourable terrain and on the enemy being taken by surprise. Such conditions, argued Hoepner, no longer prevailed on the main road to Leningrad. In the direction of Novgorod, resistance would be greater and the threat to our right flank would be considerable. It was there that we expected the most powerful enemy presence. We could not simply bypass the forces there, and the panzer group was not in the position to fight its way through them. Finally, Hoepner emphasised the necessity of freedom of action for the panzer group in its own zone of operations. Brennecke asserted that the commander of the army group was in substantial agreement with Hoepner's view.[13]

The fighting of 12 July confirmed the impression harboured by the 1st Panzer Division that the point of main effort of the enemy lay on the main road. Engaged in fierce forest fighting, the division ploughed slowly through the undergrowth beyond the road fork in Nikolayevo. By the end of the day, the division had advanced approximately ten kilometres. An envelopment group of the division had peeled off to the

13 This is according to a note in the war diary of the panzer group on 12 July 1941.

left and had taken Plyussa by 4 pm, after which it proceeded a few more kilometres in the direction of Zapolye. The village, which lay amidst extensive marshland, was seized on 13 July. Immediately to the north sat the enemy behind a firm defensive line. Further progress in this direction could only be promised by a powerful attack. The XXXXI Panzer Corps possessed neither the strength nor the intention to do this. It had already started to turn to the left so as to approach the lower Luga. The 1st Panzer Division was to be relieved in Zapolye by the 269th Infantry Division so that it could, with artillery support, continue its advance. The corps saw to it that the rather slow infantry division was brought as close as possible to the front with the temporary help of motorised transport vehicles. It was the excellent organisation of the panzer corps, the good cooperation between it and the 269th Infantry Division, and the extraordinary push of the infantry division that enabled the bulk of the 1st Panzer Division to be released in the course of 14 July. The 269th Infantry Division assumed responsibility for the occupation of Zapolye on the same day. The mobile troops of the panzer corps could now set their sights on the lower Luga.

The XXXXI Panzer Corps, led by reinforced reconnaissance units, had started to veer to the left early on the morning of 12 July. Where possible, the other combat units of the corps also set off. The 36th Motorised Infantry Division was already in the area and, providing flank protection on the left, had commenced its advance to the northwest in the direction of Gdov. The 6th Panzer Division, no longer required south of the main road due not only to the arrival there of the LVI Panzer Corps but also to the northeastward retreat of enemy units that had previously been located in Yamkino, was split into two groups and sent to the north as far as the main road. Beginning on the morning of 13 July, the division was to cross the road and proceed further north on the left-hand side of the 1st Panzer Division. The precise details as to the route to be taken would depend upon what was revealed by our reconnaissance units on 12 July.

All units were underway on 13 July. The advance of the corps was led by three spearheads: on the right were the initially weak elements of the 1st Panzer Division, in the middle was the 6th Panzer Division, and on the left was the 36th Motorised Infantry Division. By the evening, these spearheads had advanced to the north as far as the heights of Gdov. The 6th Panzer Division thrust through territory that was only sparsely occupied by the enemy and reached a point 20 kilometres beyond Lyady. Our impression that the enemy would not foresee an advance in this direction and that his forces would only be concentrated on the main roads had been confirmed. Only on the east bank of Lake Peipus did there seem to be a strong enemy presence, and the 58th Infantry Division of the XXXVIII Corps (Eighteenth Army) was already on its way there to deal with them. It looked as if we were going to succeed!

What was the view of the army group at that time? A telephone conversation between Leeb and Hoepner on the morning of 13 July indicated that the field-marshal had not expected so rapid an advance by the panzer group.[14] He was astounded, but also most pleased. He agreed to the envelopment manoeuvre of the XXXXI Panzer Corps over the lower Luga and emphasised the necessity of finding the weak point of the enemy. There was, however, one aspect of this evasion of strong enemy forces that caused him some concern, and that was the vulnerability of the right flank of the panzer group. He was worried that the Sixteenth Army would be stretched too thin and that, as a result, the gap between it and the right flank of the panzer group would become too wide. His fears regarding this gap led to a new Army Group Order on 15 July. It made clear that the Sixteenth Army needed to be committed further south and that the ever-greater gap would need to be filled at a later stage by the X Corps. The army group found itself in a dilemma here, as its northern wing still needed to be supported. After all, it was in the north that our operational objective lay.

We at the headquarters of Panzer Group 4 were unable to understand why the Sixteenth Army needed to be committed to the south, especially since the army group order also emphasised that the point of main effort was in the north. We did not have the impression at that time that the army group regarded the advance as hopeless or as something that needed to be abandoned. The measures we took were still well coordinated with the army group. The problem was that the infantry,

14 See the discussion of the situation in Appendix 9.

even that of the Eighteenth Army, was making disappointingly slow progress. We had been counting on their support, but this had yet to emerge in any effective form. We had no news on what the Sixteenth Army was up to. Our hopes that the appearance of the infantry would coincide with our approach on the lower Luga had been dashed. It was possible that their absence would be enough to endanger our final push on Leningrad. The headquarters of the panzer group therefore came up with the idea of asking the army group to shift the I Corps from its current position at the rear of the Eighteenth Army to a new one on our right wing, in the vicinity of Porkhov and Dno. This was of great importance given that the 290th Infantry Division, which had originally been earmarked for the protection of our right flank, was no longer at our disposal.

The XXXXI Panzer Corps had already set off on 13 July, and we had now done as much as we could with regard to the gap to its right. The 6th Panzer Division continued its rapid advance on 14 July, covering a distance of 70 kilometres and reaching the Luga in the vicinity of Porechye. Both bridges there were taken intact, and a small bridgehead, approximately three kilometres in depth, was established that evening on the north bank. Further to the southeast, the leading elements of the 1st Panzer Division arrived at the river near Sabsk. They found the bridge there in ruins, but still managed to cross the river and form a bridgehead on 15 July. Russian forces in the area were weak. It was quite clear that they had been taken by surprise, and only from 15 July did they start to receive reinforcements. We could assume that the enemy would somehow bring everything he had to this endangered position, so the springboard we had created would have to be exploited without delay. A few days would be necessary to assemble our forces, to repair the sole supply route that led from the main road through Strugi Krasnye and Lyady, and to top up our provisions. The panzer corps hoped to be able to resume the advance on 20 July.

Any concern about our left flank, where Lake Peipus lay, gradually faded away thanks to the passage of the 58th Infantry Division through Pskov on 14 July. The division took Gdov on 18 July with the assistance of elements of the 36th Motorised Infantry Division from the east and northeast. The XXXVIII Corps had advanced further towards Narva so as to be able to cut off Russian forces retreating before the Eighteenth Army in Estonia. Even so, Hoepner urged the army group to send one of the divisions of the corps, the 1st Infantry Division, in a more north-easterly direction so that it could approach the Porechye bridgehead.

The thrust in the direction of Novgorod stops dead

After the capture of Porkhov on 11 July at 1 am, the 3rd Motorised Infantry Division continued its advance further to the northeast towards Borovichi. On the outskirts of the town, a reinforced regimental group had to be formed to defend the eastern and southern flanks against enemy forces that would begin to apply constant pressure over the course of the next few days. Once in Borovichi, the 3rd Motorised Infantry Division was to turn in the direction of Malaya Utorgosh and Utorgosh, leaving the main route of advance open for the 8th Panzer Division. The latter reached the front on 12 July, and in one swift movement it was in the Sitnya sector, 20 kilometres west of Soltsy. For the 3rd Motorised Infantry Division, however, there were significant delays, for it had to proceed through extensive woodland on roads that were in poor condition. The skilful fighting of the enemy had also contributed to such delays. Fresh enemy forces had appeared in the area, and there were in addition parts of the Russian 3rd Tank Division that had evaded the 6th Panzer Division by moving from Yamkino to the northeast. The LVI Panzer Corps had only a very narrow front at the moment, as both of its divisions drove forward with one formation each. To the south of the Shelon River, for example, none of our forces were to be found. Our troops were sticking together along the main line of advance. The gap yawned wider and wider, but we expected that the X Corps would soon arrive there. Until that time, at least a few elements of the SS-Totenkopf Division would need to be committed there. This would be possible given that the division was no longer required near Opochka. The leading regiment of the division was also assigned the task of relieving those units of the 3rd Motorised Infantry Division that were still pinned down near Porkhov.

Towards noon on 13 July, shortly before the planned continuation of our advance, the enemy carried out an attack against the forward group of the 8th Panzer Division. He achieved some success, but was quickly repelled. The division counterattacked the retreating enemy forces, taking them by surprise and smashing most of them to pieces. A considerable quantity of materiel fell into our hands in the process. The division pushed further, entering and capturing the city of Soltsy. Meanwhile, the advance of the 3rd Motorised Infantry Division on this day became ever slower. By the evening, it trailed the 8th Panzer Division by approximately 20 kilometres. The enemy forces scattered throughout the impenetrable woodland had been thrown back, but there was still very little progress. The northern battle group of the 3rd Motorised Infantry Division was able to reach the Nikolayevo–Utorgosh road immediately to the southwest of Malaya Utorgosh, but it did not quite manage to seize the village itself. Positioned here and further west along the road were strong Russian forces, and although the division became embroiled in heavy fighting with these forces over the course of the next few days, it was unable to gain further ground. The units of the division still near Porkhov were only free again later on 14 July, for the Russians had carried out heavy attacks throughout 13 and 14 July in an attempt to retake the town. The SS-Totenkopf Division assumed command of the area on 14 July.

Early on the morning of 14 July, the 8th Panzer Division set off towards the Mshaga sector, 12 kilometres to the east of Soltsy, with the intention of seizing the crossing over the river. The division pressed forward through fierce resistance, destroying several enemy tanks and guns. It reached a point very close to the river, but it would no longer be possible to take the bridge there intact. Our forces were now spread out and simply too weak; the enemy, on the other hand, had concentrated his troops in a number of well-prepared emplacements. He also had a vast quantity of artillery at his disposal. Road and rail transport from Leningrad allowed the enemy to further reinforce his position. Similarly strong Russian forces were observed to the south of the Shelon River (south of Soltsy and in the vicinity of Dno), so we could expect him to carry out countermeasures here. Earmarked for panzer group reserve was the second regiment of the SS-Totenkopf Division, which from noon on 15 July was to be brought forward to Borovichi via Porkhov. Meanwhile, the army group had made the decision to send the I Corps (with the 11th and 21st Infantry Divisions) to Porkhov rather than through Pskov. The corps was temporarily placed under the command of the panzer group, for it was to cross our own line of advance (Ostrov and Pskov) in its eastward march on the night of 14/15 July. This meant that we would finally have infantry support on our right wing. This was all the more important given that it had been necessary for the Sixteenth Army to pivot the northern wing of the X Corps (the 126th Infantry Division) to the southeast in the course of 14 July. This 'delay for a few days' lasted until 22 July. Only then did the divisions of the X Corps appear in the vicinity to the south of Porkhov.

There was already cause for concern on the evening of 14 July. The 8th Panzer Division had thrust along the Soltsy–Mshaga road into terrain that was heavily occupied by the enemy and had been brought to a standstill. Only the road was under our control. The Russian forces on either side had not yet been pushed back. Any sort of enemy action over the Shelon from the south would be particularly unpleasant due to the fact that the road mostly ran along the north bank of the river. Almost the whole road could be observed from the south bank, and it was along this same road that our entire supply was conveyed. The distance from Borovichi to the spearhead of the 8th Panzer Division amounted to at least 60 kilometres. The situation of the division would be unenviable should enemy activity intensify! This was precisely what eventuated. On 15 July, shortly before 3:30 am, the panzer group received a message from the LVI Panzer Corps:

> Rear units of the 8th Panzer Division near Opoka (three kilometres east of Borovichi) have come under enemy machine-gun and mortar fire. Parts of the Scheller section are being committed here just in case the tanks being sent back cannot stabilise the situation on their own.

Precisely from where the attack came remained unclear at first. It was assumed at the headquarters of the panzer group that it was coming from over the river, and this was confirmed later on. The division temporarily lost contact with the corps, as could be expected in a situation like this. For some time, there was no news from the division whatsoever. We only received repeated messages in the next few hours from the headquarters of the LVI Panzer Corps: first for the dispatch of a regiment of the SS-Totenkopf Division, then for the dispatch of the whole division, and after that for an advance of forces from Porkhov towards the east.

At the same time, the 8th Panzer Division was under attack from the north in the area near and to the east of Soltsy. The enemy also crossed the Shelon from the south, and he succeeded in infiltrating the town. Communications within the division were thereby interrupted. Since no forces could be brought forward from the rear to rectify the situation, and since the supply of munitions could not be guaranteed, the division was pulled back to the west of Soltsy. After an orderly retreat, the division adopted a defensive position. A small reversal like this could always be expected in mobile warfare, and the division overcame this one in an exemplary manner. A reinforced regiment of the SS-Totenkopf Division had arrived near Borovichi, and on the night of 15/16 July it repelled additional Russian forces that attempted to cross the river. There were nevertheless some Russian tanks that had appeared on the northern side of the river, and on the southern side the enemy remained strong. The commander of the panzer group believed that we would be in a position to carry out countermeasures should the army group agree to place the I Corps at our disposal, for we would then be able to send this corps through Dno to Soltsy and further beyond. Hoepner therefore made his request to the army group. The assessment of the situation by the panzer group on the evening of 15 July was that the LVI Panzer Corps was confronted by such strong enemy forces that even the Mshaga sector would not be within our reach. The 3rd Motorised Infantry Division had made no progress on this day, and several Russian counterattacks had to be repelled. Strong reinforcements would be required for the continuation of the advance; it would otherwise be doubtful whether the LVI Panzer Corps could get anywhere near the lower Luga.

Looking back on the period of rapid advance

It was clear on the evening of 15 July that the rapid breakthrough on the two main roads that had been envisioned on 10 July had not come to pass. Only gradual progress was being made on the road towards Luga. Given that the terrain would remain quite unfavourable here, no increase in the speed of our advance could be expected. Yet the attack would have to be continued, for we would be unable to do without such an important supply road in the long run. In the sector of the LVI Panzer Corps, particularly strong enemy forces had been encountered. It was because of this that, despite the hopes of the commander of the panzer group, the line of advance that had been taken by the corps could no longer be regarded as one that could be executed with rapidity. There were also significant difficulties of supply in this direction. The one success that we had achieved had been that of reaching the lower Luga, so it was here, bearing in mind also the better terrain, that we had the best prospects of being able to approach Leningrad quickly. We had to exploit this opportunity by concentrating as many of the mobile forces of the panzer group as possible.

Unfortunately, the situation developed in such a way that prevented this from being carried out as quickly or on as large a scale as had been intended by the commander of the panzer group. This day, 15 July, had to be regarded as the end of the period of rapid advance on Leningrad for Panzer Group 4. Up until the middle of July, the mobile divisions of the panzer group had stormed forward uninterrupted and had reached a point just a little more than 100 kilometres away from their operational objective: Leningrad. After a short stop, they were ready to renew the advance on 20 July. A distance of 750 kilometres, from the East Prussian border to the Luga near Porechye, had been overcome in 23 days. This corresponded to a daily average of 32.5 kilometres. Although aided by the poor initial deployment of enemy troops, the performance of the panzer group had been marvellous. The diagram on the next page illustrates the distance covered by the panzer group over time. Enemy resistance had been crushed everywhere. If delays occurred, they were due not so much to the enemy but rather to the terrain and to the dependence on our ever-lengthening supply lines. Our successes can only be described as extraordinary. Almost without exception, these successes were achieved thanks to the element of surprise and the ability of our mobile troops to manoeuvre swiftly and decisively. Also advantageous for us was the scattered deployment of the enemy's forces, enabling us to deal him one blow after another. Only in this manner had the relatively weak forces of Panzer Group 4 managed to strike into the vicinity of Leningrad. It should not be assumed that the materiel at our disposal had ever at any

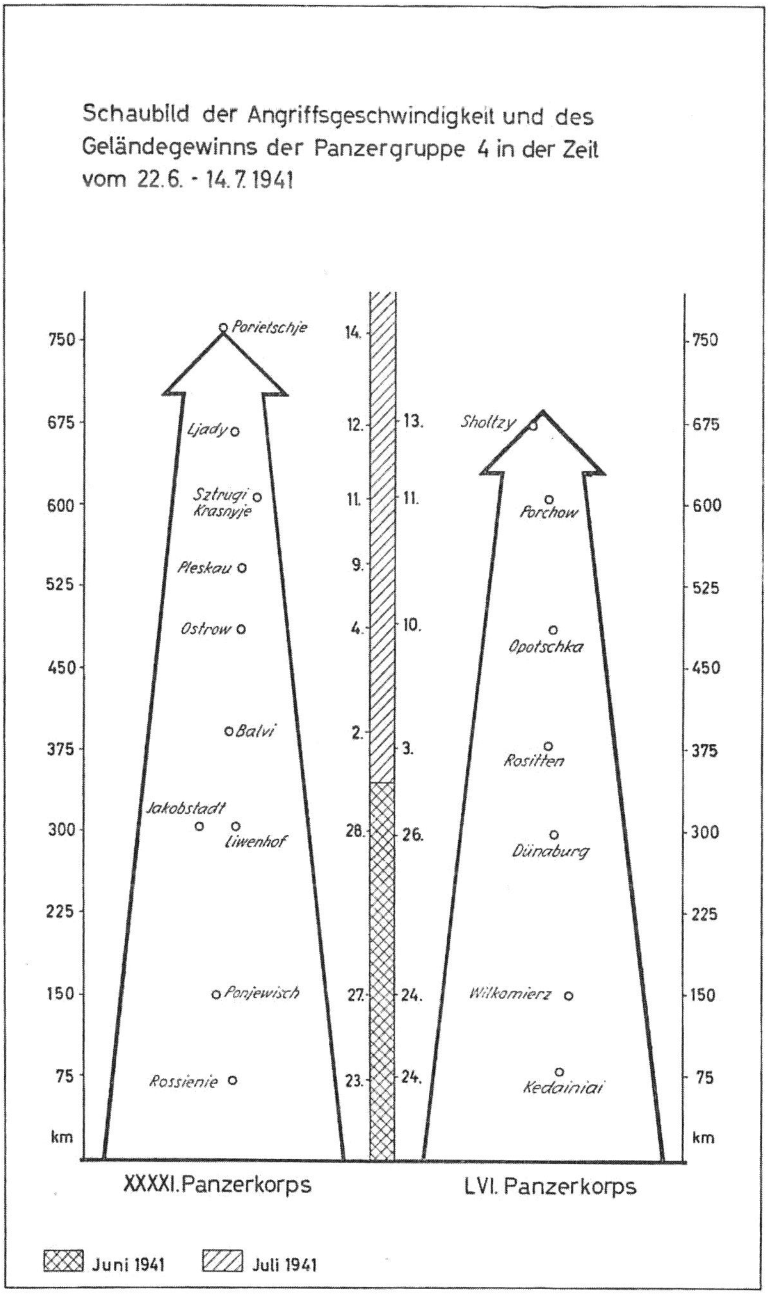

Diagram showing the rate of the advance of the XXXXI Panzer Corps and of the LVI Panzer Corps

stage been sufficient. Indecision and lack of unity of leadership on the Russian side very much worked in our favour.

The speed of our advance should not obscure the fact that we had to fight tooth and nail for our victories. The tenacity of the Russian soldier in defence became apparent very early on. Yet it can be said that we benefitted from superiority in tactical leadership in mobile warfare. Our losses during this period of rapid advance were bearable enough for us so that, in the middle of July 1941, our mobile divisions still possessed considerable striking power. What became much more noticeable at this time were the signs of fatigue in our troops.

The losses suffered by the six mobile divisions of the panzer group between 22 June and 16 July 1941 were as follows:

killed	2,025, including 150 officers
wounded	6,450, including 280 officers
missing in action	315, including 6 officers
total	8,790, including 436 officers

We had been unable to replace our losses during this period. Replacement transports had not yet been sent from the Fatherland. It was envisioned that the divisions would receive some troops from their replacement training battalions, but they had yet to arrive.

CHAPTER 5

The panzer group is brought to a halt

The intentions of Panzer Group 4 for the renewal of the advance

With the establishment of a couple of bridgeheads over the lower Luga, there were still good prospects of being able to carry out a rapid thrust on Leningrad. The XXXXI Panzer Corps stood here in readiness and in its entirety, for the 269th Infantry Division had relieved the 1st Panzer Division at Zapolye. However, the corps would be too weak to be able to overcome the 100-kilometre distance to Leningrad on its own. The commander of the panzer group would have to make every effort to ensure, if possible, that the entire LVI Panzer Corps also partook in the advance. It would need to do so either directly, by following the XXXXI Panzer Corps, or indirectly, by pushing further on Luga. We would be able to make such efforts in the next few weeks. This would include the security and the relief of both flanks, as the I Corps was due to arrive on our right and the XXXVIII Corps on our left. In a discussion by telephone with Field-Marshal von Leeb at 1 am on 15 July, Hoepner requested that the I Corps be sent to Porkhov. The field-marshal approved this. According to a note made at the time of the telephone conversation, Hoepner also reported his appraisal of the situation and his intentions regarding what to do next:

> The situation at the moment is such that the XXXXI Panzer Corps is leading the thrust on Leningrad whilst the LVI Panzer Corps is simply protecting the right flank. The LVI Panzer Corps must, however, advance on Leningrad together with the XXXXI Panzer Corps.

In other words, everything was to be sent to the point of main effort with the goal of carrying out a major thrust! That this was already very much on Hoepner's mind on 15 July is highlighted by the multiple requests he made on this critical day for the SS-Totenkopf Division to be placed under the command of the LVI Panzer Corps. His requests were repeatedly rejected. The position of the corps was difficult, and the situation reports and the inevitable rumours at that time (the afternoon of 15 July) made the position seem even more unfavourable. Yet Colonel-General Hoepner insisted quite explicitly that the regimental group of the SS-Totenkopf Division near Borovichi should be subordinated to the corps, if only temporarily. After the relief of another one of its regiments near Porkhov by the I Corps, the entire division would be available for panzer group reserve. The division could well be employed on the right, but it would be put to even better use if it were to be positioned on the left, behind the XXXXI Panzer Corps. It had already been assigned the task of conducting road reconnaissance in this direction and of repairing a couple of bridge sites at Yamkino.

On 15 July, it looked as if the thrust on Leningrad would be able to start again by 20/22 July, provided the supply road via Strugi Krasnye and Lyady could be used. Log carpets were required for long stretches of this road, so the bulk of the road-construction forces of the panzer group were hard at work there. It was absolutely necessary that our combat troops be fully supplied again. The I Corps would be in the vicinity of Porkhov by 17 July, and the panzer group continued its efforts to arrange to have the 1st Panzer Division of the XXXVIII Corps reinforce the Porechye bridgehead, as it was from this position that we planned to advance further north and northwest. It was also imperative that we proceed with the attack on Luga. Because of the terrain in this direction, infantry would be most suited to this attack. Yet there were none available, or at least not anytime soon, so elements of the LVI Panzer Corps had to be committed here. As for Novgorod, the commander of the panzer group had no intention of tying down our mobile forces in this direction. And where was Panzer Group 3, which was supposed to be cooperating with us in the thrust on Leningrad?

Hoepner had been preoccupied on 11 July with the question of a 'point of main effort on the right', for this was an operational requirement that had been laid out by the high command for the battle for Leningrad. At that time, Hoepner had decided to pivot the panzer group towards the lower Luga. Now, on 15 July, this question was once more on his mind. It was one that he did not regard as promising. The available forces were simply insufficient. Rather, the success that had been achieved on the lower Luga now had to be exploited with all the forces that could be mustered. Our mobile forces would be most effective there; they would not be in the terrain southeast of Leningrad.

A change in the point of view of the army group

Until 14 July, the commander of the army group had supported the outlook and plans of the panzer group. He had even agreed with the probing of what he called the 'weak point' along the lower Luga, despite the emphasis that the OKH had placed on the 'point of main effort on the right' in its directive to the army group on 9 July. However, a change occurred on 15 July. Some researchers (although none from Panzer Group 4!) have since attributed this change to the influence of the OKH.[15] Evidence of this change can be found in the army group order of 15 July.[16] Enemy resistance was now regarded as a 'united front'. The OKH had advised that a reorganisation of the main command of the Russian armed forces had taken place a few days previously. The result of this was that the enemy was less likely to conduct withdrawals from now on. The OKH therefore had doubts about an advance by Panzer Group 4 on its own. It would no longer be possible to proceed without the infantry; their arrival would have to be awaited. The new restraint on behalf of the army group was particularly apparent in the third paragraph of its order. The left wing of the panzer group was to hold back. This was where the Luga bridgeheads were located, the one area where the panzer group had attained success! The next topic in the order was that of the 'point of main effort on the right'. This came as a surprise to the panzer group, as our intention of advancing on the left with the LVI Panzer Corps was well known to the army group. A clear change was the task that was now assigned to the

15 See also the discussion on this in Chapter 8.
16 See Appendix 10.

Sixteenth Army. It was to coordinate its efforts with the northern wing of Panzer Group 3. Its commitment to the right (i.e. to Army Group Centre) would become stronger and would compete with the desire of Panzer Group 4, which had until this point enjoyed the support of Army Group North in its outlook, to advance from the lower Luga towards Leningrad, which was after all the operational objective of Army Group North! The previous task of the Sixteenth Army, that of providing important flank protection for the panzer group, was addressed in the order as follows: 'The ultimate goal of the forces of the Sixteenth Army will remain the same.' Even so, this meant that the flank protection we needed would be postponed. The army group promised the I Corps as a temporary measure.

It was not obvious to the panzer group at the time that there had been a change in the point of view of the army group. It could not be easily seen from the way in which the order was formulated. The focus of the panzer group was firmly on the lower Luga. We felt that there would only be a small delay, and we hoped that the I Corps would prove effective during the temporary diversion of the Sixteenth Army. We had of our own accord requested that this corps be sent to us! The army group order did not mention that we had to wait for the arrival of the infantry armies. The panzer group still expected that it would be able to resume its advance at any moment. Hoepner described in great detail his opinion and the developments that had led to the current situation to Hitler's Wehrmacht adjutant, Colonel Rudolf Schmundt, during the latter's visit to the command post of the panzer group on the afternoon of 15 July. Hoepner hoped that this would make the hard facts and the existing opportunities known to the supreme command and that, as a result, there would be no more wishful thinking.

The army group wishes to tread more carefully

Leeb visited the command post of the panzer group on the afternoon of 16 July. The field-marshal took the opportunity to elaborate on his order of 15 July. Although Hoepner outlined his intentions, among other things the plan of resuming the advance from the lower Luga from around 20 July, Leeb simply pointed out that, as a result of the urgently executed rotation of the left wing of the Sixteenth Army towards the southeast, a wide and open flank had come into being in the northern sector of the army group. The withdrawal of the 8th Panzer Division, Leeb added, was therefore of no harm to us. The panzer group had to refrain from making any major leaps forward for the time being. The I Corps had yet to arrive, and the gradual repositioning of elements of the Sixteenth Army would also require some time. A hasty advance by the LVI Panzer Corps on the left would increase the vulnerability of the flank. It was thus best to stay put for now! He then spoke of the future zones of responsibility of the formations of the army group. There were two possibilities. The sector between Lakes Ilmen and Peipus could be divided, or it could just be left under the control of the panzer group, with the Sixteenth Army on the right and the Eighteenth Army on the left. The field-marshal preferred the latter.

Not at any stage did the field-marshal mention the 'point of main effort on the right' as a task for the panzer group. He did not object to the thrust planned by the panzer group from the lower Luga; he simply deemed it necessary to decelerate the shift of the LVI Panzer Corps to the left. He had no thoughts of giving up the Luga bridgeheads or of regrouping part or all of the XXXXI Panzer Corps on the right wing in the direction of Novgorod. Such thoughts, as will be seen, only arose later from the OKH. The hesitant acceptance by the army group of the wishes of the OKH regarding the 'point of main effort on the right' indicates that the field-marshal still agreed with the combat intentions of the panzer group. He perhaps even hoped that success on the lower Luga in the direction of Leningrad would allow him to push aside the rather unpromising idea of a 'point of main effort on the right'. When he spoke more clearly of the wishes of the OKH at a later stage, he did not seem to be particularly convinced. For this reason, he sought and finally found another solution which, although it did not make sense to the panzer group at the time, provided some context to his remarks on the future zones of responsibility.

The fighting up until 25 July 1941

The first effect of the increasing restraint on the part of the army group was that the planned northward advance of the LVI Panzer Corps became dependent on a satisfactory development of the situation on the southern flank. That meant that the enemy to the south of the Shelon had to be removed by the I Corps and that, as was soon demanded by the army group, the Russian forces facing the LVI Panzer Corps had to be thrown back behind the Mshaga sector. Only then might the panzer corps be permitted to regroup in the north. The renewal of the advance from the Luga bridgeheads was therefore delayed, but the army group still reserved for itself the decision as to whether or not this advance would go ahead. We can thus see how the different points of view between the army group and the panzer group were playing out. In any case, the intervention of the I Corps had to be awaited, and on 16 July it was placed under the command of the panzer group.

In accordance with the task that had to be carried out by the panzer group, the I Corps, with the 21st Infantry Division on the right and the 11th Infantry Division on the left, was to proceed on both sides of the railway line from Porkhov through Dno and Morina so that it could then turn to the northeast to strike over the Shelon on either side of Soltsy. The corps would then advance further in the direction of Novgorod. The right flank to the southeast had to be made secure, so parts of the SS-Totenkopf Division on the southern and eastern sides of Porkhov were relieved on the night of 16/17 July, after which the 21st Infantry Division gained some space by carrying out a minor attack to the south. The I Corps was then able to commence its push to the east at 3 pm on 17 July. Enemy resistance was strong at first, but both divisions, especially the 21st Infantry Division, soon made good progress. There were even a few spots where the enemy seemed to have been taken by surprise. The 21st Infantry Division was already fighting to the south of Dno at noon on 18 July, although it was immediately faced with a strong Russian armoured counterattack that had to be repelled. Dno itself was taken early on 19 July by the 11th Infantry Division, which was then to turn to the northeast and approach the Shelon upstream from Soltsy. The leading elements of the division approached the river and, by the evening, were approximately eight kilometres away from Ryelbitsy. They crossed paths with Russian columns fleeing from west to east and badly mauled them. The 21st Infantry Division had on the same day arrived at a point about halfway between Dno and Morina, but had unfortunately been compelled to detach several security units to cover the ever-lengthening right flank. The corps had nevertheless made good headway and had forced numerically superior Russian forces to give ground. Many prisoners and much materiel were taken. On 20 July, following the seizure of Morina, the 21st Infantry Division also pivoted to the northeast. It was to approach the Shelon downstream from Soltsy. On the same day, the 11th Infantry Division created two small bridgeheads over the river near Ryelbitsy. These merged into one large bridgehead on 21 July, and by noon even a bridge had been constructed.

From 20 July, the SS-Totenkopf Division took a hand in the action along the north bank of the river. It was placed at the disposal of the LVI Panzer Corps so that it could release the 8th Panzer Division, which was due for a short period of rest. The SS-Totenkopf Division assumed its position on the frontline on the night of 18/19 July. The 3rd Motorised Infantry Division stood directly alongside from 21 July. The objective of the now united attack of the I Corps and the LVI Panzer Corps was to take the Mshaga sector, which was to serve as the springboard for the further advance on Novgorod. After the 21st Infantry Division, on the right flank, managed to cross the Shelon downstream from Soltsy on 22 July, with Soltsy itself being taken on the same day by the 11th Infantry Division, the attack by both corps got going. The advance reached a point approximately six kilometres away from the Mshaga sector by the evening of 24 July. On the northern wing, the 3rd Motorised Infantry Division took Utorgosh on 23 July and thrust further north along the road leading to Luga. Some of our forces even arrived at a point just ten kilometres away from Luga, but they had to be withdrawn due to the overwhelming numerical superiority of the enemy. It was a fleeting success that, with our lack of forces, was unable to be exploited. Wherever we now encountered the enemy, he was simply too powerful.

This was also the case to the south of the Shelon, where the I Corps had been managing with meagre security forces. From 22 July, it had come under increasing enemy pressure from the southeast and had to be withdrawn ever further to the northwest and thus ever nearer to the bridgeheads. On the afternoon of 24 July, our forces near Ryelbitsy had to retreat to the north bank, and we had to do away with the bridgehead there so as to hinder the enemy's pursuit. The danger to our right wing did not last for long, though, for the divisions of the X Corps had finally reached the combat zone. On the evening of 24 July, the spearhead of the 30th Infantry Division stood immediately before Morina, whilst the 126th Infantry Division had reached Dno. A regiment from the latter neared Ryelbitsy from the south.

On the main road leading to Luga, the reinforced 269th Infantry Division had been exposed to strong enemy countermeasures since 18 July. Plyussa was lost on 19 July, although elements of the 1st Panzer Division and 36th Motorised Infantry Division were able to retake the town on 20 July. The fighting subsided here after that. Yet without further reinforcements, the prospects of pushing through the woodland terrain as far as Luga were quite poor. In the view of the commander of the panzer group, the LVI Panzer Corps ought to take over the attack in this area. The 269th Infantry Division was therefore subordinated to the LVI Panzer Corps. The idea behind this measure was to relieve the XXXXI Panzer Corps so that it could devote its attention to preparing for the resumption of the advance from the Luga bridgeheads.

An approximately 80-kilometre gap existed between the main front of the XXXXI Panzer Corps (the Luga bridgeheads) and the 269th Infantry Division. Nothing stood in or behind this gap. The 36th Infantry Division would be sent to the vicinity southeast of Osmino only after it had completed its task of combing through the area between the panzer group and the XXXVIII Corps. Although the supply road ran past quite closely behind the bridgeheads, the risk posed by this gap so close to Leningrad had to be accepted. We lacked the forces needed to plug it at that moment.

The Luga bridgeheads had been established and seemed, at first, to provide a good base from which we could thrust onward. The enemy hardly had anything there to begin with, but he soon hurled into the area whatever he could somehow find. There were officer cadets from Leningrad, a proletarian division, and then even more units. From 18 July, transport trains ran with such relentless frequency along the Krasnogvardeysk–Narva railway line that each would have been within sight of the next. Our long-range fire and occasional air raids barely had any effect on them. In contrast, the Russian air force was far more active, operating from a number of airfields that lay nearby. Russian aircraft were playing the main role in the enemy defence on the lower Luga. They attacked incessantly from 15 July, causing our combat troops heavy losses and our roads significant damage. Russian tanks appeared on the scene on 16 July. Enemy artillery was noticeably reinforced over the next few days, with both of the bridges over the river at Porechye coming under heavy fire. The bridges were hit multiple times and constantly had to be repaired. Strong enemy counterattacks were launched from 20 July, which, due to the small size of the bridgeheads, caused us excessively high losses. We would have to go on the offensive soon if we wanted the advantage we had attained to pay off. Staying put in our current position would be costly. The XXXXI Panzer Corps and the panzer group pointed out this fact quite clearly to the army group. We recommended 25 July, and after that 27 July, as the deadline for the renewal of the advance, but the army group was not yet ready.

Further west, extending to Lake Peipus, the situation had become more secure thanks to the arrival of the XXXVIII Corps. The 36th Motorised Infantry Division could be pulled out from there and sent to take over the protection of the northern part of the gap between the Luga bridgeheads and the 269th Infantry Division. To ensure unity in the conduct of operations in this zone, the XXXVIII Corps was placed under the command of the panzer group from the evening of 18 July. Its 58th Infantry Division secured the Narva River, towards the west, from 19/20 July with four battalions. The division arrived there just in time. Four Russian bridgeheads were in the process of being established over the river between Lake Peipus and the confluence of the Plyussa and the Narva. Russian forces evacuating Estonia planned to cross the river here, but the 58th Infantry Division destroyed the bridgeheads and then set up a line of defence along the river. Unfortunately, the division was unable to push further north to take the Plyussa bridge, through which the main road led, just to the south of the city of Narva. The bridge was blown up by the enemy. Our efforts to form a bridgehead on the north bank failed, so we had to give up here for the time being. It was intended that the second division of the corps (the 1st Infantry Division) proceed to the Porechye bridgehead via Zaruchye, but it was unavailable at that time. Some of its forces were mopping up in the area east of the Gdov–Narva road and heading towards Kingisepp.

Differences of view between the army group and the panzer group

> It remains the intention of the commander of the panzer group to concentrate our forces for the renewal of the advance. This means that the LVI Panzer Corps is to turn north, leaving the thrust on Novgorod to the I Corps alone. The army group, under pressure from the OKH, urges for a joint attack on Novgorod by the I Corps and the LVI Panzer Corps. The commander of the panzer group refuses to carry this out due to the complete unsuitability of the terrain to the west and north of Novgorod for motorised units.

This short note from the war diary of the panzer group on 21 July regarding the future role of the LVI Panzer Corps demonstrates how the change in the outlook of the army group, as referred to earlier, now had an effect on the headquarters of the panzer group. It could only be seen as a result of the influence of the OKH, for it seemed to us that this new attitude of the army group was inconsistent with what we had experienced previously.

As the commander responsible for the advance from the Luga bridgeheads, Hoepner could not allow it to proceed with insufficient forces; otherwise, the attack would lack penetrative power. As an experienced panzer commander, Colonel-General Hoepner knew that dividing his already weak armoured forces ought not to be permitted. To do so under current circumstances would be disadvantageous. As a matter of fact, it would mean a violation of the fundamental idea of the concentration of armoured forces against a point of main effort. Hoepner therefore strove to the utmost to minimise the impact of the clearly incorrect decision of the army group and, if possible, to unite the forces of the panzer group for a single thrust. The headquarters of the panzer group did not fail to notice that the commander of the army group had already decided that the attack on Leningrad was to be carried out together with the infantry. Field-Marshal von Leeb had yet to order the commencement of the attack, and it seemed that we might at the very least have to await the arrival of the Sixteenth Army.

The result was that the LVI Panzer Corps, as we have seen, continued to push towards the Mshaga sector in conjunction with the I Corps. This meant that the renewal of the advance from the Luga bridgeheads had to be delayed. On 22 July, Hoepner had estimated that the advance could resume on 26 July; however, on 23 July, he had to change his estimate to 28 July. Leeb had revealed to Hoepner on 22 July that the right wing would be reinforced by the X Corps and that perhaps another infantry division would follow afterwards. The panzer group would have to see to it later on that this corps could continue to protect the right flank on the northern side of Lake Ilmen. Hoepner wrote down his 'intentions for the continuation of operations' on 22 July and sent them to the army group.[17] His old plan can again be recognised. He foresaw the LVI Panzer Corps heading towards the Luga, with the SS-Totenkopf Division staying behind in panzer group reserve. He strongly emphasised quick deployment so that the attack could begin on 26 July. On 23 July, just to be on the safe side, the panzer group named 28 July, 'if not earlier', as the date for the attack. We hoped, given all of our discussions with the army group, that we would soon be able to continue with the attack. Yet the army group decided at that time to set 3 August as the date for the attack.

There was a surprising and unusual intervention by the OKH on 23 July. It demanded that the mobile forces of the army group focus on the 'point of main effort on the right' and that, therefore, some or all of the units of the XXXXI Panzer Corps be shifted from the lower Luga to the right wing. The commander of the army group decided not to pass this order on to the panzer group. Instead, he ordered that the LVI Panzer Corps extend its attack slightly to the east, in the direction of Lyuban, which lay 35 kilometres northwest of Chudovo, on the main road towards Leningrad. The mobile forces of the corps would advance in this direction via Novgorod and Chudovo. That Leeb had his heart set on this line of advance is clear from a record of a telephone conversation on 23 July between the chiefs of staff of the army group and of the panzer group.[18] The conversation revolved around the prospects of the new plan. Leeb wanted the OKH and the panzer group to meet one another halfway. He had explained to the OKH that the terrain on the right flank was ill-suited to mobile units and that he was attempting to find other solutions. The OKH reconsidered the situation and issued new orders: the XXXXI Panzer Corps would remain on the lower Luga. We

17 See Appendix 11.
18 See Appendix 12.

at the panzer group were most grateful for the support the field-marshal demonstrated towards us.

The reorganisation of our offensive forces

The fighting in the Mshaga sector cost much more time than had been anticipated by the headquarters of the panzer group. It later became apparent that it was here the point of main effort of the Russian forces lay. The headquarters of the Russian army group under Marshal Kliment Voroshilov was situated in Novgorod. Only on 28 July did both divisions of the I Corps, having ploughed through near impenetrable terrain, reach a point approximately two or three kilometres away from the Mshaga sector, but by that moment it had become necessary for them to top up their supplies. Shortage of ammunition was becoming a concern. Such great demands had already been made on the infantry that they had only been able to advance with strong support from our artillery. To the north of the I Corps, the SS-Totenkopf Division of the LVI Panzer Corps had reached the Mshaga sector near and to the north of Stary Myedved (18 kilometres east of Utorgosh). Immediately further to the north was the 3rd Motorised Infantry Division. The frontline therefore extended in the direction of Luga as far as the southern tip of Lake Cheremenets. In the vicinity of the lake was the 269th Infantry Division, which now belonged to the LVI Panzer Corps. The front had become stationary here. In tough fighting, the 269th Infantry Division had gradually approached Luga and was approximately 15 kilometres away from the town by the end of July. Yet the division was constantly exposed to Russian counterattacks along and to the west of the main road. The 8th Panzer Division, which had temporarily been in panzer group reserve, thus had to be made available to the LVI Panzer Corps so that it could be employed on the left flank of the corps.

Further delays ensued. It had been intended that the X Corps would advance on the northern side of Lake Ilmen, but it was instead compelled to proceed eastwards on the southern side of the lake so as to get rid of the enemy forces near Staraya Russa. Taking the place of the X Corps in the advance on Leningrad was the XXVIII Corps, although it had only just started to march from the south towards its destination.

Given the strength of Russian forces at the end of July, the army group was not prepared to unleash Panzer Group 4 on Leningrad on its own. The thrust from the lower Luga now had to be incorporated into the entire offensive plan of the army group. Unfortunately, it seemed to us that the army group was taking too long to reorganise its forces in the current position. The change of plan with regard to the X Corps is an example of this, and the result was that Russian forces along the lower Luga had ample opportunity to be reinforced. Our aerial reconnaissance revealed that the enemy was constructing a number of defensive fortifications to the rear. Particularly grave, though, was how costly the daily fighting in this area was. The headquarters of the XXXXI Panzer Corps reported in the first few days of August that the losses in the bridgeheads since their establishment on 14/15 July would soon reach the grand total that had been lost before that point. But the arguments of the panzer group fell on deaf ears. Given these circumstances, we even wondered if it would be better to abandon the bridgeheads. We had, after all, been waiting a long time to resume the advance. The wait originally ought only to have been a few days, but it had now in fact been three-and-a-half weeks. It was now too late. The army group had held back due to the difficulties encountered by the Sixteenth Army, which had been unduly delayed and had only just started to approach from the south. Another factor that may have contributed to the desire of the army group to wait was that the OKH had promised support in the form of Panzer Group 3, even though the OKH had advised that such support would hardly be effective before 5 August. The OKH then decided on 30 July that Panzer Group 3 would not be sent to provide assistance; the army group would once more have to rely upon the forces at its disposal. This meant that the OKH was giving up the idea of an envelopment to the east of Lake Ilmen. It had before now placed great value on this idea despite the bad terrain there and the weakness of our forces! The thrust of the X Corps was currently aimed in this direction. Army Group North could finally limit its commitment of forces on the east flank along the Volkhov River.

Following a meeting at its headquarters in Malnava on 27 July, the army group laid out its intentions for the new zones of attack in its 'Army

Group Order No. 2 for the Continuation of the Offensive'.[19] The attack on the Leningrad area was to be carried out by both the Sixteenth Army and Panzer Group 4. Both divisions of the I Corps would cross the path of the Sixteenth Army and would assume primary responsibility for the push on Novgorod. A new infantry corps (the XXVIII, with two infantry divisions) would be inserted in the dense woodlands between the I Corps and the LVI Panzer Corps. The SS-Totenkopf Division would also be placed under the command of the XXVIII Corps, whose line of advance would be towards the north. The LVI Panzer Corps would remain committed to its advance on Luga. The reinforcement of this corps with another infantry division was considered. In this regard, the police division that was assigned to army group reserve in the order of 27 July was a possibility, for its equipment and strength was equivalent to that of an infantry division. In the zone of Panzer Group 4, the task of the XXXXI Panzer Corps and the XXXVIII Corps would remain the same as before. The Sixteenth Army still intended to advance on either side of Lake Ilmen, with the X Corps carrying out an envelopment on the eastern side, but this plan would have to be given up later on. The army group would keep the 8th Panzer Division back as a mobile reserve that would be used to exploit any success. The attack was to commence as soon as the XXVIII Corps had arrived at the front.

We at the headquarters of the panzer group were disappointed with this rearrangement of forces. Not only the 8th Panzer Division but also the SS-Totenkopf Division would be detached from the panzer group. The former had been the only reserve for the panzer group, but it was now available for use at any point along the entire front of the army group; the latter was being handed over to the XXVIII Corps. A 100-kilometre thrust from the Luga bridgeheads to Leningrad could not be effectively conducted with only three mobile divisions. Both flanks would be highly vulnerable. The southern flank would at best be covered by some rather weak security forces. While the minimum requirement would be four mobile divisions, the thrust would have far better prospects with the participation of all six divisions of the panzer

19 See Appendix 13.

group. That is why we strove right from the very beginning to have the LVI Panzer Corps, or at least strong elements of the corps, assigned to this sector. Our concern about lack of forces was described in a short report I wrote on 31 July after a visit by Field-Marshal von Leeb.[20] Such concerns were not unfounded, even though we could understand the point of view of the field-marshal. The army group foresaw 6 August as the date for the renewal of the offensive.

Despite the somewhat averse attitude of the army group, Colonel-General Hoepner felt duty-bound to make every effort to have sufficient mobile forces allocated to the panzer group. He had some success in this regard a couple of days later. After giving a report to the commander in chief of the German Army, Field-Marshal Walther von Brauchitsch, at the headquarters of the army group in Pskov, the 8th Panzer Division was once more placed under the complete control of the panzer group. The SS-Totenkopf Division would therefore be assigned to army group reserve. The detachment of the division from the XXVIII Corps at least created the possibility of it being made available to the panzer group in the event of a successful breakthrough from the Luga bridgeheads. The panzer group also sought to have the 3rd Motorised Infantry Division placed under its command. Aside from the aforementioned police division, another infantry division was very much needed for the push of the LVI Panzer Corps towards Luga. The panzer group even considered relieving the LVI Panzer Corps with an infantry corps so that the panzer corps could be given the task of carrying out a second strike, behind the XXXXI Panzer Corps, against Leningrad and thereby bringing about the decisive victory. Perhaps the panzer group would yet receive the reserve forces it needed for the seizure of Leningrad!

20 See Appendix 14.

CHAPTER 6

Renewal of the advance on Leningrad

The starting point for the offensive of the army group

The directive of the OKH on 30 July had indicated that a defensive flank still needed to be formed on the southern side of Lake Ilmen. In accordance with this directive, Army Group North decided to place greater emphasis on its 'point of main effort on the right'. Forces that were on their way to the front would therefore be sent to the right flank. The 96th Infantry Division and one-third of the 126th Infantry Division were to reinforce the right wing in the sector of the I Corps. Further south, the Sixteenth Army, which had been relieved of pressure, would continue to play an important role. To be placed under its command was the XXVIII Corps, which initially included the SS-Totenkopf Division. This organisation of forces created a clearer separation of zones of responsibility and enabled the panzer group to devote greater attention to the offensive effort from the Luga bridgeheads. The panzer group shifted its headquarters from where it had been in Strugi Krasnye to a position further north, near Lake Samro, so as to be near the attack sector (that of the XXXXI Panzer Corps). Nonetheless, the panzer group also remained responsible for the advance on Luga (the LVI Panzer Corps) and Narva/Kingisepp (the XXXVIII Corps). Cooperation with the Eighteenth Army could not yet be counted on, as it was still engaged in fighting near Reval. Those elements of the Eighteenth Army that advanced eastwards were still approximately 90 kilometres away from the Narva River on 7 August.

The organisation of the forces of Army Group North on 7 August was as follows:

Formation	number of divisions	width of sector
Sixteenth Army, defensive wing	5⅔ infantry divisions	approx. 140 kilometres
Sixteenth Army, offensive wing	5⅓ infantry divisions, 1 mobile division	approx. 50 kilometres
Panzer Group 4	4 infantry divisions, 5 mobile divisions	approx. 150 kilometres
Eighteenth Army	5 infantry divisions	approx. 120 kilometres

A corps headquarters and 4⅓ infantry divisions (XXVIII Corps, 96th Infantry Division, 121st Infantry Division, 122nd Infantry Division, one-third of the 126th Infantry Division, and the SS-Police Division) were additionally inserted into the frontline between Lakes Ilmen and Peipus. This organisation of forces indicated that the army group gave little thought to the way in which the situation might develop after 7 August. Its distribution of mobile forces demonstrated that it was not sticking to its plan of sending a mobile corps through Novgorod. Only the SS-Totenkopf Division, in the sector of the XXVIII Corps, was available for a short time to head in this direction, but the division was soon reassigned to army group reserve. The army group had not been able to ignore the arguments of the panzer group to have stronger mobile forces sent to the Luga bridgeheads. It was only from these bridgeheads that the objective of Leningrad could be reached, provided that the flanks of the advance did not become eroded. And it was not to be denied that the terrain the XXXXI Panzer Corps sought to control was well-suited to our mobile forces; they would be able to showcase their superiority there.

The commander of the army group, Field-Marshal von Leeb, even spoke optimistically about the prospects of a thrust from the bridgeheads when he visited the panzer group on 6 August. He was of the view that there were no longer enemy reserves in and around Leningrad. Should the attack run smoothly, he thought it possible that a defensive front could be established for a short time before Leningrad and that an assault could be carried out to the south and southeast of the city so as to help both the LVI Panzer Corps and the left wing of the Sixteenth Army in their advance. The commander of the panzer group, Colonel-General Hoepner, also hoped that there would be good progress, but he emphasised once more the necessity of a sufficient commitment of forces. He particularly desired the SS-Totenkopf Division so that it could cover the sector before Leningrad. The field-marshal promised that this would be done should the panzer group perform well. He added that the L Corps would soon become available. It was his intention to give the corps to the panzer group so that it could be sent to area near Luga. This meant that the LVI Panzer Corps could be released for the second decisive strike against Leningrad. We at the headquarters of the panzer group found the open-mindedness of the field-marshal to be rather a pleasant surprise, especially given that there had generally been little support for our ideas in the last few weeks. The task of the XXXXI Panzer Corps had not been an easy one thus far. It had been required to advance rapidly and to penetrate thick woodlands, but it had pulled through! The terrain would finally be much friendlier than it would have been in the direction of Novgorod and Luga. The army group now seemed to be in full agreement with our point of view.

The areas in which the Luftwaffe was to be committed for the upcoming attack highlighted the points of main effort that had been chosen by the army group. The VIII Air Corps had recently been allocated to the army group to provide support for the ground troops on the left wing of the Sixteenth Army. That meant that it would be assisting the I Corps in its objectives. Parts of the I Air Corps, which had already been assigned to Army Group North for some time, were also on the left wing of the Sixteenth Army, but the rest was in the vicinity of Panzer Group 4. The importance that the army group attached to Luftwaffe support was shown by its decision to await the arrival of all air units before the commencement of the attack. These air units were also to be fully supplied, so this would require additional time. Luftwaffe cooperation further necessitated consideration for weather and visibility, yet another factor of uncertainty for the timing of the attack.

As we have seen, since 20 July the panzer group had been eager to renew the advance, but the army group remained hesitant and continued to delay the date of the attack. Between 20 July and 6 August, the army group went through the process of selecting a date and then postponing it no fewer than five times. The delay in the approach of a number of units had been the reason thus far. After that, the Sixteenth Army had reported that it lacked supplies, especially ammunition. With neither ammunition nor Lufwaffe support, infantry attacks had little chance of success. We therefore had longer to wait, even though the units of the panzer group were already fully supplied. On the evening of 4 August, the date of the attack was postponed to 7 August and then 8 August. On 6 August, Leeb explained to Hoepner that the postponement was due to the ammunition shortage of the Sixteenth Army and the unpreparedness of the VIII Air Corps. The dilemma for the panzer group was that we would need to start assembling the troops in the bridgeheads two days prior to the commencement of the attack. On the late afternoon of 7 August, preparatory movements had already been underway for a whole day when the army group informed us that there would be yet another delay. Aerial support would be impossible in the current weather conditions. The panzer group immediately raised objections. As a result, we were told at 6 pm that 8 August would be kept as the date of the attack, although the Sixteenth Army might possibly commence its advance a few hours later. Yet at 7 pm, the chief of staff of the army group informed us that there might still be a postponement of one or two days. When the commander of the panzer group protested that the advance from the bridgeheads could no longer be put off, he was assured that the panzer group could still attack at 9 am on 8 August, albeit without the LVI Panzer Corps. We were told that the LVI Panzer Corps would need to head towards the right. But this meant that a gap would open up between the XXXXI Panzer Corps and the right wing of the army group! This right wing, with the LVI Panzer Corps, set off at 4:30 am on 10 August despite the fact that 11 August, due to the weather conditions, had been discussed as a possibility the day before. Field-Marshal von Leeb even made the astonishing statement to Colonel General Hoepner that 'the XXXXI Panzer Corps might have to remain where it is if the situation is too difficult and the weather fails to improve'. That would simply not do after the heavy fighting of 8 August! The panzer group urged for an immediate start, particularly as the Russians had been withdrawing forces from before the LVI

Panzer Corps and sending them to the lower Luga throughout the day on 9 August. That would put the XXXXI Panzer Corps at a serious disadvantage.

These developments have been described so that we can understand, on the one hand, the increasing and justifiable impatience of the panzer group and, on the other, the difficulties for the army group in ensuring the harmonious coordination of the formations under its command. The situation was not to be mastered easily; on top of that, the weather had taken a turn for the worse. Would it be best under such circumstances to do without the help of the Luftwaffe? The army group believed that this might put too much pressure on the infantry. It very much seemed that the demands of the situation would be tough to meet.

Preparations for the advance from the Luga bridgeheads

The offensive of the XXXXI Panzer Corps from the Sabsk and Porechye bridgeheads had to succeed. Both bridgeheads were small, and we had only intended to pause there for a short time. We had not foreseen that we would be compelled to stay put for three-and-a-half weeks. The casualties suffered from defending these bridgeheads were excessive. Not even the army group had wanted or counted on such a long delay. Rather than remaining in a state of costly inactivity, it would have been more practical for the XXXXI Panzer Corps to be given the task of seizing Narva and setting up a line of interdiction. The corps could have begun this task immediately, in the middle of July, and, in conjunction with the XXXVIII Corps, it would have probably been able to carry it out in eight to ten days with little difficulty. Russian land forces in Estonia would have thereby been cut off. Unfortunately, the army group had not considered such a course of action; neither had the panzer group, whose focus at that time was solely on Leningrad.

What was the terrain like in and around the bridgeheads? The Sabsk bridgehead on 22 July was approximately three kilometres in width and three kilometres in depth. The forces there at that time were keen to attack straightaway. Their defensive capability was reasonable. The situation was different in the Porechye bridgehead. It was the most important bridgehead thanks to the two bridges there, and the troops in this area had already thrust further north as far as a small reservoir which promised to act as a natural obstacle against the enemy. The three-kilometre stretch of road in the bridgehead led through impenetrable terrain with forests on either side. This meant that the lines of security to the east and west were only about 500 metres from the road. This deep and narrow corridor was difficult to defend, and the only way for reinforcements to enter it was from the south bank of the river. To relocate the line of defence within the woodlands was beyond the ability of our available forces. The one advantage in this almost impossible defensive position was that the enemy could only attack from the east or west; otherwise he would be exposed to German fire. Nonetheless, the defence of this bridgehead resulted in heavy losses for the 6th Panzer Division. Given the long period during which we were stationary, it would have been far better to give up the bridgehead. But this had not been foreseen.

To the north of the bridgeheads, the terrain still very much resembled the conditions encountered to the south of the Luga. This was the case for the first 20 kilometres on the right and the first 12 kilometres on the left, although it was at least a little less marshy. There was much forest (mostly mixed forest) with almost impenetrable shrubland, a number of small streams, and narrow roads. Settlements were few and far between. The terrain undulated such that the high points could be up to 10 metres above the surrounding territory. Glades were rare; any that existed tended to be small. While the infantry would be able to plough through shrubland, it would be a lot of trouble. It would also make it difficult for them to find their bearings. But the ground would gradually rise after that and become open country. The roads would no longer be narrow and would be in much better condition. We would be entering territory with cultivated land and with a well-developed road network, quite different to what we had experienced in Russia thus far.

The terrain before both bridgeheads possessed the right characteristics for the preparation of an effective defence. The enemy had exploited the time given to him to strengthen his system of defensive installations. Several antitank ditches, makeshift bunkers of various designs, and extended field emplacements now had to be overcome. As an example of the difficulties that we would encounter, a 7-kilometre advance to the north from the Porechye bridgehead would require our troops to cross five antitank ditches. These ditches featured 1-metre high embankments and then dropped down steeply by about 3 metres. The width at the bottom was at least 6 metres. It was clear that the Russians had put in a tremendous effort and that the ditches posed difficult problems for us. The transportation of the vast quantity of materiel that had been needed to construct concrete and log bunkers, gun emplacements, tank traps, and so on was nothing short of remarkable.

Two phases were envisaged for the offensive of the XXXXI Panzer Corps from the bridgeheads. The first phase was the expansion of the bridgeheads in order to allow the assembly of the troops. The expansion of the Sabsk bridgehead had already taken place in July; that of the Porechye bridgehead had started on 6 August. The second phase would be the offensive itself, which was to begin from the bridgehead on the right on 8 August. The 1st Panzer Division was to thrust to the north and northeast, roughly in the direction of Moloskovitsy, whilst elements of the 36th Motorised Infantry Division were to head to the northwest and establish contact with the Porechye bridgehead. From the eastern part of this bridgehead, the 6th Panzer Division was to advance to the east and northeast; from the western part, the 1st Infantry Division would proceed northwest along the road to Opolye and west along the north bank of the Luga. The task of the infantry division was twofold: to carry out the attack through Kingisepp in conjunction with the XXXVIII Corps and to secure the left flank of the XXXXI Panzer Corps in the vicinity north and northeast of Opolye. The panzer corps itself wanted to make it through the forest terrain as quickly as possible and then pivot to the east so as to reach its first objective, the Volosovo–Begunitsy line, which was halfway along the route to Krasnogvardeysk and Krasnoye Selo. A major concern for the panzer corps and the panzer group during this advance would be the ever-lengthening flanks. It would be quite some time before the arrival of the XXXVIII Corps from Narva. The entire 1st Infantry Division would not reach Opolye in one go. At best, a few small units would arrive there to begin with. The flanks would somehow have to be covered with our own forces. We decided to assign the 36th Motorised Infantry Division to the left flank. The 8th Panzer Division would be responsible not only for the security of the right flank but also for the execution of an envelopment that would support the advance of the LVI Panzer Corps (and later the L Corps). It was with these forces that the panzer group hoped to be able to reach the Krasnogvardcysk area. For the final thrust on Leningrad, though, more mobile forces would need to be allocated to the XXXXI Panzer Corps, the northern wing of which would absolutely have to be covered by the XXXVIII Corps.

It was clear to the troops and their commanders that the attack would not be easy under the current circumstances. Even if the troops did not know exactly what had yet to be overcome, their commanders paid close attention to the defensive preparations of the enemy. It was our intention to commit our forces where they could make progress with as little difficulty as possible. We hoped that the I Air Corps could provide effective support despite the weather in recent days. In contrast to the beautiful conditions of the past few weeks, the sky was now grey and sometimes rainy.

The offensive of the XXXXI Panzer Corps

The divisions of the XXXXI Panzer Corps rolled forward on 8 August at 9 am. They had to do so without air support at this stage due to the pouring rain. The advance from the Sabsk bridgehead seemed to proceed smoothly, with the 1st Panzer Division making especially good progress towards the northeast by noon. In the area of the Porechye bridgehead, heavy Russian artillery fire had been encountered. By the afternoon, we realised that the advance was going to be slow. The enemy resisted stubbornly. The impact of Russian artillery in the Porechye area was immense; the northern bridge in particular had received multiple hits and could only be used by foot soldiers or motorcyclists. Although the advance on the outer right and left had made good headway, the panzer group had gained the impression that the fighting was going to be tough. The corps released its detailed daily report at 11:30 pm, and it provided a rather unfavourable appraisal of the situation:

> The enemy initially stayed put in his field fortifications and defended tenaciously. He then counterattacked throughout the afternoon, presumably with fresh forces, against the 36th Motorised Infantry Division and the 6th Panzer Division. Only by using all of the forces at its disposal could the 6th Panzer Division hold its

> ground. Despite the good start made by the 1st Panzer Division and the 1st Infantry Division, a continuation of the offensive cannot succeed with such pressure against the 6th Panzer Division. The strength of the enemy counterattack is bound to increase, and the corps on either side of the XXXXI Panzer Corps have yet to make their presence felt.

The wings of the corps had managed to thrust forward by three to five kilometres, but the enemy seemed to be most active between the bridgeheads. The 6th Panzer Division had already lost up to one-third of its forces! Such was the impression made on the corps that it ended its appraisal of the situation with the following words:

> The XXXXI Panzer Corps will halt at and fortify the line that has been reached and will go over to the defensive.

This came as a surprise! The commander of the panzer group was unable to agree with this decision, even though he and the commander of the corps had faced a number of crises together and had developed a relationship of trust. He conveyed his opinion in a telephone conversation on 9 August at 12:45 am. An account of the conversation was written down shortly afterwards. Hoepner said that the intention of the corps to go over to the defensive was out of the question. A defensive stance could naturally be adopted at specific points where the enemy was particularly strong, but the offensive momentum otherwise had to be maintained. Strong enemy resistance had been expected from the outset. The prior assessment of the enemy by the corps must have been inaccurate if it now had to give up the attack. The commander of the corps had been of the view before the offensive that it would be the wings that would manage to push forward. He had stated this in a telephone conversation on the evening of 7 August and had said the same thing in person two days before that. Now the wings were indeed forging ahead, so this had to be exploited. We had to keep going!

It was difficult for Hoepner to have to urge a commander so high in his estimation to keep going. Was it possible that the enemy had become too strong, as was what seemed to be the conclusion of the corps? Were we sacrificing the lives of our men in vain here? It was not unjustifiable that such questions might arise. And now Hoepner was countermanding the order of the commander in charge of the corps! Although a tough call to make, Hoepner regarded it as necessary. But then the commander of the army group telephoned and spoke of his intentions, as described earlier, of drawing upon the forces of the panzer group for the offensive on the right wing. He wondered whether the advance of the XXXXI Panzer Corps ought to indeed be brought to a halt. So even the army group wanted to hold back rather than push forward! Yet Hoepner did not halt the advance. And with the XXXXI Panzer Corps fighting on its own at the moment, he thought it crucial that the LVI Panzer Corps drive forward with all the energy it could muster.[21]

The reason for the difficulties encountered in advancing from the Porechye bridgehead became apparent later. According to evidence gathered from POWs, the Russians had ordered a counterattack for midnight on 8 August so as to eliminate the bridgehead. This explained the strong presence of enemy artillery, their high expenditure of ammunition, the tenacity of infantry resistance, as well as the immediate counterattack. Had our own attack not already begun, the enemy would have disrupted our preparations in the confined space of the bridgehead with his artillery fire and his mass of ground troops. A situation could have arisen in which the German side was put at a disadvantage from the word go. We could therefore count ourselves lucky that we had not further delayed the commencement of the offensive.

For several hours on 9 August, we waited anxiously for news from the front! It eventually became clear that the 1st Panzer Division was making progress. It had penetrated the front on our right wing and had advanced northeastwards as far as Izvoz via Gankova. It now wanted to pivot to the west with the intention of striking from behind the enemy forces on the road there. It succeeded in re-establishing contact with a battalion of the 36th Motorised Infantry Division that had been encircled near Pustoshka the previous evening. The troops of the motorised infantry division otherwise pressed slowly towards the northwest. Russian fire on the bridges of Porechye had eased off. The corps reported: 'Enemy forces on the wings have been defeated; those to the north have fallen

21 Refer to the discussion earlier regarding the proposal of the army group for the XXXXI Panzer Corps to stay put and for the LVI Panzer Corps to be sent to the right.

back.' It was now the plan of the corps for the 1st Panzer Division to head north and then pivot to the west to assist the 6th Panzer Division. The crisis that had arisen in the opening phase of the offensive would thereby be overcome!

Even if only on the wings to begin with, our forces were once more on the move. We therefore had the opportunity to take advantage of the superiority of our mobile troops in firepower, speed, and manoeuvrability. The panzer corps sought to penetrate the woodlands, and should the 1st Panzer Division succeed in doing this, the elimination of the remaining enemy resistance would probably only be a matter of time. The envelopment of enemy units and their destruction from behind would soon wear down enemy resistance, as this was the most effective tactic that could be employed in combat by mobile forces against an opponent lacking in manoeuvrability. The results of such a tactic are most clearly demonstrated by the development of the situation for the 1st Panzer Division. It was already nearing Moloskovitsy on 11 August; it had exited the woodlands and had entered the terrain most ideal for combat. An envelopment group of the division had turned west upon reaching Yablonitsy on 10 August and had reached a position to the north of Lopets on 11 August, from where it could strike the rear of the enemy and contribute to the relief of the 36th Motorised Infantry Division and the 6th Panzer Division. The latter only managed to take the village of Yurka, which lay very close to the Porechye bridgehead, on 12 August. Further details, including dates, regarding the advance from the Luga bridgeheads can be found in Map 7. The fighting in the central and western sectors remained difficult until 12 August. Even the 1st Infantry Division, like the 6th Panzer Division, suffered heavy losses.

Because of the rapid advance of the 1st Panzer Division, the commander of the panzer group decided on the morning of 11 August to place the 8th Panzer Division at the disposal of the corps. The plan from the beginning had been to thrust through the woodlands as quickly as possible, and it was hoped that the assistance of the 8th Panzer Division would hasten this process. The division was under the command of the corps by 2:45 pm. In the course of 14 August, our units reached open ground. A 20-kilometre stretch of the Volosovo–Kingisepp road was in our hands. The 1st and 6th Panzer Divisions were now grouped together for the further thrust towards the east. The 36th Motorised Infantry Division had advanced behind the 1st Infantry Division via Yurka and Ivanovskoye so that it was now on the left wing. It had reached the area east of Opolye and was to assume responsibility for the protection of the northern flank.

The enemy forces had been utterly decimated. Only a few weak elements remained before the front of the corps. Not a single Russian unit seemed to be intact. Brand-new tanks had been disabled and captured; it was the first time that their crews had sat in tanks. The prospects of a breakthrough to Leningrad were good. We just needed the forces to carry it out! We were once more of the view that, despite our success, we were too weak on this front. The 3rd Motorised Infantry Division and the SS-Totenkopf Division needed to get to the front quickly!

The development of the situation for the XXXVIII Corps

The rather weak XXXVIII Corps was thinly spread out at the beginning of the offensive. A regimental group of the 58th Infantry Division covered the front to the west along the Narva. A second regimental group, which had already made a futile attempt to take Narva, stood to the south of the Plyussa in readiness to launch another attack. The third regimental group was further east. It was advancing towards the Luga upstream from Kingisepp and was to take this town in conjunction with the 1st Infantry Division, which was approaching from the east. The second division of the XXXVIII Corps, the 1st Infantry Division, was temporarily subordinated to the XXXXI Panzer Corps and, as we have seen, was making good progress. It was the task of the XXXVIII Corps to take Kingisepp and Narva and thereby secure the northern flank of the panzer group. It would also be necessary for pressure to be applied against Opolye, where only weak forces of the 1st Infantry Division remained, as well as further east.

The attack on Narva would be difficult, as the terrain appeared to offer few possibilities for the positioning of our troops. The corps, to the dismay of the panzer group, chose to hold back so as to await the approach of the 1st Infantry Division from Kingisepp. It was also unwilling, despite the advice of the army group and of the panzer group, to draw upon the forces that it had committed to the line of security along the Narva to the west. So the 58th Infantry Division lay rather idle where it was whilst the panzer group urgently sought to reinforce its northern flank with infantry forces. On 17 August, Kingisepp was seized from the east by the 1st Infantry Division and from the south by one of the regimental groups of the 58th Infantry Division. The attack on Narva, originally planned for 14 August, had not been carried through. Instead, the city fell on 17 August into the hands of the German forces approaching from the west (the XXVI Corps of the Eighteenth Army). The panzer group still wanted a strong infantry presence on its northern flank. In particular, it was keen to be given back the 1st Infantry Division as soon as possible. The division had worked very well together with the XXXXI Panzer Corps, yet it had been placed back under the command of the XXXVIII Corps on the morning of 15 August. As of 18 August, the XXXVIII Corps was subordinate to the Eighteenth Army, which on the orders of the army group was now to partake in the attack on Leningrad.

The situation in the vicinity of Luga and the measures of the panzer group

At 4 am on 10 August, the LVI Panzer Corps commenced its attack on Luga with the SS-Police Division and the 269th Infantry Division. The point of main effort lay on the western side of the main road. To the right and further behind stood the 3rd Motorised Infantry Division. With the right flank open, it had yet to start its advance and was awaiting the arrival of its right-hand neighbour, the XXVIII Corps. After some initial territorial gain, the attack had run into a deep, well-constructed, and heavily mined Russian defensive front. A renewed and carefully prepared attack at 3 pm on 11 August brought about little progress, and throughout 12 August we were unable to force a breakthrough. It was unlikely that the 3rd Motorised Infantry Division could change the situation, so in a discussion between the commanders of the panzer group and the corps it was considered whether the division ought to be detached and sent to support the successful thrust of the XXXXI Panzer Corps. The LVI Panzer Corps itself was soon to be relieved by the L Corps, with the latter to take over the attack on Luga in conjunction with the XXVIII Corps on the right and, possibly, with elements of the XXXXI Panzer Corps to the north.[22] By 15 August, the L Corps had taken over.

The question of whether the 3rd Motorised Infantry Division should follow in the wake of the XXXXI Panzer Corps had become quite urgent, for the efforts of the commander of the panzer group to have the SS-Totenkopf Division sent there had come to nothing. After the arrival of the 8th Panzer Division at the front of the XXXXI Panzer Corps on 11 August, Hoepner had reported on the situation to Field-Marshal von Leeb and requested that he be given the SS-Totenkopf Division, as had been promised on 6 August. Yet the field-marshal felt unable to fulfil his promise at this moment. The division was engaged in combat and could only be released in the event of good progress by the XXVIII Corps. This was most disappointing! Hoepner again conveyed his opinion to the army group on 12 August, this time in writing. It was essential that a mobile division be allocated to the XXXXI Panzer Corps so as to fully exploit the momentum that the corps had picked up.[23] The XXXXI Panzer Corps was in the best position to achieve final victory. It was highly likely that it would reach Leningrad in a single thrust! This was not the case at any other point along the front. In the area of the XXVIII Corps, where the SS-Totenkopf Division was still located, the terrain on the way to Leningrad was thickly wooded and unsuitable for mobile forces. The commander of the army group was at that time considering a thrust in the direction of Novgorod to be carried out by the SS-Totenkopf Division in the area of the I Corps. He had in any case already ordered that the division be detached from the XXVIII Corps and placed in army group reserve. His appraisal of the situation was clearly somewhat different to that of the panzer group. As we will see, this was quite unfortunate! The army group was clearly aware on 12 August of the successful breakthrough of the XXXXI Panzer Corps. Because of the refusal of the army group to hand over the SS-Totenkopf Division, Colonel-General Hoepner ordered early on 13 August the detachment of the 3rd Motorised Infantry Division from the front before Luga so that it could move into the area of the XXXXI Panzer Corps. This would

22 Refer to Map 8 for the subsequent advance on Luga.
23 See Appendix 15.

require a temporary suspension of the offensive in the vicinity of Luga, although this had already become necessary given that the XXVIII Corps had yet to arrive. The police division relieved the 3rd Motorised Infantry Division and would later, after the arrival of the XXVIII Corps, envelop Luga from the east. The advance on Luga would resume on 22 August and would be carried out by the L Corps, with the police division on the right and the 269th Infantry Division on the left.

Decisive intervention by the army group

The advance of the right wing of the army group (the Sixteenth Army) that had commenced on 10 August immediately encountered fierce enemy resistance. With good support from the VIII Air Corps, the divisions of the I Corps had to carve their way through a deep defensive zone. On the evening of 14 August, the 21st Infantry Division, reinforced with a regimental group of the 126th Infantry Division, was situated five kilometres to the southwest of Novgorod, while the 11th Infantry Division, with its entire front facing north, had reached the Novgorod–Luga railway line.[24] The eastern wing of the 11th Infantry Division was approximately 15 kilometres to the west of Novgorod and was heading due north. On the left and slightly behind was the 96th Infantry Division. The XXVIII Corps, with the 121st Infantry Division on the right and the 122nd Infantry Division on the left, had crossed the upper Luga and had almost covered the same distance as the 11th Infantry Division. By the evening of 14 August, the corps stood approximately eight kilometres to the south of the Batetskaya railway junction. Enemy resistance had diminished, so it seemed as if the seizure of Novgorod was in the offing.

In contrast, the situation to the south of Lake Ilmen on the evening of 14 August appeared to be less favourable. The X Corps was there, and its original task had been to conduct an encirclement to the northeast. However, it was completely on the defensive in its position to the east and south of Staraya Russa (see Map 1). On its southern front in particular it had to fight off a number of powerful Russian attacks. This put the corps

---

24 The front of the division ran almost along the entire length of this railway line. See Map 8 for the western part.

at a serious disadvantage, for Russian motorised forces were threatening to outflank it from the southwest.[25] The X Corps had no forces whatsoever at its disposal with which to meet this threat, which seemed to be aimed towards or to the west of Morina. In its report to the army group on the evening of 14 August, the headquarters of the Sixteenth Army painted a particularly gloomy picture. It strongly emphasised how the troops of the corps were suffering from battle fatigue, something that the corps itself had already reported previously. This development would turn out to have a psychological impact upon the army group and would also play a considerable role in how events would unfold for Panzer Group 4.

When Field-Marshal von Leeb visited the command post of the panzer group early on the morning of 15 August, Colonel-General Hoepner told him of his intention to detach the 3rd Motorised Infantry Division from the LVI Panzer Corps so that it could be sent to help maximise the progress being made by the XXXXI Panzer Corps. The field-marshal agreed with this, but, as had been the case with the SS-Totenkopf Division, he rejected the request of the colonel-general for support from the VIII Air Corps. He still had in mind the idea of the point of main effort on the right. On top of that, his thinking was probably influenced by the development of the situation in the vicinity of Staraya Russa, even if only subconsciously. The panzer group now began to feel the effects of this, although not yet at a level that could be regarded as critical. Towards 6 pm, the army group ordered the panzer group to hand over the LVI Panzer Corps, with the 3rd Motorised Infantry Division, to the Sixteenth Army. This news struck the headquarters of the panzer group, which was situated near the peaceful Lake Samro, 'like a bombshell':[26]

> This is the second time that the army group has stopped the panzer group from achieving its objective. The first occasion was on 18 July when we wanted to strike northwards from the Luga bridgeheads; now it is when we want to fully exploit the breakthrough of the XXXXI Panzer Corps.

---

25 The Russian motorised forces (the 168th Motor Rifle Division) were reported to be approximately 15 kilometres to the southeast of Morina. In addition, Russian cavalry was approaching from the south.

26 See my short report on 15 August in Appendix 16. The command post of the panzer group had by this time been shifted from Strugi Krasnye to Usadishche, near Lake Samro.

This excerpt from my short report on 15 August summarises how we at the headquarters of the panzer group felt at that time. It was particularly disappointing given that the field-marshal had only that morning approved of our plan to reinforce the XXXXI Panzer Corps, and that would be with forces already under the command of the panzer group. The situation near Staraya Russa must have been fairly bad! To abandon the advance on Leningrad, an objective for which we had striven so hard since the beginning, due to what could only be a diversionary attack would result in the initiative being taken by the enemy. The Russian leadership would be able to congratulate itself for such a result. The XXXXI Panzer Corps, our main-attack group, would then find itself in a rather difficult position. As illuminated in my report, the commitment of the corps was a risk that had been taken so as to lead the army group forward towards its objective. Yet we had taken this risk in the belief that the panzer group would at the very least still have six mobile divisions at its disposal, even if they were quite weak. Now it would all be over! The headquarters of Panzer Group 4 was bitterly disappointed over the decision that had been made by the army group, but what added fuel to the fire was our subsequent discovery that the OKH had made available to the army group a panzer corps from Panzer Group 3 on the very same day – 15 August! It would, however, take a few days for the panzer corps to arrive. On the evening of 15 August, towards 9:30 pm, Leeb telephoned Hoepner to express his regret that the detachment of the LVI Panzer Corps had been necessary. He had given the order 'only with the utmost reluctance'. He said that he hoped that those elements of the 3rd Motorised Infantry Division that would not be ready to leave their operational area until 17 August, and that had therefore not yet been detached, might still be allowed to remain with Panzer Group 4. We at the headquarters of the panzer group would not be holding our breath.

The XXXXI Panzer Corps must slow down its advance

The intervention of the army group compelled the commander of the panzer group to order the XXXXI Panzer Corps, whose progress had been dramatic, to halt at the Volosovo–Begunitsy line on 16 August. This was not just a quiet demonstration against the army group, which seemed to attach no particular value to the hazardous thrust that the corps was carrying out for its benefit; the decision to halt was also made in the recognition that the corps could no longer carry out its task as planned. What use would it be to take Krasnogvardeysk or even Krasnoye Selo if our success could not be exploited? Volosovo, only 40 kilomotres away from Krasnogvardeysk, was occupied by the 1st Panzer Division on the morning of 16 August. There was barely any enemy presence before the front, and the few small Russian groups that remained were in the process of disintegrating. It might have been possible to reach and occupy both Krasnogvardeysk and Krasnoye Selo on 17 August, and perhaps even the outskirts of Leningrad, if we had only possessed the forces necessary to do it. But we did not have those forces. Our mobile units were far too weak to be able to see through the combat that could be expected at the gates of Leningrad; the enemy was bound to put up as much resistance as possible, be it with regular forces drawn from the Finnish front or with militia forces drawn from the city of millions. If the XXXXI Panzer Corps were to drive on Leningrad now, there would be little with which to defend the flanks! The 36th Motorised Infantry Division and the bulk of the 6th Panzer Division would be in the north, where enemy activity could be expected to increase; the 1st Panzer Division and the rest of the 6th Panzer Division would be in the east in the vicinity of Krasnogvardeysk; and the severely depleted 8th Panzer Division, as the only other available unit, would be in the south or southeast in the rear of the Russian front before Luga. This meant that there would exist a southern flank approximately 60 kilometres in depth with little or no cover. Of course, there might have been almost no risk in such a position, for the enemy forces facing the XXXXI Panzer Corps had been smashed to pieces (though not yet on the northern flank!), whilst those in the vicinity of Luga were threatened from the rear. Indeed, on 20 August, roughly 15 kilometres south of Krasnogvardeysk, the 8th Panzer Division had pushed eastwards beyond the Luga–Krasnogvardeysk road and had turned southwards to assist the L Corps in its advance. The commander of the panzer group had permitted the XXXXI Panzer Corps to continue its advance, albeit only at the slow pace of approximately 10 kilometres per day. After all, we still wanted to be able to take advantage of the vacuum that had been left by the enemy. The area west and south of Krasnogvardeysk was thereby reached on 21 August. Three mobile divisions (the 36th Motorised Infantry Division, 1st Panzer Division, and 6th Panzer Division) were at that time tied down in the defence of the front and flanks. The only attack group that remained was the 8th Panzer Division, which was driving south along the main road towards Luga.[27] The front of the XXXXI Panzer Corps extended to more than 150 kilometres. In those last few days of August, it was extremely difficult for the corps to scrape together any attack forces at all. Its weakness is demonstrated by the struggle of the 8th Panzer Division on either side of the Krasnogvardeysk–Luga road in its attempt to establish contact with the L Corps. Only on 31 August could contact be made approximately 25 kilometres to the north of Luga. The Russian forces there comprised the 41st Rifle Corps with around five divisions. These forces were pushed back into the marshland east of the main road, where they would later be encircled, split into three pockets, and eventually annihilated (see Map 9). The main road was therefore open for the northward advance of the infantry of the L Corps, but, more importantly, the route of supply we had needed was now in our hands. It was with a great sense of relief that our military leadership and supply stations could begin to make use of this road from 3 September.

The precarious situation on the northern flank of the XXXXI Panzer Corps

It had thus far been the southern flank that had been negatively affected by the advance of Panzer Group 4, but the successful breakthrough of the XXXXI Panzer Corps in the open terrain north of the lower Luga brought about a similarly debilitating development on the northern flank. Here, to the south of the Gulf of Finland, the enemy forces were retreating from Estonia, predominantly the Russian 8th Army. These forces were falling back towards the east in the direction of Leningrad, although they could at any moment pivot to the south to threaten the security of the

27 The L Corps, having been temporarily brought to a halt, was to renew its advance on 22 August.

panzer group. The failure thus far of the XXXVIII Corps to take Narva and cut off the retreat of the enemy had now come home to roost. It could not be the task of the panzer group to put up resistance against these forces. On the contrary, the panzer group had to make use of its superiority in speed and advance on Leningrad as quickly as possible so as to prevent the retreating forces from reaching the city. It was important in this regard that the Eighteenth Army, with 2⅓ infantry divisions of the XXVI Corps beginning to arrive from Estonia, drive to the east as swiftly as it could in order to release the 36th Motorised Infantry Division and the 6th Panzer Division, both of which were currently committed to the protection of the northern flank of the panzer group. In the opinion of the panzer group, the XXVI Corps ought not to try to charge into the rear of the enemy; rather, it should avoid combat and proceed quickly along the Narva–Kingisepp–Opolye road with the idea of relieving the divisions of the XXXVIII Corps or of marching behind them towards the northeast. Speed was of the essence! The earlier this could happen, the greater the striking power of the panzer group would be and the sooner it would be able to reach Leningrad. We therefore requested from the army group that the Eighteenth Army be given the role of protecting the northern flank of the panzer group. The army group issued this order on 17 August, but it also gave an additional task to the Eighteenth Army: the destruction of the forces of the Russian 8th Army and the seizure of the coastal fortifications along the southern side of the Gulf of Finland right up to Leningrad. This twofold task resulted in the Eighteenth Army fighting its own battle in the area to the north of the Narva–Kingisepp–Opolye road between 18 and 29 August, so it was only thereafter that the so eagerly awaited relief of Panzer Group 4 could take place to the east of Opolye. It is of interest to note that the panzer group had foreseen this development and had drawn the attention of the army group to it prior to the time the order was issued. I had also visited the headquarters of the Eighteenth Army in an attempt to coordinate our efforts. The disappointing development of the situation with regard to the security of our northern flank is clearly illustrated in a report from the panzer group on 29 August.[28] It had taken the Eighteenth

28 See Appendix 17.

Army eleven days to cover the distance of 40 kilometres between Narva and Opolye, and this was at a time when every single man was needed for the assault on Leningrad. Unfortunately, the army group even took away the XXXVIII Corps from the panzer group and placed it back under the command of its original army. This created further delays and, as noted in our report, put both infantry corps in the forests north of Kingisepp, where they were engaged in costly yet worthless combat. The report concluded in resignation:

> What must be strongly emphasised is that the panzer group had been given no opportunity to withdraw forces from its northern front until the arrival of parts of the Eighteenth Army on 29 August. The result is that the offensive against Leningrad and the assault from the north against Luga have been unable to be carried out to the extent desired or with the rapidity needed.

Had the XXVI Corps been subordinated to Panzer Group 4 upon its crossing of the Narva, and had the Eighteenth Army not been tied down in useless fighting, we would have by this time been much closer to Leningrad and Luga. While this is an observation we can make in hindsight, it is also a demonstration of how personal considerations in the assignment of units can have a decisive influence over the unfolding of events. The army group wanted to make maximum use of the Eighteenth Army in the destruction of enemy forces. However, as noted in our report, the result was that the Eighteenth Army was stuck in a position far away from Leningrad. This was what it amounted to! If the task being undertaken by the Eighteenth Army was regarded as absolutely necessary, then it might even have been better to place Panzer Group 4 under its command. The retreating enemy forces would then have been obliterated expeditiously. Yet this could well have been asking too much of the accomplished commander of the panzer group.

CHAPTER 7

The offensive in the lead-up to the encirclement of Leningrad

The first plans of the army group for the encirclement of Leningrad (Map 10)

The imminent opening of the Luga–Leningrad road and the resulting possibility for the L Corps to advance on Krasnogvardeysk compelled Field-Marshal von Leeb, during a visit to the command post of the panzer group near Lake Samro on the morning of 27 August, to express his intentions for the attack on Leningrad to Colonel-General Hoepner. At that point in time, the 12th Panzer Division, the leading unit of the XXXIX Panzer Corps (which had been sent to the north by Panzer Group 3), had entered Tosno along the Chudovo–Leningrad road. This meant that the XXXIX Panzer Corps would soon reach the Neva, upstream from Leningrad, and would probably also get very close to the city itself. Although the protection of the left flank of the panzer group had been painfully delayed, we were now in the position to make effective use of the units there thanks to the approach of both infantry corps of the Eighteenth Army. The encirclement of Leningrad was soon to take place. In the opinion of the army group, all recent signs indicated that the Russians had resigned themselves to the loss of Leningrad. They maintained only a defensive stance along the entire front of the army group. It was unlikely that they would launch an attack, especially after their defeat at Staraya Russa.

As far as the further plans of the army group were concerned, the Sixteenth Army was to 'keep its front facing to the east'.[29] To the north of Lake Ilmen, the I Corps was to establish a defensive front near Volkhov. The Schmidt Group, composed of the XXXIX Panzer Corps and the XXVIII Corps (a total of three mobile and two infantry divisions), was to assume responsibility for completing the southeastern side of the encirclement of Leningrad and for isolating Volkhov (north of Chudovo).[30] It was planned that the Schmidt Group be placed under the command of Panzer Group 4 at a later date. Unfortunately, we would have to do without the LVI Panzer Corps from now on. After the victorious conclusion of the counterattack south of Staraya Russa, we had expected that the corps would be returned to us. It turned out, quite astonishingly, that the corps was to remain to the south of Lake Ilmen, where it was given the task of pushing further eastwards. Panzer Group 4, now with four corps under its command, was to approach Leningrad from the southeast, south, and west with the goal of establishing a firm ring of encirclement around the city. The panzer group would commence from a line running along the Neva River downstream from Shlisselburg to Ivanovskoye, then along the east and southeastern edge of the marshland east of Kolpino, through Izhora, then upstream along the Izhora River to the area northwest of Krasnogvardeysk, and then along the Krasnogvardeysk–Pudostya–Prokovsina–Ropsha road all the way to Peterhof, on the southern side of the Gulf of Finland. The 20th Motorised Infantry Division of the XXXIX Panzer Corps was to assume responsibility for the Neva front and attempt to force a crossing of the river. Three divisions of the Eighteenth Army were to thrust directly towards Leningrad.

Once this starting line had been reached and there were sufficient forces at our disposal, the assault on Leningrad would begin. The army group order of 29 August referred to an 'outer' and an 'inner' line of encirclement. The outer line of encirclement would run along the Neva,

29 For more on the intentions of the army group, as well as on the progress of the panzer group, especially in the vicinity of Luga, see the assessment of the situation by Panzer Group 4 on 27 August 1941 in Appendix 18.

30 General of the Panzer Troops Rudolf Schmidt was the commander of the XXXIX Panzer Corps.

as before, between Shlisselburg and Ivanovskoye with bridgeheads over the river, and then along a line connecting Izhora, Detskoe Selo, Pulkovo, and Uritsk. The inner line of encirclement would be close to the eastern and southern outskirts of the city centre, with the southern part running through Alexandrovskaya, Kupchino, and Uritzk. The army group reserved for itself the decision as to when the assault would commence.

Measures taken by the panzer group on 27 August 1941

On 27 August, in accordance with the instructions issued by the army group, the commander of the panzer group issued his 'directive for the further advance of the corps on Leningrad'. Owing to the rapid advance of the 8th Panzer Division from the north, the division would soon be united with the L Corps and, as a result, the vital road leading to Leningrad would be open. With ever-worsening weather, we needed this road to ensure the continuous flow of supplies. The supply route over the lower Luga had only been regarded as a temporary measure at first, but we had thus far had to make extensive use of it due to the long-drawn-out combat near Luga. Although the delivery of some supplies via the waterway from Pskov through Lake Peipus to its northeastern tip helped and were most welcome, the security of the existing supply lines for the XXXXI Panzer Corps remained uncertain. The panzer group now devoted its attention to the rapid repair of the newly acquired main road, for the fighting had taken its toll on that part of the road in the vicinity of Luga. Even the bridge over the river had been destroyed.

Priority would now be given to reinforcing both divisions of the L Corps as soon as possible so that they would be able to thrust further in the direction of Leningrad in conjunction with the units of the Schmidt Group, which would very soon be within striking distance of the city. It was by no means certain, based on previous experience, whether the forces of the Eighteenth Army would arrive in time. The commander of the panzer group was in favour of continuing the attack, be it with or without the divisions of the Eighteenth Army. Indeed, he regarded it as absolutely necessary. The L Corps was therefore to mop up any remaining enemy forces on either side of the road, as well as on either side of the railway line, all the way up to and to the east of Krasnogvardeysk. The corps would then prepare itself for the final assault from this position, i.e. between the Soltsy–Leningrad railway line and the Luga–Krasnogvardeysk road. The zone of operations for the corps included the road, but not the railway line. The security forces of the XXXXI Panzer Corps that were still in this zone would be reallocated to the L Corps, whose point of main effort would lie on the right once the attack continued. The XXXXI Panzer Corps was assigned the sector between the Luga–Krasnogvardeysk and Kingisepp–Krasnoye Selo roads. It was to push further forward towards the starting line and scout out the most ideal points from which to launch the attack. It was not to engage in heavy combat. Given that it might take time for the Eighteenth Army to arrive, two panzer divisions were detached from the corps and were to stand ready to the west of the Luga–Leningrad road. The panzer group decided that it would shift its command post to the area south of Krasnogvardeysk, whereupon the Schmidt Group would come under the command of the panzer group, as had been negotiated with the Sixteenth Army.

The commander of the panzer group did not intend to commit strong forces against the Russian 41st Corps, which had been so severely battered in the fighting near Luga. The enemy corps had been driven into the extensive marshland east of the road and railway line and no longer represented a threat (see Map 9). A few security forces would therefore be sufficient to deal with it. An encirclement of the enemy there had not been our original plan, but this was the situation that arose after the disturbing reappearance of enemy units on either side of Lake Orlinskoye. They were attempting to push to the northwest so as to disrupt the flow of traffic along the road. Astonishingly, even a handful of Russian tanks had appeared on the scene. We later discovered that they had entered the northern part of the pocket via a corduroy road from the Lugi area, the assembly point of the Russian 41st Corps before it had retreated into the marshland. As the 8th Panzer Division was nearing Yashchera from the north along the main road, it had to turn to the east at Divenskaya Station and proceed to the southern tip of Lake Orlinskoye in order to safeguard the road. Our few forces were thus spread out more thinly and were robbed of their striking power. They found themselves stuck in the middle of the enemy forces. Although the enemy presence had been anticipated after their retreat from the main road, the degree of their strength had not been foreseen. It was therefore becoming clear that the main road would require protection for an extended period of time. Yet the entire L Corps, led by the 269th Infantry Division and with elements of the SS-Police Division in the rear, had to move forward along the road towards Krasnogvardeysk in accordance with the instructions of the panzer group. The rest of the SS-Police Division (at first two regiments and then only one) had advanced via Lugi into the enemy pocket from the south, but they were to be relieved by the battle group of the 285th Security Division and other emergency units.[31] It was imperative that we commit as many forces as possible to the decisive battle for Leningrad!

The development of the situation up to 8 September 1941: approaching the jump-off line

After motorised elements of the 21st Infantry Division had been thrown forward on the attacking wing of the Sixteenth Army and had taken Chudovo on 20 August, the XXXIX Panzer Corps (from Panzer Group 3) had thrust onward and had entered the area southeast of Leningrad on 24 August, from where it would hopefully deliver the coup de grace. The disadvantageous combat conditions that could be expected were already beginning to have an effect, for the I Corps found itself tied down to flank protection along the Volkhov between Novgorod and Chudovo. The enemy was becoming increasingly active on the east bank of the river. The 18th Motorised Infantry Division, at this stage the leading formation of the XXXIX Panzer Corps, had to pivot to the north from its position between Chudovo and Lyuban on 25 August so as to hurl back enemy forces that were threatening the main road there. The division was placed under the command of the I Corps and entrusted with the establishment of a predominantly defensive position. From 26 August, the 12th Panzer Division took over as the lead formation of the XXXIX

31 The 285th Security Division had recently been assigned to the rear area of the panzer group by the army group, and had already played a role in mopping-up operations west of Luga.

Panzer Corps. Its thrust along the road from Chudovo in the direction of Leningrad was executed with such relative ease that, by 28 August, it had reached a point very close to Izhora. The village was soon taken, but after that the division made no further progress into territory that was increasingly suburban in character. The 20th Motorised Infantry Division, which was the third division of the XXXIX Panzer Corps, was near Lyuban and heading due north towards the Neva River. Its objective was to secure the position along the river between Shlisselburg and Ivanovskoye in preparation for the continued advance on Leningrad.

By 31 August, the XXXIX Panzer Corps had come to a halt. It was unable to get closer to Leningrad for the time being. The Russian forces near Izhora were not particularly strong, but it would be pointless for the 12th Panzer Division to push forward on its own. The 20th Motorised Infantry Division had reached the Neva near and downstream from Shlisselburg, although it found itself ever more bound down in the east in the area of Mga (see Map 1). A momentary crisis had arisen for the division when, on 1 September, the enemy launched multiple surprise strikes against the Mga railway junction from the northeast, east, and south. He even attacked from the north, over the Neva. Fortunately, the situation was under control by 4 September thanks to the efforts of parts of the 122nd Infantry Division (from the XXVIII Corps). It was clear that the enemy sought to reopen the land connection to Leningrad. He would make a more concerted effort in the near future! On 3 September, the XXXIX Panzer Corps, whose task was not only the thrust over the Neva but also the security of the front in the east and the elimination of enemy forces up to the mouth of the Volkhov, reported that it would only be able to carry out the last of these tasks with the help of the 12th Panzer Division. This division currently stood in the vicinity of Izhora and was the only mobile division of the panzer corps that was still earmarked for the attack on Leningrad. Nevertheless, enemy pressure from the east resulted in the division being moved to a new position. The subordination of the XXXIX Panzer Corps to the panzer group that had been planned for noon on 3 September would not take effect, for the corps would no longer partake in the battle for Leningrad. It had been ever more forced by the enemy to defend itself in terrain characterised by impenetrable marshland, in which it could not bring its firepower or mobility to bear. In the opinion of the panzer group, it would have been better had the three mobile divisions of the XXXIX Panzer Corps been kept in the open terrain south of Leningrad, where they could help to ensure our success, whilst the infantry of the XXVIII Corps should have been sent into the unfriendly terrain as far as the Volkhov River, where they would be perfectly capable of establishing a defensive line. Our advice regarding the inability of armoured forces to engage in combat in marshland went unheeded. The XXXIX Panzer Corps would be made to suffer in poor conditions!

The XXVIII Corps, which had come under the command of the panzer group as planned on 7 September, was to proceed with the attack on Leningrad from the southeast and was to do so without the armoured support it so badly needed. It had advanced relatively easily through the thick woodland in its attack sector near Mshaga, and had been able to help the L Corps in the fighting near Luga from the east. The right wing of the XXVIII Corps had reached and occupied Lyuban on 25 August shortly before the arrival of the spearhead of the XXXIX Panzer Corps, and had then pivoted to the northwest so as to approach the starting line for the attack on Leningrad. It had reached this line by early September. The 96th Infantry Division relieved the 12th Panzer Division near and to the south of Izhora, while the 121st Infantry Division, further southwest, slowly fought its way through forest and marsh to get to the Izhora River. Small elements of the 122nd Infantry Division, the third division of the XXVIII Corps, assumed responsibility for the Ivanovskoye–Izhora sector. The bulk of the division remained in the area of the XXXIX Panzer Corps for the time being, but it was intended that it be released as soon as possible.

The movements of the L Corps and the XXXXI Panzer Corps towards the starting line proceeded without any particularly strong enemy countermeasures. However, the first alteration to the plans of the panzer group occurred at the beginning of September, as the enemy in the Luga pocket proved to be far more troublesome than had been anticipated. The elimination of the pocket required additional forces as well as more time and effort. This meant that the 8th Panzer Division could not be placed, as had been intended, in panzer group reserve. On 1 September, the division was instead given the task of destroying the enemy pocket. Unfortunately, our efforts there suffered not only due to the shortage of forces but also to the fact that they had to be shifted around. Both infantry regiments of the Police Division had to be detached, the reconnaissance battalions of the L Corps that would partly take their place would still take a few days to arrive, and so on. In this desperate situation, we had no choice but to rely upon our rear supply units to contain the encircled Russian forces. As it turned out, the 8th Panzer Division executed its task so effectively that it managed to split up the enemy pocket into three smaller ones on 7 September. The southern pocket was eliminated on 9 September, but it took until 15 September for the last 'remnant pocket' to be destroyed. In the end, more than 20,000 prisoners of war were taken, and, from 14 September, the 285th Security Division was entrusted with mopping-up operations.

The units of the Eighteenth Army, on which the army group placed great importance for the assault on Leningrad, started to arrive from 29 August. The leading formation of the army, the XXXVIII Corps, endeavoured to maintain the momentum in its advance on the city, while the XXVI Corps was to assume responsibility for the protection of the northern flank. At the request of the army group, the Eighteenth Army reinforced its attack forces with another infantry division from Estonia. The XXXVIII Corps thereby had three divisions at its disposal for the assault on Leningrad (the 1st, 58th, and 291st Infantry Divisions). So as to ensure that these forces had time to get into position, the army group set 9 September as the date for the commencement of the assault on the city.

Order of battle for the assault on Leningrad

From the starting line that had been reached in the few days leading up to 8 September, Panzer Group 4 was to be divided into two groups for the attack. The XXVIII Corps was to attack from the east, whilst the L Corps and the XXXXI Panzer Corps were to strike from the south and west. Immediately to the left of the panzer group, the three divisions of the XXXVIII Corps of the Eighteenth Army were to participate in the drive on Leningrad. The splitting up of the panzer group was a result of the way in which events had unfolded over the past few days and was also demanded by the features of the terrain that lay ahead of us. The original plan of the commander of the panzer group, whereby the point of main effort of the attack of the L Corps was to be on its right wing (i.e. along the Susanino–Leningrad railway line) so as to facilitate cooperation with the XXVIII Corps, had to be abandoned, as it had become apparent that the terrain there would be difficult to traverse. Our attempt to bring the artillery of the SS-Police Division into position to the east of Pustoshka failed completely. The panzer group therefore had to abandon its plan of enveloping rather than taking Krasnogvardeysk. The town lay on high ground and was a fully developed stronghold for the enemy, so we wanted to avoid it altogether. On the recommendation of the L Corps, the bulk of the 269th Infantry Division advanced northwards on the eastern side of Krasnogvardeysk, whilst the remaining elements of the division turned to face the town itself. In the meantime, the SS-Police Division was diverted: the point of main effort of its attack now lay along the northern foothills of the town, but some of its forces would also attack from the west and southwest to pin down the enemy there. The shift in the point of main effort of the L Corps meant that that of the XXXXI Panzer Corps could also be altered. In view of the terrain ahead, as well as the disposition of the enemy troops, the commander of the XXXXI Panzer Corps had wanted to place the main emphasis of the attack on the northern wing, and the commander of the panzer group was now able to approve this. Of course, this meant that the corps would no longer play a role in the envelopment of Krasnogvardeysk. The corps would instead turn towards the imposing hills where Duderhof lay so that it could work in conjunction with the XXXVIII Corps (of the Eighteenth Army), whose main attack wing was on the right and aimed towards Krasnoye Selo. The objective of this combined effort was to take the high ground in this region. Duderhof had been the location of the parade ground in tsarist times, and at the foot of the hills, so to speak, on the other side lay Leningrad and the Gulf of Kronstadt. It was unlikely that the enemy would want to relinquish this high ground. Nevertheless, the 6th Panzer Division (of the XXXXI Panzer Corps) was to support the L Corps in its advance north of the Izhora, for there was a strong Russian artillery presence in the triangular road junction north of Krasnogvardeysk.

It was our plan that the western (and main) attack group of Panzer Group 4 strive to meet with the eastern group (the XXVIII Corps) in the area to the north of Detskoe Selo. Of the eastern group, the 96th Infantry Division was to attack westwards and the 121st Infantry Division northwards. Whilst covering the western flank against enemy forces near Slutsk and Detskoe Selo, the advance would proceed further towards the northwest. Since enemy forces and bad roads delayed the deployment of the XXVIII Corps, especially that of the 121st Infantry Division in its approach from the south, there was no guarantee that the corps would be ready by 9 September. Colonel-General Hoepner therefore granted the corps an additional two days before its attack on Leningrad was to begin. This postponement seemed to be acceptable, as the corps was already getting quite close to where it needed to be. Moreoever, the staggered assaults on Leningrad would offer an advantage to the XXVIII Corps in that it would be able to receive support, even if somewhat limited, from the Luftwaffe. Indeed, we attached such great importance to aerial support that we later made the decision to postpone the commencement of the attack of the corps by yet another day. This meant that the corps was now due to set off on 12 September. Another factor in this decision was that the delivery of ammunition to the corps along the very long supply route via Novgorod could not be carried out safely until 11 September. The shortening, and with it the security, of the supply route to the corps was becoming ever more urgent. In short, the corps needed access to the Luga–Krasnogvardeysk road, so steps were taken by the western group to make contact with the eastern group as soon as possible. The panzer group reported to the army group that the corps ought to be able to have this access from 10 September. A challenge that remained, however, was the significantly reduced striking power of our infantry. Their success could only be ensured if they were supported by bombers and artillery.

The first offensive success

On 9 September at 9:30 am, the final and decisive attack on Leningrad was launched from the south and southwest. The objective, as ordered by the army group, was no longer the capture of the city. Instead, a tight ring of encirclement was to be formed around it. This corresponded to the intentions of the supreme command and, as pointed out in the assessment of the army group, was probably all that could be achieved by the combat troops anyway, given their condition and numerical disadvantage. Colonel-General Hoepner, not to mention the officers and men of the units under his command, still cherished the hope that Leningrad could be taken. The 8th Panzer Division was being held in army group reserve at that time, and we were of the view, not unjustifiably, that it could be employed to provide extra impetus to the assault on the city. But the army group chose to hold back the panzer division due to a decision that had been made by the supreme command and of which the panzer group was not yet aware. We will come back to this later, but at this particular point in time the panzer group felt less confident about the prospects of the XXVIII Corps, whose divisions were now completely lacking in striking power. The strongest of these, the 96th Infantry Division, had only two regiments at its disposal. The last two-and-a-half months of combat had been taxing, more so for the infantry than for the mobile divisions. The troops were exhausted, a factor that should never be overlooked in warfare.

We shall focus first on the mobile forces of the XXXXI Panzer Corps. Ground mist meant that it initially had to do without aerial support from the VIII Air Corps, but from 11 am this was no longer a problem. The 36th Motorised Infantry Division, all by itself on the northern wing, breached the Russian fortifications on either side of Starokvoritsy in one swift and expertly executed motion and advanced approximately four kilometres into the gradually rising terrain. Although enemy resistance was fierce to begin with, it abated throughout the day, so it looked as if the way had been paved for further success here. The corps therefore decided that the 1st Panzer Division, which had been held back in readiness for a follow-up strike on the right or left, would be sent forward on 10 September immediately on the southern side of the 36th Motorised Infantry Division so as to exploit the situation there. The 1st Panzer Division drove right up to the Krasnogvardeysk–Krasnoye Selo road, although a few elements had to turn to face the Taytsy salient to guard against the possibility of the division being outflanked. The 36th Motorised Infantry Division then thrust further eastwards and reached a position well beyond the road. Despite bitter enemy resistance, the division took the Duderhof barracks and entered the wooded hills on the southeastern side of Lake Duderhof. We were thereby able to gain a foothold in the western part of the range of hills of the Duderhof Heights, a strategically important area that dominated further terrain to the north and east. If we could gain full control of this area, it would offer us a significant advantage. As the 6th Panzer Division was urgently needed for the fighting in the vicinity of Krasnogvardeysk, our thoughts turned to the 8th Panzer Division. Unfortunately, it was not yet available.

The 6th Panzer Division had been engaged in heavy fighting near and to the northwest of Pudostya on 9 and 10 September, destroying 32 bunkers and two steel and concrete fortifications. It wanted to push further eastwards on 11 September. The L Corps had just regrouped on 10 September in response to strong enemy resistance, with the SS-Police Division having barely achieved anything the day before. This division would therefore shift its attention further north so as to work more closely with, and exploit the progress of, the 6th Panzer Division. Even the territorial gain of the 269th Infantry Division had been insignificant on 9 September. It had been outflanked to the east and was also facing a fiercely defended Krasnogvardeysk. We would need to regroup here, too, and the infantry there would require the help of a panzer battalion from the 8th Panzer Division in order to sweep through the open terrain before them. We would have to wait and see whether such help arrived!

On 11 September, the main attack group of the 269th Infantry Division pushed forward on the right wing, with the support of tanks and aircraft, as far as Bolshaya Samostye and was able to cross the railway line to its north. The left attack group of the division infiltrated the southeastern area of Krasnogvardeysk, which was still being toughly defended from all quarters. The SS-Police Division attacked Krasnogvardeysk from the west and northwest on the same day, but was unable to force its way in and remained approximately two kilometres away from the western outskirts of the town. However, the eastward thrust of the 6th Panzer Division from Pudostya reached as far as the Krasnogvardeysk–Krasnoye Selo road at a point roughly four kilometres to the north of the town. The division would then continue its advance to the east on the next day.

Better progress was made in and around Krasnogvardeysk on 12 September. The 269th Infantry Division advanced further northwards, despite the heavy counterattacks of Russian armour, and reached the Krasnogvardeysk–Detskoe Selo road in the vicinity of Romanova. The left group of the division had paused on this day so as to await the arrival of the left group of the SS-Police Division from the southwest. The two groups were to work together the next day to force an entry into Krasnogvardeysk. The left group of the SS-Police Division had in the meantime been approaching the town from the northwest and had closed in to within one kilometre. To the north of Krasnogvardeysk, elements of the 6th Panzer Division had turned southwards to form a front against the town whilst the rest had lunged as far as the Krasnogvardeysk–Pulkovo road. The Russian forces in the town were thereby denied their last route of retreat. The distance between the 6th Panzer Division and the 269th Infantry Division (in Romanova) now amounted to a mere three kilometres. The assault on the town would very soon take place, and it turned out that the fighting on 13 September was very brief. The headquarters of the L Corps reported at noon that Krasnogvardeysk had been seized. Most fortunately, the bridges in the area of the town fell into our hands without any damage whatsoever. The corps immediately continued its advance to the northeast. Its task was to drive on Slutsk and Detskoe Selo and to establish contact with the XXVIII Corps.

Following the success of the 36th Motorised Infantry Division on 10 September, Colonel-General Hoepner granted the XXXXI Panzer Corps freedom of action with regard to the direction in which it chose to advance next. The corps could proceed against whichever of Leningrad or Detskoe Selo seemed to offer the greatest prospects of victory. Hoepner himself had visited the command post of the 36th Motorised Infantry Division early on 11 September. He had requested on the evening of 10 September that the Eighteenth Army, as a part of its role of providing protection on the northern flank of the XXXXI Panzer Corps, be responsible for the rapid capture of Krasnoye Selo. Hoepner had become somewhat concerned by the fact that the northern neighbour of the XXXXI Panzer Corps, the 1st Infantry Division, had pivoted to the north prior to reaching the town. The Eighteenth Army promised that the 58th Infantry Division would be sent into the town. This meant that forces would not have to be diverted from the XXXXI Panzer Corps, as had been feared by Hoepner. Nikolayevka was the objective of the day for the 36th Motorised Infantry Division on 11 September, and the division reached it with little difficulty. The impression we had gained of the enemy was as follows: there was no systematic defence, there existed little artillery activity, and the Russian 3rd Rifle Division had been hastily thrown in from Moscow. The northern battle group of the 1st Panzer Division had taken the Duderhof Heights in the face of only weak Russian resistance. The southern group of the division was still embroiled in fierce fighting near the Taytsy salient. A gap opened up in the enemy front between Duderhof and Nikolayevka on the evening of 11 September, but unfortunately we lacked the forces needed to exploit it. The 8th Panzer Division was still unavailable, although its release was underway. The first few elements of the division would be at our disposal on the evening of 12 September.

The advance on Leningrad from the southeast

Before we go into the promising prospects for the advance on Leningrad from the southeast, we will first examine the situation of the XXVIII Corps at that time. The 121st Infantry Division had only managed to reach the Izhora River from the south throughout the course of the day on 10 September. The toing and froing as to when the attack should begin became only worse throughout 11 September, when the question arose as to whether the corps ought to attack at all. Towards 10 am, Field-Marshal von Leeb told us over the phone that he was worried about the situation of the XXXIX Panzer Corps. He would probably need to send some help to the corps, and would need either the 96th Infantry Division or the 8th Panzer Division to do this. He preferred the latter due to its greater mobility. I pointed out to the field-marshal that the 8th Panzer Division was fully engaged in fighting and could not be made available at all. The panzer group agreed to the detachment of the 96th Infantry Division, but this meant that the attack of the XXVIII Corps would have to be cancelled. By the evening, the army group had decided that it was able to do without the extra forces, for the XXXIX Panzer Corps had managed to master the situation. The headquarters of the panzer group nevertheless remained in a state of concern, as the army group seemed to be in the habit of drawing upon the forces that were needed for the main attack, and this was moreover at the very moment when victory was within our grasp. The army group ended up taking away the 8th Panzer Division, even though it was well aware that the panzer group regarded the division as a reserve unit to be used by the XXXXI Panzer Corps in the final thrust on Leningrad. Why did the army group not make use of the mobile forces to the south of Lake Ilmen instead? There were two corps committed there in what the panzer group saw as an insignificant zone without any good prospects. Before Leningrad, on the other hand, an important battle was about to take place which could very well be decided in our favour. To make matters worse, the 8th Panzer Division was being thrown into the marshland in the vicinity of Mga despite the fact that the panzer group had already advised that the division would be ill-suited to such terrain. An infantry division, with its greater strength in foot soldiers, would be far better. The bad experience to be endured by the XXXIX Panzer Corps would be a lesson!

So it transpired that the attack of the XXVIII Corps was to go ahead. Supported by the VIII Air Corps, both divisions of the corps set off on 12 September at 8:30 am with the initial goal of capturing Fodorovskoye-Posad. It was an important town that could not be bypassed. The corps formed a tight ring of encirclement around it, and by the evening the town was in German hands. On the morning of 13 September, Russian tanks ploughed into the assembly area of the 96th Infantry Division. We were able to repulse the Russian attack, but by the end of the day we had made no further progress whatsoever. The next day bore no fruit either, especially since the Luftwaffe was grounded by bad weather. In the morning hours of 15 September, we lost the northern part of Fodorovskoye-Posad when the enemy launched a powerful strike supported by tanks. We counterattacked, retook the area, and pushed the frontline right up to the strongly built-up Slutsk. But then the attacking power of the XXVIII Corps petered out. The only chance of success would be if a simultaneous attack were carried out against Slutsk from the west. The conspicuously large number of Stalin tanks that we came across could be explained by the fact that the nearby Kolpino was the location of their manufacture. They were the heaviest type of Russian armoured vehicle. Brand-new tanks with garrisoned factories close by existed not only here but also at other points along the front of the panzer group. It was therefore rather difficult for the XXVIII Corps to fulfil its task of pressing the attack.

The panzer forces are to be detached

Army Group North had already received OKW Directive No. 35 on 6 September. It stated that the main offensive on the Eastern Front was to be conducted against Moscow. The mobile and aerial forces of Army Group North were therefore to be redirected from 15 September. The army group had initially refrained from passing on this news to the panzer group, as the attack on Leningrad was about to take place. It understandably remained the desire of the army group to more or less bring the battle for Leningrad to a conclusion, which meant at least the establishment of a tight ring of encirclement around the city. If only the army group had been able to press for an early start to the attack! We were now in a severely disadvantageous position. The enemy had been given time to prepare a stubborn defence, so it seemed unlikely that we would be able to conduct an extensive and victorious offensive operation against the city in a period of less than one week. Yet it was very much the case that the enthusiasm of the army group for the attack on Leningrad was far less pronounced than that of the panzer group. On the evening of 10 September, Field-Marshal von Leeb told Colonel-General Hoepner that it would all come down to the progress made by the L Corps. This was only the second day of the assault on Leningrad, and our success near Duderhof was already underway. This was also the day on which we at the headquarters of the panzer group learnt of the detachment of the mobile forces planned for the middle of the month. Interestingly enough, one effect of this news was to increase the urgency and speed with which we sought to attain victory with the XXXXI Panzer Corps. Maximum use had to be made of the corps whilst it was still available for the assault on Leningrad. And it was now more important than ever that the 8th Panzer Division be committed to the assault!

It certainly might have been the case that the army group thought it possible to temporarily postpone the handing over of its units, for in my telephone conversation with the commander of the army group on 11 September at 10 am, the same one in which the question arose as to whether the XXVIII Corps ought to launch an attack, I gleaned from the field-marshal the following: 'Field-Marshal von Leeb is in complete agreement with our intention of fully exploiting the success of the XXXXI Panzer Corps that is currently underway and says that under these circumstances the detachment of Panzer Group 4 for use elsewhere cannot be considered for the time being.' However, there was no way the OKH would agree to this. Regardless of what the commander of the army group truly wanted, the fact was that there now existed a prevailing attitude of restraint and limitation with regard to the objectives before Leningrad. After the order had been made to focus on the attack on Moscow, Leningrad could no longer be top priority! This explains why the army group had decided to do without the exploitation of the success in the Duderhof Heights and to emphasise instead the necessity of the advance of the L Corps. They would be the only troops available following the detachment of the XXXXI Panzer Corps, and the army group was now interested in shortening the front and in closing the gap to the XXVIII Corps. Having been informed that the detachment of the XXXXI Panzer Corps was required, the panzer group, which had at first been otherwise inclined, chose to adopt the position of the army group. For sure, the initial efforts of the army group to conceal the plans for the detachment had caused misunderstanding and differences of opinion, but it is understandable why the army group had done this. It would have been a psychological error for the army group to announce such plans prior to the launch of the assault on Leningrad.

The conclusion of the advance on Leningrad

As we have seen, the imminent detachment of the mobile forces required that we refrain from exploiting the success in the Duderhof Heights and instead focus on closing the gap to the XXVIII Corps in the east. Despite the disorderly retreat of the enemy and the lack of resistance he was expected to put up, the 36th Motorised Infantry Division was instructed not to cross the Detskoe Selo–Peterhof road to the north. The division was to remain behind this road unless there was some indication that the Eighteenth Army was approaching Uritsk. The Eighteenth Army and Army Group North still harboured the intention of breaking through here to the Gulf of Finland and thereby cutting off the route of retreat of those Russian forces located further west. The panzer group was prepared to partake in this effort despite the looming detachment of the XXXXI Panzer Corps, as it was still, until 13 September, counting on being able to make use of the 8th Panzer Division. When giving consideration to this attack, the panzer group expressed its desire for the 254th Infantry Division, which had been sent forward by the Eighteenth Army from Estonia, to be inserted on the right-hand side of the 36th Motorised Infantry Division. In the opinion of the panzer group, it was there that the best chances of success lay. It would at least mean the availability of an infantry division should either the 36th Motorised Infantry Division or the 1st Panzer Division need to be released. However, the army group followed the recommendation of the Eighteenth Army and approved the commitment of the 254th Infantry Division between the 1st and 291st Infantry Divisions. The advance towards the Uritsk–Peterhof line commenced early on 15 September with a front approximately 18 kilometres in width, but only on the right wing was there sufficient penetrative power. Uritsk was swiftly taken by the 58th Infantry Division, and German forces managed to reach the Gulf of Finland to the west of the town. It probably would have been more practical in this situation for the Eighteenth Army to take charge of the advance of the 36th Motorised Infantry Division so as to fully maximise the point of main effort on the eastern wing and take advantage of the lack of enemy resistance that existed at that time. What actually happened, though, was that this sector of the front stayed where it was right up until the mobile forces were pulled out.

The non-stop efforts of the panzer group to have the 8th Panzer Division placed under its command finally came to nought on 13 September. We had intended to place the division somewhere between Pulkovo and Uritsk, but this would no longer be possible. We received the order of the army group in the morning: the division was to be ready by 15 September as the first mobile formation to be transferred to Army Group Centre. After everything that had happened until now, this was a great disappointment for the panzer group. Our disappointment was all the greater when, on the late afternoon of 14 September, Army Group North ordered the immediate dispatch of the division to the Sixteenth Army 'to support the XXXIX Panzer Corps'. It was with regret that the war diary of the panzer group concluded: 'The result of this decision is that the division, no longer available for the assault on Leningrad, is going to the neighbouring army and will probably not at all have a chance to be used by Army Group Centre.' Perhaps Army Group North was only speaking of the 'temporary' subordination of the division to the Sixteenth Army, but the unstable situation of the XXXIX Panzer Corps meant that, unfortunately, the prediction of the panzer group was proved to be correct. The terrain there was simply not good for mobile troops! The panzer group had foreseen the disadvantageous situation that would develop there, but no attention had been paid to our concerns. On 15 September, the supply vehicles of the XXXIX Panzer Corps were forced to use the supply route of the panzer group via Luga, as the road through Novgorod was endangered by an enemy breakthrough between the 18th Motorised Infantry Division and the 12th Panzer Division. This was the very spot which was supposed to be secured by the employment of the 8th Panzer Division.

From 12 September, the panzer group, aside from planning to make use of the 8th Panzer Division, was focused on uniting its eastern and western attack groups in the vicinity of Detskoe Selo. The advance of the L Corps towards the northeast was to be supported by the 6th Panzer Division, even though it had originally been planned that the division, after its seizure of Krasnogvardeysk, would be employed in the sector of the XXXXI Panzer Corps. The 1st Panzer Division had in the meantime pivoted towards the east and had been assigned the objective of reaching the road junction southwest of Pulkovo. It had to withstand a number of fierce counterattacks on 14 and 15 September that were conducted by heavy Russian tanks – yet again the Stalin type from Kolpino! As had been the case near Raseiniai, it was evident that the penetrative power of the bulk of our armour was inadequate in the face of these Russian tanks. The division was able to continue its eastward thrust on 16 September, taking Alexandrovka on the same day. As a result of these developments, it was decided that the 6th Panzer Division, instead of the 1st Panzer Division, would be removed from the front on 16 September and would set off on the evening of 17 September behind the 8th Panzer Division towards the south via Luga and Pskov.

In the area of the L Corps, the 269th Infantry Division, following its crossing of the Izhora, had to veer ever more eastwards. Enemy troops stood on both sides of the railway line leading to Leningrad, between Susanino and Detskoe Selo, and we had thus far been unable to attack them, due not only to lack of forces but also the fact that the terrain there was covered with marsh and forest. Two-thirds of the 269th Infantry Division were already tied down to the security of its eastern front. It was therefore becoming increasingly urgent that something be undertaken against this pocket, which had taken on the shape of a sack 25 kilometres in depth. With the fighting in the Luga pocket having just come to an end, the 285th Security Division, reinforced with SS and other auxiliary units, was given the task of emptying this sack of enemy forces from 16 September. The main combat forces of the corps could then strike towards Maryino and Detskoe Selo. The latter was taken on 17 September, a parting gift, as it were, from the panzer group to the Eighteenth Army, which was to assume responsibility for this area from noon. The emptying of the sack lasted a few more days, and Slutsk would eventually be captured by the XXVIII Corps.

The advance of Panzer Group 4 on Leningrad was over.

CHAPTER 8

The effects of the operational measures of the OKW and OKH on the conduct of operations of Army Group North

The operational plans of Hitler and those of the OKH for the Russian campaign were very much the same and corresponded almost word for word on paper. Hitler's Directive No. 21 for Operation Barbarossa and the OKH Deployment Directive for Barbarossa had been issued on 18 December 1940 and 31 January 1941 respectively. However, the development of the campaign quickly revealed differences of opinion whose effects we experienced due to the intervention of the higher levels of command, primarily the OKH, on the conduct of battle in the northern sector of the Eastern Front. These differences of opinion revolved around what the operational objective ought to be. Even though Hitler was increasingly plagued by indecision, he generally gave Leningrad priority over Moscow, as had been outlined in both aforementioned directives. The decisions of the OKH, on the other hand, as the campaign unfolded revealed a strong desire for the seizure of Moscow. Amidst the tense atmosphere of this fundamental operational disagreement, Army Group North swiftly got on with its advance. Its victories came to nothing when the main operational objective in the Russian campaign switched to Moscow, and the unsatisfactory outcome there in November and December 1941 added insult to injury. The operational possibilities for Army Group North and its freedom to make decisions were thereby curbed, influenced, or altered. The effects of this on Panzer Group 4 have been described in detail. Army Group North was unable to carry out its own plans, and the compromises that it made resulted in half-measures that could have very easily been avoided.

It is not the aim of this book to examine the reasons for the disagreement at the highest levels of command, nor is it to investigate the measures they took or the changes of plans they made. Rather, to be examined are the limitations imposed on Army Group North so that its conduct of command and that of Panzer Group 4, which often felt it had gotten a raw deal, can be justified or understood. The two main limitations were as follows:

(1) The close relationship between Army Group North and its right-hand neighbour, Army Group Centre, often resulted in delays in the advance on Leningrad and in decisions being made which ran counter to the idea of taking the city quickly.
(2) The lack of clarity with regard to how and where Panzer Group 3 would be employed in the area of Army Group North made it difficult for any long-term plan to be made and led to half-measures being pursued whose success depended on the wishes of the army group coming true.

On point 1: The Sixteenth Army suffered the most from the relationship between Army Group North and Army Group Centre. According to the instructions it had originally received from Army Group North, the Sixteenth Army was supposed to place the main emphasis of its advance on its northern wing so as to make full use of the thrust of Panzer Group 4 on Leningrad. The Sixteenth Army would then also be in the position to provide protection to the southern flank of the panzer group. However, on the order of the OKH, the Sixteenth Army had become involved in the fighting on the northern wing of the Ninth Army in the Western Dvina area. On top of that, it had been required to hand over the XXIII Corps and to 'temporarily' extend its combat sector by 20 kilometres towards the south.[32] Against the operational intentions of Army Group North, as much as 60 per cent of the fighting power of the Sixteenth

32 Details on the demands made by the OKH of the Sixteenth Army can be found in Appendix 5.

Army had become committed to the fighting on the southern wing, and this was at the time when Panzer Group 4, the spearhead of the army group, launched its decisive thrust from Pskov towards Leningrad. Only the X Corps pushed forward towards the northeast on the northern wing of the Sixteenth Army in the first half of July, and it became ever farther away from the rest of the forces of the army. This was how the gap to the south of Panzer Group 4 came into being, the very one that the panzer group was eventually ordered by the commander of the army group to deal with on the lower Luga. In view of the fact that the objective of Army Group North was Leningrad, the fighting on the southern wing of the Sixteenth Army was completely worthless. It led to considerable delays and much attrition. The Russian forces there could have been eliminated after a successful outcome in Leningrad, and their sacrifice would have been just as great as that of the Russian forces in the vicinity of Kiev when Panzer Group 2 was ordered by Hitler to pivot to the south at the end of August 1941. However, the armoured thrust of Panzer Group 4 could not build up the momentum needed to secure victory, for the Sixteenth Army was not in the position to secure its southern flank. With enemy forces flowing into any gaps that had opened up, the Sixteenth Army was similarly exposed and had to carve out its own path to the northeast in the direction of Lake Ilmen. The shock that the Russian forces in the north had received at the outset of the campaign had lasted only a very short time!

On point 2: Hitler had wanted to dispatch Panzer Group 3 to Army Group North from the beginning, and it was with the belief that this would take place that the army group made its operational calculations, especially for the battle for Leningrad. Although Hitler repeatedly, from the end of June, suggested this reinforcement of Army Group North to the OKH, he always allowed himself to be fobbed off by the assessment of the OKH to the effect that it was the rapid advance of Panzer Group 4 that would prove to be the decisive factor. On 8 July, the day on which a decision about the dispatch of Panzer Group 3 had to be made, the OKH yet again chose to put it off. It was on 9 July that Army Group North learnt from the OKH that it would still be denied Panzer Group 3. This did not meet with Hitler's approval. He urged for the dispatch of Panzer Group 3 a couple more times (on 13 and 17 July), and, during his visit to the headquarters of Army Group North on 21 July, he promised that this would be done. The fulfilment of this promise was forestalled by Field-Marshal Walther von Brauchitsch, the commander in chief of the German Army, who did not like the idea of sending Panzer Group 3 far from the zone of Army Group Centre. He decided that Panzer Group 3 would only support Army Group North with a flank attack in the Valdai Hills so as to 'cut through' the lines of communication between Moscow and Leningrad. In carrying out this attack, Panzer Group 3 was to remain under the command of Army Group Centre. It would not be handed over to Army Group North! Yet this plan was cancelled by the OKH on 30 July, and Army Group North was yet again in the position where it would have to take Leningrad with its own forces alone. This refusal by the OKH to dispatch Panzer Group 3 to Army Group North seemed to be final, for the OKH wanted to keep Panzer Group 3 ready for the assault on Moscow! It was clear that this still did not correspond with Hitler's intentions to resolve the situation in the Leningrad area. Further considerations at the highest levels of command ended when, during the Russian counterattack in the vicinity of Staraya Russa on 15 August, Hitler ordered that any available panzer forces be handed over to Army Group North. The result was the diversion of the XXXIX Panzer Corps to the north in the middle of August.

Aside from the burdensome commitment of the Sixteenth Army in the south and the uncertainty regarding whether or not Panzer Group 3 would be sent northwards, Army Group North was repeatedly subjected to the influence of the high command in the conduct of operations in Estonia. This was because there was little agreement on how to assess the situation there. Field-Marshal von Leeb, on the one hand, wanted to commit as few forces as possible to Estonia. He was of the view that victory in Leningrad would seal the fate of any Russian forces still in Estonia; if the former fell quickly, then so too would the latter. The OKH, on the other hand, pressed for the reinforcement of German forces in Estonia. Even Hitler's Directive No. 34 of 30 July specifically mentioned: 'Estonia is to be mopped up with all of the forces at the disposal of the Eighteenth Army; only after that may its divisions proceed further in the direction of Leningrad.'

Army Group North, the only one of the three army groups that from the outset had its concentrated mobile forces directly under its command and that therefore managed to achieve a number of successes in quick succession, maintained its focus on the rapid thrust on Leningrad and did so, despite all the interference, for as long as victory still seemed possible. The army group soon found that it would have to do without a rapid thrust. Panzer Group 4 had been subjected to the effects of the limitations described above and had ended up in a position where it had to halt for an extended period of time, isolated and in great danger, before resuming the advance on Leningrad. All of this was because a rather unusual situation had arisen. Despite the major successes thus far, the highest levels of command had become more anxious and restrained (e.g. the reorganisation within the Russian high command had caused some concern). In the meantime, confidence, morale, and initiative at the front had only been increasing. It was no wonder that there was a lack of understanding over the behaviour of the high command. There were no fears or reservations on the part of Panzer Group 4, and not even on the part of Army Group North. The situation did not present any reason to panic, certainly not for as long as we continued to make rapid progress. The OKH and Hitler judged the situation here according to the experiences of the other army groups. It is also possible, as far as the OKH was concerned, that the fixation on Moscow may have played a role. The OKH was only interested in the seizure of Leningrad to the extent that it did not draw upon the forces of Army Group Centre. The fact that so significant forces of the Sixteenth Army had been sent to the south in an utterly worthless direction instead of to the north, as had been preferred by Army Group North so as to cover its own ever-widening front, underlines the intense focus of the OKH on Moscow.[33] Even though this corresponded to the operational intentions of Field-Marshal von Brauchitsch, it did not at all match Hitler's conception of the campaign in Russia. Hitler, who knew that the Leningrad area needed to be eliminated quickly, had not prevented the obstructive influence of the

33 The resolution on the Western Dvina in the Polotsk–Vitebsk–Nevel area was of great benefit to the advance of Army Group Centre!

OKH, nor did he refuse any of its recommendations. He was probably unable to see the effects of the decisions of the OKH! Indeed, he often accepted and even sometimes built upon those decisions, something which the OKH could only interpret as his agreement with their outlook. This was what led to the emphasis on the worthless sealing off of Leningrad, with the point of main effort from the southeast, and the positively pointless idea to 'cut through' the lines of communication between Leningrad and Moscow. The latter could have quite easily been left to the Luftwaffe; the army lacked the forces to carry it out, and, as was what transpired, the terrain did not make rapid movement possible. To commit forces to the Valdai region was also operationally worthless. Getting as far as or even occupying this area would have made no impression whatsoever on the Russian leadership in Leningrad more than 300 kilometres away! The dissipation of our forces would have been the only result!

A word will be said here about the way in which the high command evaluated the terrain. Knowledge of the terrain is of the utmost importance for panzer troops, whereas it is less so for the infantry who, marching on foot, are able to put up with difficult ground. For mobile units, bad terrain causes delays and thus reduces operational effectiveness and combat firepower. Just as a cavalry charge would fail amidst water, marsh, or forest in times past, so would a tank assault today. The German panzer arm was at that time much stronger than its Russian counterpart, but it still needed the right preconditions to be able to fully exploit its superiority.

The terrain factor was something that Hitler was unable to assess, but, unfortunately, even the OKH did not adequately recognise its importance. This was demonstrated in the assignment of operational objectives in the north. The Opochka area had been selected as the first operational objective for Army Group North. This was supposed to be, as it were, the springboard for the assault on Leningrad. Yet no roads led to Opochka from the west, and the town itself possessed no road junction, so it was no surprise later on when the LVI Panzer Corps ground to a halt to the west of the town. Ostrov and Pskov would have been far better objectives in every respect. Opochka was probably chosen by the OKH because, at first glance, it might have looked like a good point from which to carry out an envelopment manoeuvre against Leningrad (i.e. from the southeast).[34] Further northeast from Opochka, in the direction that was probably imagined by the OKH, there were no roads, not even any that would be somewhat adequate, and no terrain that would lend itself to a decisive tank battle. It would be difficult, and indeed worthless, to attempt to carry out this operational plan with neither roads nor good terrain. Both were absolutely necessary for the decisive employment of panzer troops! The commander of Panzer Group 4 and the panzer leaders under his command therefore chose, and in fact had to choose, the best roads for the advance. It was thus that the panzer group drove forward and bypassed the Opochka area to the north. The practicalities of the situation meant that the theoretical planning of the OKH had to be disregarded. As the advance proceeded smoothly, no objections were raised.

Rather more of a stir was caused when the commander of the panzer group made the decision to place, wherever possible, the emphasis of the advance not on the right wing, as had been foreseen by the OKH, but on the left wing, in the direction of the lower Luga. The terrain on the left was far more suitable for tank warfare. We have described the difficulty of this decision for Colonel-General Hoepner. He not only made this decision but also accepted, in full awareness, responsibility for the consequences that, in the eyes of the unpredictable layman Hitler, might have appeared to be most disadvantageous. Field-Marshal von Leeb belatedly approved this decision. It was by no means unalterable, but he had come to the conclusion that Hoepner had made the correct decision. In contrast, the OKH demonstrated little understanding of the decisive importance of the terrain and continued to demand that the point of main effort be placed on the right.

Army Group North constantly found itself caught between the OKH on the one hand, whose rigid demands completely disregarded the terrain, and the realities of combat on the other. The army group sought to support the position of Panzer Group 4 wherever possible. Nonetheless,

---

34 In the Deployment Directive for Barbarossa, the following intermediate objectives were assigned: the area northeast of Opochka for Panzer Group 4, Opochka itself for the Sixteenth Army, and Ostrov–Pskov for the Eighteenth Army.

the final result, among other things, was the abandonment at the last moment of a concentrated tank thrust on Leningrad, the operational objective. Subsequent developments highlight not only how disadvantageous the misjudgement of the terrain was when it came to combat with the panzer arm, but also how insignificant any theoretically advantageous operational envelopment would be. The XXXIX Panzer Corps, whose contribution was supposed to be decisive, was held up by enemy forces southeast of Leningrad amidst forest and marshland. The corps could therefore play no role whatsoever in the battle for Leningrad. The unification of the two attack groups before Leningrad that was planned by the army group did not materialise. This was detrimental to the chances of success. The difficulties of supply for the XXXIX Panzer Corps have already been described. As we have seen, its precarious situation in the marshland southeast of Leningrad meant that we were eventually compelled to hand over the 8th Panzer Division to it. This was the division that was supposed to be the spearhead of Panzer Group 4, which by this time was already being transferred to the Smolensk area for the assault on Moscow. As had been the case for some time, the panzer group would have to go into combat without the division!

It is clear that little attention was paid from above to the judgements and warnings of the commander of the panzer group. It is also worth pointing out that Hoepner had only made the decision to proceed over the lower Luga in anticipation of a further rapid thrust on Leningrad in which the infantry would fully participate! With the delay of this rapid thrust beyond the river and the ever-increasing displacement of German forces for the 'point of main effort on the right', we at the headquarters of the panzer group remained convinced that the only chance for the mobile forces would be where the terrain was favourable. We therefore stuck to our plan of renewing the advance from the bridgeheads we had established on the north bank of the Luga. We have seen how the commander of the panzer group strove to gather together all six mobile divisions here, albeit unsuccessfully due to the measures of the army group. His refusal to shift the point of main effort of the panzer group further east was due not only to the terrain factor but also to the impossibility of supplying forces concentrated so far away. Also to be emphasised is the danger that would have been ever present from the east bank of the Volkhov. The envelopment plan of the OKH, with the main emphasis on the right, was bound to fail from the outset, especially because it gave no consideration whatsoever as to how the units involved were to be supplied.

All of these repeatedly reported grounds against shifting the point of main effort to the right were ignored by the OKH. It remained committed to its theoretical idea of where the emphasis of the advance should be and completely disregarded the actual conditions of the situation, be it our position, the enemy position, the terrain, the question of supply, or even the severe exhaustion of the troops (approximately 30 per cent killed or wounded without any replacements at all). Unfortunately, the high command trusted its own judgement more than that of the commanders in the field. It was the commanders of the army group, of the panzer group, and of the various corps who experienced with the troops under their command the true conditions at the front and whose recommendations and warnings were informed by their sense of responsibility and by their understanding of the way in which events were unfolding. Did the high command concern itself too much with daily operations and too little with reaching a position from which the final decisive battle could be fought? It was the interference of the high command that had made it difficult for Army Group North to reach Leningrad. The operations did not unfold as planned, and the support we needed from the OKH failed to materialise. The intense focus of Field-Marshal von Brauchitsch on Moscow may have been the reason why our needs were disregarded, and this might also explain why the OKH misunderstood the situation in the northern sector of the Eastern Front. Another contributing factor to this misunderstanding was the seemingly easy advance of Panzer Group 4. Although the advance had yet to reach any important objectives, its rapidity and depth gave the high command the impression that the power of resistance of the enemy had been broken and that Army Group North therefore ought to be able to carry out the assault on Leningrad with the forces currently at its disposal. The tremendous progress that had been made by the mobile forces of the army group, through both skill and good fortune, had thus turned out to be disadvantageous rather than advantageous. The OKH saw and valued our progress only within the framework of its Moscow plan. It therefore underestimated the enemy in the area of Army Group North and overestimated our own performance there. The unfortunate result of this was that the OKH believed it could draw upon the forces of Army Group North (the Sixteenth Army) to reinforce Army Group Centre and thus make the advance in the direction of Moscow easier. Army Group North, despite its weakness before this time, had still hoped to be able to exploit the deep and rapid thrust of Panzer Group 4, but this would no longer be possible. The question then arose as to whether we could still reach Leningrad quickly and whether its capture would even have a decisive effect.

CHAPTER 9

Could Leningrad have been taken?

For the duration of the advance on Leningrad, the hope that the city could be taken had filled the officers and men of Panzer Group 4 with courage and had spurred them on. This hope had given rise to the determination with which the headquarters of the panzer group, despite many obstacles and disappointments, adhered to and carried out its decisions, which had already been made based on what it regarded as correct and most promising. Even the army group was inspired by this desire to drive forward in the direction of Leningrad, and it made this clear in its first order for Barbarossa, outlining the task to be carried out by the panzer group:

> Panzer Group 4 is to create the conditions for a deep and rapid penetration in the direction of Leningrad. In order to achieve this overall objective, it is necessary to exploit any opportunity that arises and to deny the enemy the time he needs to form a united defensive front further back from the border.

These words indicated that the leadership of the panzer group was to make a concerted effort to reach Leningrad and that it would be given the freedom of action needed for the attainment of this goal. Field-Marshal von Leeb, in full awareness of the importance and potential of the panzer arm, sought to maximise what it could achieve to the greatest extent possible. He placed the panzer group immediately under the command of the army group so that he could issue orders directly to it at any time. The panzer group was to be the spearhead of the army group, and he wanted the headquarters of each to work together closely. A decisive factor for the drive on Leningrad was the distribution in depth of the enemy forces in the combat sector of Army Group North, which was in stark contrast to the situation along the rest of the Eastern Front. This hardly allowed an immediate overthrow of the enemy, but he could still be taken by surprise and eliminated piece by piece.

The army group pushed for the continuation of the thrust on Leningrad following the crossing of the Western Dvina, but it became more cautious later on when the panzer group was prepared to proceed from the Ostrov bridgehead. In the event, Colonel-General Hoepner acted more or less independently and the panzer group continued its drive. After all, almost two-thirds of the distance to Leningrad had been covered. On 10 July, after just two-and-a-half weeks, only 300 kilometres separated us from the city. This greatly motivated the panzer group, but the army group was much more apprehensive due to the extended frontline and the dependency of the Sixteenth Army on its northern neighbour. In hindsight, such apprehension can be seen as the influence of the OKH. The army group had become worried that the panzer group might find itself isolated and that the unity of the army group itself would be endangered. Its desire for the rapid thrust on Leningrad and the exploitation of the unpreparedness of the enemy began to wane.

The army group had been given insufficient forces with which to reach Leningrad, but it seemed as if the city was no longer the objective! As envisioned by the OKH, the point of main effort of the entire operation was to be applied in the direction of Moscow! The only compensation for our lack of forces was the attainment and full exploitation of the element of surprise. Only a rapid thrust could take the enemy by surprise, so it was of great importance that no time be lost. It was a matter of course that the mobile forces be concentrated together so as to guarantee a swift advance, and it therefore made sense that both infantry armies place the emphasis of their advance on their inner wings!

Yet very soon, in fact still in June, Army Group Centre pivoted to carry out an encirclement of the enemy and thereby temporarily abandoned its advance to the northeast. This was bound to have a significant effect on Army Group North, whose direction of advance was supposed to circle ever more to the north. The OKH ordered that Army Group

North was to maintain contact with Army Group Centre, the result of which was that the axis of advance of Army Group North would very much become dependent on the pull of its southern neighbour. It was from this point on that a number of obstacles began to be put in our way! This development would put a great strain on Army Group North and distract it from carrying out its original plan.

While the thoughts of the army group began to drift towards a deceleration of the advance, the panzer group made the decision on 10 July to grant both panzer corps freedom of action in their drive beyond Novgorod and Luga in the direction of Leningrad. From this moment, the lack of a third (reserve) panzer corps would begin to be felt. The panzer group confronted this decisive situation without any reserves at all; the infantry had yet to arrive. It was then that both panzer corps ground to a halt. The northern corps, in an attempt to cover the final 100 kilometres to Leningrad, had proceeded over the lower Luga in order to find a weak point to break through. But an immediate renewal of the advance was not possible there. The situation in the area of the LVI Panzer Corps needed to be resolved first, after which the flow of supplies and the improvement of the main road had to be awaited. A third panzer corps would have enabled us to maintain greater momentum! But it was now that the army group stopped. It had become uncertain on both wings, especially on the right. This was again most certainly the result of the influence of the OKH. The army group wanted to at least await the arrival of the infantry of the I and XXXVIII Corps, which would mean a delay of approximately ten days. In the meantime, the panzer group had taken steps to shift the LVI Panzer Corps to the left so that it could advance either via Luga or in the wake of the XXXXI Panzer Corps.

Differences in opinion were beginning to become clearer! The army group now wanted to place greater emphasis on the right wing. A great deal of toing and froing was taking place, with the line of the OKH being toed the one moment and then ignored the next. This delayed the attack from the Luga bridgeheads by more than three weeks (15 July to 8 August), granting the enemy valuable time and making our eventual attack all the more difficult. The army group was no longer keen on the idea of shifting the LVI Panzer Corps to the attack wing of the panzer group. Any effort on the part of the panzer group to proceed with this shift became pointless once the corps was detached and sent to carry out a counterattack in the vicinity of Staraya Russa.

Staraya Russa proved to be the turning point in the Leningrad operation! By making the decision to counterattack near Staraya Russa on 15 August, the army group finally abandoned the rapid thrust on Leningrad. It had taken away one-third of the forces of the panzer group and had thereby reduced the chances of a successful strike from the Luga bridgeheads. More serious was the fact that the relocation of two mobile units from the attack front to the Staraya Russa area played into the hands of the enemy. The Russian diversionary attack near Staraya Russa achieved its goal of weakening the German attack on Leningrad. This was a successful move by the Russian leadership and almost certainly meant the rescue of Leningrad. The second period of time that was gained by the enemy lasted for three-and-a-half weeks, from 15 August until 9 September. This enabled him to organise a decent defence which had not existed in the middle of August and which, although somewhat makeshift in nature, was more than enough to confront the weakened German forces.

Had Army Group North got itself into a predicament? Even though Field-Marshal von Leeb had only just, on 15 August, promised to place the 3rd Motorised Infantry Division at the disposal of the panzer group, the suddenness of his decision to focus on Staraya Russa indicates that the situation must have seemed rather dire there for the X Corps. It was a decision made, so to speak, in the heat of the moment. On the late afternoon of 15 August, shortly after the decision had been made, it turned out that the army group was promised the XXXIX Panzer Corps. Its arrival would take a few days, but even the 3rd Motorised Infantry Division, in the vicinity to the south of Staraya Russa, would not be ready to attack before 19 August. The XXXIX Panzer Corps arrived there on 20 August, a strong indication that the idea of the point of main effort on the right was what prevailed in the minds of the German military leadership. The OKH had not at any stage envisioned sending the panzer corps to the Luga bridgeheads. It stuck to its old plan. Army Group North, in making the decision to focus on the right, had probably not been enjoying complete freedom of action.

This day, 15 August, was probably the only one on which the army group behaved in this way. It was probable that it once more valued the advance on Leningrad by 16 August. Indeed, on this day, the XXXXI Panzer Corps had a good chance of being able to reach Krasnogvardeysk, for there were barely any enemy forces that could oppose it! Elements of the 3rd Motorised Infantry Division would have already been crossing the lower Luga by this time. As mentioned, the XXXIX Panzer Corps was now available to support the X Corps if necessary. In fact, the OKH came to the conclusion on 17 August that the situation in the area of Staraya Russa was under control. This was before the arrival of the LVI Panzer Corps there! The disappointment we felt at the headquarters of Panzer Group 4 was not only understandable but also justifiable. In any event, the enemy had been given more time to organise his defence of Leningrad. This need not have been the case if the army group had not intervened on 15 August and had instead allowed the LVI Panzer Corps to follow in the wake of the drive of the XXXXI Panzer Corps. The panzer group would have then avoided every OKH order to stop. Krasnogvardeysk could have been taken on 16 August, or on 17 August at the very latest, and then the German armoured forces would have stood before Leningrad on 18 August, poised to attack with a minimum strength of two mobile divisions.

It was only from the north that our rapid thrust could be endangered, if at all, for that was where any remaining Russian units retreating from Estonia could be expected to appear. This could be taken into account as a part of mobile warfare and ought not to have posed much of a risk if the forces of the Eighteenth Army had focused more on maintaining contact with Panzer Group 4 (its primary task!) and less on frontal warfare with the retreating enemy. An extra week could very well have been gained here, not to mention the earlier release of at least one mobile division for the battle for Leningrad.

It can only be guessed how victory at the gates of Leningrad would have then manifested itself. The degree of morale on the Russian side would have played a significant role. His defence might have collapsed completely, or he might have tried to hold out in what was a hopeless situation. What is certain is that the panzer divisions that had only just entered the battlefield would have plunged right through the severely demoralised enemy forces. The Russian troops and their leadership would have been in an overwhelmingly disadvantageous position. We would have been able to reach Leningrad much more quickly (gain in time!) and could have established a tighter ring of encirclement around the city (economy of manpower!). And perhaps more could have been achieved. Right up until the last days of the drive on Leningrad, the commander of the panzer group had in mind the seizure of the city, especially in the case of the collapse of the enemy defence.[35] But in the conditions that prevailed in September, this would probably no longer be possible. It had been intended, and was indeed necessary, that the 8th Panzer Division be sent to our sector of the front, but this was delayed. This division remained our last hope that the battle for Leningrad could be decided in our favour. We were therefore greatly disappointed when the army group chose not to place the division at our disposal. The XXXXI Panzer Corps had made excellent progress in its charge towards Leningrad since the middle of August. Two more mobile divisions behind the XXXXI Panzer Corps, be they with the LVI or the XXXIX Panzer Corps, would have significantly accelerated the approach to the city. While the army group eventually carried out an assault on the city in September, we could have done this three weeks earlier and with far less attrition. Such a gain in time would have come in useful for the thrust on Moscow or enabled further success in the Leningrad region. For example, we could have pushed on and made contact with the Finns, or we could have annihilated the enemy forces retreating from Estonia rather than allowing them to embed themselves in the Oranienbaum pocket, a major headache for Army Group North which lasted for years.[36]

That a major and rapid success did not take place, and that Army Group North gave up the advance far too soon, was primarily the result

---

35 Despite Hitler's order that Leningrad be besieged, Colonel-General Hoepner was determined to take the city should the situation make it possible. Any military success ought to be exploited to the utmost; otherwise, the long-term consequences can be costly.

36 Oranienbaum lay on the coast, 10 kilometres west of Peterhof and opposite Kronstadt.

of the influence of the OKH. It would have been better if the OKH had been interested in resolving the situation in the Leningrad area quickly, for this would have corresponded to Hitler's wishes and would have created a far more advantageous position from which to carry out the decisive operation against Moscow. The refusal of the OKH to recognise or accept this highlighted the already existing tension between Hitler and the commander in chief of the army. The advance on Leningrad therefore ended with a rather limited victory. The German forces had reached the city without actually taking it.

Conclusion

An objective analysis requires some closing remarks on the performance of our leadership during this extensive and rather complex campaign. As emphasised in the foreword, what has primarily been described in this book is the point of view of the headquarters of Panzer Group 4 at that time. This includes the facts as we saw them, the impressions we formed, and the way in which we appraised the situation. We may not have been in a position to fully take into account the broader concerns of the high command. A general observation can be made here: even the leadership of a military organisation can form an impression of a situation that is shaped not only by bare facts and requirements but also by interaction and disagreement between various personalities. This is a phenomenon that can always be seen in politics. It is therefore often the case in military events that any given position is not the best that could have been achieved. Because of the need to compromise with others, the result is usually an intermediary position rather than one whose full potential has been realised.

Each participating personality wanted to achieve as much as possible with regard to the task he had been given to carry out. This explains the behaviour of the commander of Army Group North, Field-Marshal von Leeb – usually a calm, clear-headed, and objective personality – during the time he felt compelled to make concessions to his superior, the commander in chief of the army, in the interests of the assault on Moscow, even though this would make the conduct of his own task much more difficult. This demanded a considerable degree of self-discipline, a matter of course for this honourable soldier.[37] It was thus that, despite

37 The field-marshal was aware that far too much was being asked of the troops under his command. He consequently asked Hitler, in the course of the advance on Tikhvin, that he be relieved of command. Hitler granted this request.

the somewhat unsatisfactory development of the situation, there were never any serious disagreements between the commander of the panzer group and the commander of the army group.

To understand the way in which the panzer arm was employed during the campaign, it must be realised that there were still many figures in the German Army and even within the German General Staff who did not know how the panzer troops should be led and how their needs should be met. Perhaps the easy victories of the panzer troops in Poland and France had made the German leadership too optimistic. Neither the Polish nor the French forces had been as well-trained or as well-equipped as the German forces, but the panzer arm had yet to encounter a truly powerful enemy. The overestimation of the abilities of the panzer arm proved to be disadvantageous during the campaign in Russia. By underestimating Russian resistance, overtaxing the panzer troops, and not paying attention to what type of terrain our tanks needed, the German leadership played a role in the failure of the advance. Of course, it is only rarely that the most ideal combat terrain can be chosen, but sending armour into completely unfriendly terrain is bound to lead to disappointment. This had always been the case for the cavalry charge in times past; it would often fail if the conditions were not right. Few military commanders have fully mastered the use of both infantry and mobile (now panzer) forces. The difference between the two is considerable. Before the outbreak of the Second World War, the later Colonel Generals Guderian (the true creator of the panzer arm) and Hoepner (the old cavalryman) emerged as the most noteworthy representatives of the new panzer arm. Many other figures became interested in its development, too, but the way in which to best employ the mobile forces had not yet become common knowledge. It was not even possible at that time, and this is why the panzer troops eventually found themselves overburdened in Russia. Only a commander with a strong sense of responsibility and an ability to confront the challenges the panzer troops faced, like Colonel-General Hoepner, could lead his men in a way which he thought best. It was always easier and probably more personally rewarding to carry out one's orders to the letter, but Hoepner was not prepared to conduct the advance in a manner that went against his better judgement. As we have seen, subsequent developments proved Hoepner's assessment of the situation to be correct. Moreover, he felt duty bound to do what was right for the troops under his command. He remained true to this inner sense of duty during the advance on Moscow (the result of which was his dismissal) and right up until his death (execution on 8 August 1944 for his participation in the plot of 20 July 1944).

Hoepner's efforts to deploy the panzer troops in the most favourable terrain and to concentrate them for maximum effect, two aspects that were of the utmost importance for the use of the panzer arm, were thwarted due to the development of the situation. Although the advance on Leningrad had proceeded much more slowly than intended, the fact that 800 kilometres had been covered and that the objective had been reached was an indication of the tremendous performance of the officers and men of Army Group North.

It is worth making a remark on the comments made by Field-Marshal von Manstein in his book *Lost Victories*, in the chapter 'Panzer Drive', as they have caused some displeasure. A comparison of this chapter, which is in any case only written from memory, with the facts reveals some astonishing discrepancies and contradictions which can be explained by more than just 'subjectivity', as Manstein says in his foreword, and gaps in memory. The comments in question are those he made for 27 June, at which time he was the commander of the LVI Panzer Corps: 'Was the objective to be Leningrad, or should we turn towards Moscow? The Panzer Group Commander … could tell us nothing.'[38] Only some sort of mental confusion could have compelled Manstein to write this, for he had already been aware of the plans to advance on Moscow. Dünaburg had been the primary objective of the panzer group for the first phase of the offensive. The XXXXI Panzer Corps did not lag behind anywhere near as much as Manstein suggests.[39] Indeed, it was the XXXXI Panzer Corps that engaged, encircled, and annihilated the group of Russian tanks near Raseiniai that would have otherwise been a thorn in the side for the LVI Panzer Corps. Manstein's strong objection in his book to

38 Erich von Manstein, *Lost Victories*, tr. Anthony G. Powell, 1958, p. 185.
39 *Ibid.*, p. 184.

the halt of the LVI Panzer Corps in the Dünaburg bridgehead ignores the fact that he needed to stock up on supplies and that the enemy was conducting a number of counterattacks at that time.[40] There was, for example, no way his corps was ready to send an advance detachment from Dünaburg towards Rositten immediately. His representation of the penetration of the Stalin Line is either distorted or completely false.[41] The idea of approaching Sebezh originated with the LVI Panzer Corps and went against the intentions of the commander of the panzer group. The attempt to envelop the enemy forces near Pskov with the LVI Panzer Corps from the southeast never took place and is a figment of Manstein's imagination.[42] What is the XXXXI Panzer Corps supposed to have done in the meantime? Would it have sat there, deep in enemy territory in the vicinity of Ostrov, and done nothing, even though it had just achieved a great victory? Similar discrepancies are to be found throughout 'Panzer Drive', which means that Manstein's account of the advance on Leningrad is of no value to military science whatsoever.

Manstein, who did not oversee actual developments, has made a number of misjudgements or mistakes in his book. It would be fair to say that he has even fallen victim to imaginings. The reader can no doubt judge for himself the degree to which Manstein's personal and subjective criticism of our brilliant commanders rings true. Field-Marshal von Leeb and Colonel-General Hoepner are no longer with us. We owe it to them to point out the way in which they have been erroneously portrayed in *Lost Victories*.

The Author

40 *Ibid.*, p. 186.
41 *Ibid.*, p. 187.
42 *Ibid.*, p. 192.

APPENDIX I

The order of battle of Panzer Group 4 at the outset of the campaign

	4.	
Gen.Kdo's	XXXXI.	LVI.
Divisionen	269. 36. 6. 1.	290. 3. 8.
Den Korps unterstellte Heeres-truppen	Arko 30 Art.Rgt. St. 618 II./A.R. 67 (s.F.H.) II./A.R. 59 (s.F.H.) Art.Abt. 611 (10 cm Kan.) Art.Abt. 615 (21 cm Mörs) Beob.Abt. 2 Nebelw.Regt. 52 Fla.Btl. 601 Pi.Regt.St. 628 Pi.Btl. 52 (mot) Brüko B 52 Brüko B 2./406 (254. I.D.) Brüko B 1./430 (1. Pz.) Brüko B 661 (6. Pz.) Brüko B 37 (1. Pz.) Brüko B 57 (6. Pz.) Brüko K 57 (6. Pz.) Brüko B 36 (36. mot) Brüko B 2./411 (269. I.D.) Kdr. Bautr. 71 BrückenbauBtl. 26 BauBtl. 62 (t-mot.) BauBtl. 254 (t-mot.)	Arko 125 II./A.R. 61 (gem.) Pz.Jäg.Abt. 559 (sfl.) Pi.Regt.St. 678 Pi.Btl. 48 (mot) Brüko B 48 Brüko B 649 Brüko B 2./412 (8. Pz.) Brüko B 59 (8. Pz.) Brüko K 59 (8.Pz.) Brüko B 3 (3. mot.) Brüko B 2./505 (290. I.D.) Kdr. Bautr. 4 BauBtl. 44 (t-mot) BauBtl. 55 (t-mot) BauBtl. 87 (t-mot)
	Luftwaffe (nur taktisch unterstellt!) Grufl. 23 Aufkl.St. 4. (H) 31 Aufkl.St. 2. (H) 23 (Pz), 1. Pz. Aufkl.St. 3. (H) 23 (Pz), 6. Pz. FlakAbt. I/3 1. FlakAbt.. 83 (1. Pz.Div.) 1. FlakAbt. II./411 6. Pz.Div.)	Grufl. 13 Aufkl.St. 8. (H) 32 Aufkl.St. 3. (H) 41 (Pz), 8. Pz. FlakAbt. II/23 1. FlakAbt. 92 (8. Pz.)
Zur Verfügung der Panzer-gruppe	SS„Totenkopf"Div. Pz.Jäg.Abt. 616 (sfl. 4,7 cm) Pz.Gr.Nachr.Regt. 4 Prop.Kp. 694 **Luftwaffe** FlakRegt. St. 133 Aufkl.St. 4 (F)/33	Pi.Btl. 62 Brüko B 1., 2., 3./62 Brüko K 62 Brüko B SS„T" Sturmbootkdo. 906 Ober Baustab 32 1. Radf.Str.BauBtl. 507 1. Radf.Str.BauBtl. 508 OT. Abt. 1 (mot)

APPENDIX 2

Organisation of the 6th Panzer Division and the 3rd Motorised Infantry Division

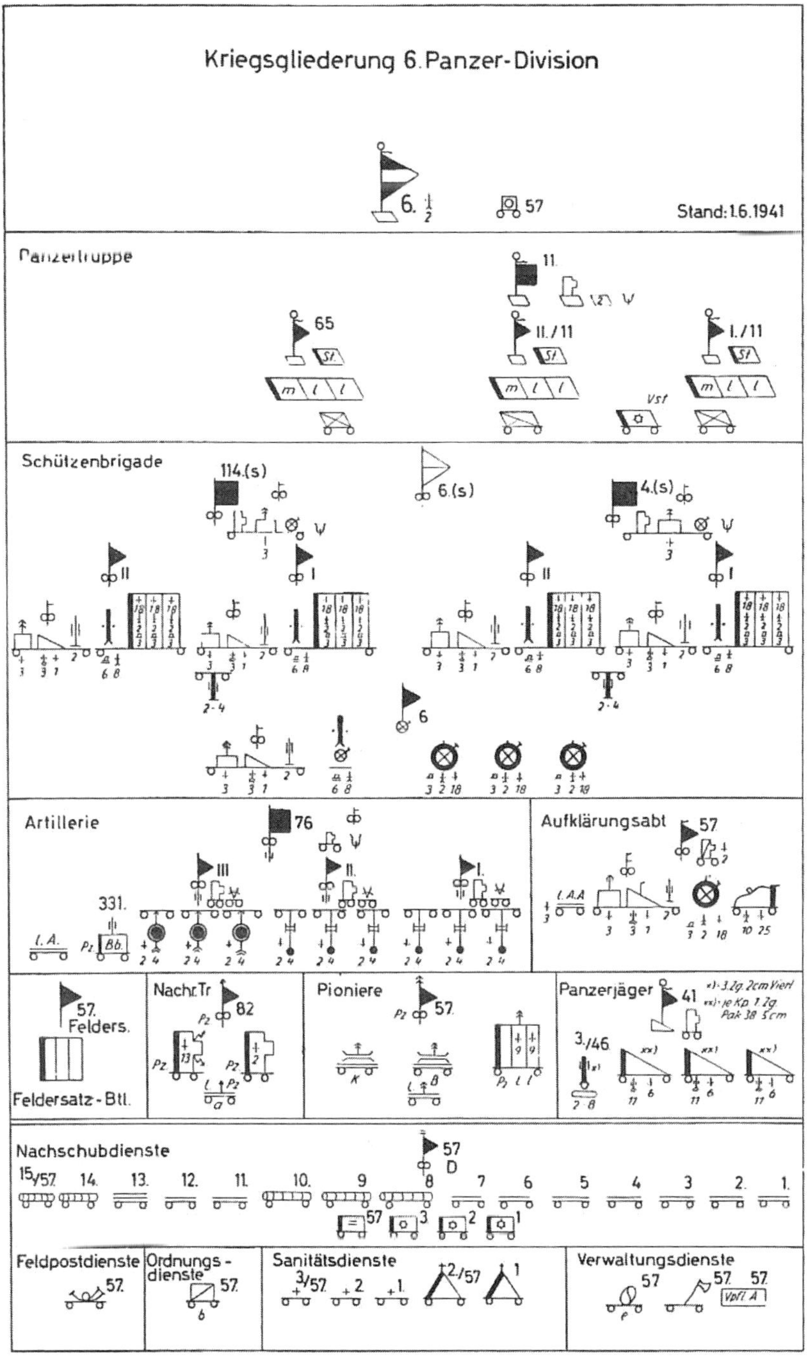
Kriegsgliederung 6. Panzer-Division
Stand: 1.6.1941
Panzertruppe
Schützenbrigade
Artillerie
Aufklärungsabt
Felders.
Feldersatz-Btl.
Nachr.Tr
Pioniere
Panzerjäger
Nachschubdienste
Feldpostdienste
Ordnungs-dienste
Sanitätsdienste
Verwaltungsdienste

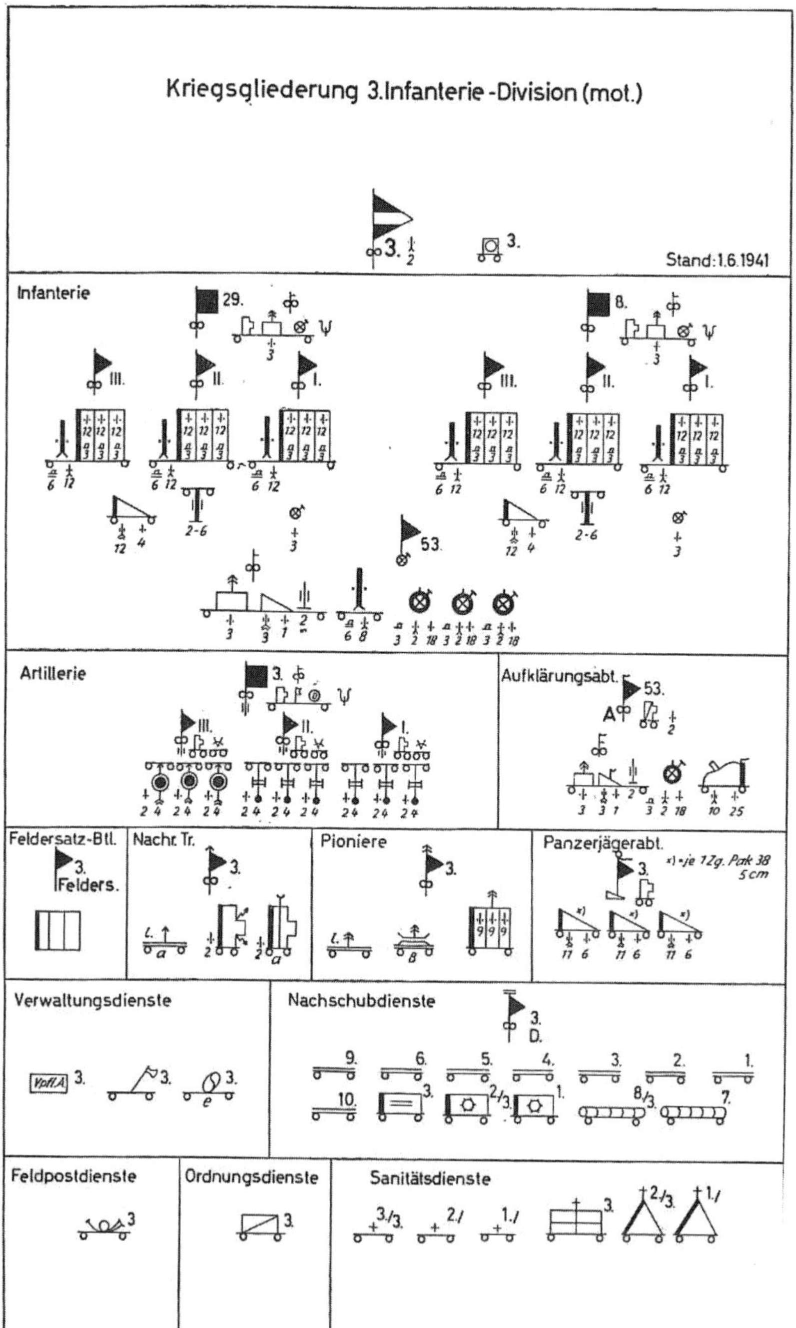
Kriegsgliederung 3.Infanterie-Division (mot.)
Stand: 1.6.1941
Infanterie
29.
8.
53.
Artillerie
3.
Aufklärungsabt.
53.
Feldersatz-Btl.
3. Felders.
Nachr. Tr.
3.
Pioniere
3.
Panzerjägerabt.
3.
x) = je 1 Zg. Pak 38 5 cm
Verwaltungsdienste
Nachschubdienste
3. D.
Feldpostdienste
Ordnungsdienste
Sanitätsdienste

APPENDIX 3

Officers at the headquarters of Panzer Group 4 on 22 June 1941 and their areas of responsibility

Commander

Colonel-General Hoepner

Chief of Staff

Colonel on the General Staff Chales de Beaulieu

Command Division (Ia) (Operations)

Leader: Major on the General Staff von Schön-Angerer
Leader (only from 13 July): Captain Litterscheid (assessment of the situation, deputy Ia)
Administrative Officer 1: First Lieutenant Wätjen (Ia reports)
Administrative Officer 4: First Lieutenant Schauwecker (distribution of orders, war diary)
Adjutant Ia: Second Lieutenant of the Reserve von Legat
Adjutant Ia: Second Lieutenant of the Reserve Dr Prinz von Hannover (Ernst-August)
Ia Surveying: Captain of the Reserve Püchel (Graduate Engineer)
Mapping Detachment: Second Lieutenant of the Reserve Klotz

Attached Officers: Major Topf (communications officer)
Cavalry Captain of the Reserve Franke (chemical defence officer)
First Lieutenant Voigts (adjutant commander)
First Lieutenant of the Reserve Schaeper (chief administrative officer)

Command Division (Ic) (Enemy Situation)

Leader: Captain on the General Staff Bruns
Administrative Officer 3: First Lieutenant of the Reserve Doctor Bothe
Intelligence Officer: Major Sobirey (procurement of information)

Adjutancy (IIa) (Officers' Personal Matters)

Adjutant: Lieutenant-Colonel von der Schulenburg (officer replacement)
IIb: Major Heinrichs (replacement of non-commissioned officers and enlisted men)
Commandant: Major Dannecker (commandant of officers' quarters)

Special commanders at the headquarters of the panzer group

Medical Service Commander: General of the Medical Corps Dr Full
Adjutant: Captain of the Medical Corps Dr Holleck-Weithmann
Pioneer Commander: Colonel Dinter
Adjutant: First Lieutenant Bohnstedt
Signal Communications Commander: Colonel Negendanck
Adjutant: Captain Poretschkin

Quartermaster's Division (Supplies)

Quartermaster: Major on the General Staff von Metzsch
Quartermaster 2: Captain Kaufmann
Administrative Officer 2: Major Herbst
Administrative Officer 5: First Lieutenant of the Reserve Freiherr Grote

Administrative Officer 6: Second Lieutenant of the Reserve Freiherr Speck von Sternburg

Commanding officers of supply areas

IVb: General of the Medical Corps Dr Full (medical supplies)
IVa: Intendant Dr Spruth (food supply)
Sub-Intendant Dr Rieger
IVb: Pharmacist Official Dr Lehmann
V: Lieutenant-Colonel Baumann (motor vehicle supply and repair)
Ammunition: Major Göckus (replacement of weapons and ammunition)

Group Judges

III: Chief Court Martial Adviser Dr Kleist
Court Martial Adviser Schumann (air corps judge)

Officers attached to the headquarters of the panzer group

Major Baldamus, head of liaison staff from the chief of transportation systems (railway matters)
Captain of the Luftwaffe Deiss, transport officer (railway construction and operation)
Luftwaffe Liaison Officer Captain Stein
Luftwaffe Liaison Officer Captain of the Reserve Dietl

Strength of the headquarters of Panzer Group 4

Staff: 59 officers, 20 officials, 51 non-commissioned officers, 222 enlisted personnel
Permanently attached: 24 officers, 7 officials, 105 non-commissioned officers, 325 enlisted personnel

---

Total: 83 officers, 27 officials, 156 non-commissioned officers, 547 enlisted personnel

APPENDIX 4

Situation report of the panzer group on 7 July 1941 regarding the use of the SS-Totenkopf Division

On the night of 4/5 July, the headquarters of the panzer group received an emergency radio call from the LVI Panzer Corps. The poor road conditions had brought the 3rd Motorised Infantry Division and the 8th Panzer Division to a halt. The situation has therefore changed for the panzer group, as the corps will be unable to continue its advance on Opochka for the time being. The commander of the panzer group drove to the headquarters of the LVI Panzer Corps early on 5 July to speak with General von Manstein. He emphasised that the corps must somehow push further to the northeast; otherwise, it would have to proceed northwards behind the XXXXI Panzer Corps, acting as the second wave to strike the enemy. Some scouting missions and road repairs will therefore need to be carried out immediately in the direction of Opochka and Krasnoi as well as to the south of Ostrov. The plans of the corps are then to be reported straightaway. The chief of staff of the panzer group had at the same time flown to the headquarters of the XXXXI Panzer Corps in Tilza in order to discuss the possibilities for the advance from the Ostrov bridgehead, which might perhaps be reinforced by elements of the LVI Panzer Corps. The panzer group learnt in the evening that the SS-Totenkopf Division would be sent by the LVI Panzer Corps from Rosenovo in the direction of Sebezh, with the idea that it would lead the corps further to the north via Opochka. The attack was to begin at noon. It was the view of the panzer group that enemy resistance in the vicinity of Rosenovo would make it difficult for the division to execute such an advance. Because of the need for artillery reinforcement, the attack of the SS-Totenkopf Division did not commence until 3 am on 6 July, whereupon it ground its way through the bunker line of the border fortifications. The commander of the panzer group expressed to the commander of the LVI Panzer Corps his doubts that the attack of the SS-Totenkopf Division could succeed. Even if it took Sebezh, it would still have to fight tooth and nail to create a path all the way to Opochka. General von Manstein requested that the results of the rest of the day on 6 July be awaited before a final decision was made regarding whether the SS-Totenkopf Division should press on with the attack or whether it would best follow in the wake of the advance of the XXXXI Panzer Corps through Ostrov. Colonel-General Hoepner reluctantly agreed to this. General von Manstein was confident in his view of the situation, and Colonel-General Hoepner did not want to forbid him just yet from continuing with an attack which had thus far been successful. On the evening of 6 July, General von Manstein, who was at that time with the SS-Totenkopf Division, gave the order that the attack be continued. The leading elements of the division reached Vasselkova and were therefore at the halfway point between Rosenovo and Sebezh. Yet by the early morning of 7 July, the opinion of the headquarters of the panzer group had not changed. The advance of the division via Opochka would simply be too long drawn out. The chief of staff of the panzer group recommended to the commander of the panzer group that preparations be made to pull the division out. In a telephone conversation shortly before 8 am, General von Manstein once more requested from the commander of the panzer group that a decision regarding whether or not to withdraw the division be delayed until the end of the day. The general regarded the prospects of a breakthrough to be good. He thought that the extraction of the division would be difficult and that it would probably consume far more time than would the continuation of the advance on Opochka. Colonel-General Hoepner agreed to await the results of the day, for any diversion of the SS-Totenkopf Division towards Ostrov could in any case only take place after the 3rd Motorised Infantry Division had completed its northward movement through Karsava. The commander of the LVI Panzer Corps was to report this evening on the progress made. During the telephone call, Colonel-General Hoepner once more expressed his view that the prospects of success for the SS-Totenkopf Division did not look good. He emphasised, as he had done before, his lack of enthusiasm for the current commitment of the LVI Panzer Corps along a 120-kilometre front between Sebezh and Ostrov. The corps has to be brought northwards as soon as possible.

Chales de Beaulieu
7 July, 10 am

APPENDIX 5

Compilation of notes on the effects of the OKH on the operations of the Sixteenth Army in July 1941

As early as the end of June, some of the forces of the Sixteenth Army (the XXIII Corps with the 86th, 206th, and 253rd Infantry Divisions) were sent into the area of Army Group Centre. The 32nd Infantry Division (from the II Corps) also came to the aid of the Ninth Army (the right-hand neighbour of the Sixteenth Army) in the fighting north of Vilnius.

On 2 July, the XXIII Corps, with the 86th and 206th Infantry Divisions, was handed over to the Ninth Army. At the same time, the L Corps, with the 253rd Infantry Division and the Police Division, was to be sent behind the southern wing of the army.

On 4 July, the boundary with Army Group Centre was 'temporarily' shifted 20 kilometres further south. It had, in contrast, been the original plan of the OKH to expand the combat zone of Army Group Centre to the north, for the frontline of Army Group North would more than double in width the further to the northeast it advanced. Both divisions of the II Corps had at that time been to the south of the old boundary!

The 126th Infantry Division, the northern formation of the X Corps, was located approximately 20 kilometres southeast of Ostrov on 13 July. It had to pivot towards the southeast to engage in combat southwest of Novorzhev, for the remaining forces of the Sixteenth Army had found themselves too strongly bound to the south. The result was that the gap to Panzer Group 4 grew ever larger and that the help the panzer group so urgently needed was lacking!

On 17 July, although its point of main effort ought to have been on its northern wing so as to cover the flank of Panzer Group 4, the

Sixteenth Army shifted its headquarters to Pustoshka. This place lay only 20 kilometres north of the boundary with Army Group Centre, yet the attack sector of the Sixteenth Army was now 180 kilometres in width. The L Corps, the II Corps, and parts of the XXVIII Corps were involved in the fighting in the boundary area in the middle of July. Only three divisions of the Sixteenth Army (the X Corps and the rest of the XXVIII Corps) covered the remaining 150 kilometres. The emphasis of the advance of the army was quite different to what had been intended!

Only from 21 July did the Sixteenth Army resume its advance towards the northeast, along the original line of attack that had been planned.

The delay in the intervention of the northern wing of the Sixteenth Army in the vicinity on either side of Lake Ilmen lasted two to three weeks. This was at a time when the rapid advance of Panzer Group 4 on Leningrad was still very much possible. The delay in the arrival of the Sixteenth Army meant that the leading elements of Panzer Group 4 could not exploit their early success. The panzer group would now have to force its way through terrain that the enemy was defending with ever-increasing tenacity.

APPENDIX 6

Assessment of the situation by Panzer Group 4 on 6 July 1941

Headquarters of Panzer Group 4, Division Ia No. 1423/41 classified. Panzer Group Command Post, Malnava, 6 July 1941.

Intentions for the continuation of operations

Intelligence on the enemy:
The enemy is throwing all of the forces at his disposal into the fighting to keep our assault in check. The thrust of the XXXXI Panzer Corps had seemingly taken him by surprise. His attempt to establish a defensive front along the Latvian–Russian border has failed thanks to the penetration near Ostrov on the northern wing of the panzer group. Enemy resistance is better organised further south, east of Kraslava and Rosenovo.

Our picture of the enemy along the new line of advance is less clear. His movements do not reveal any systematic defence. He had brought troops into the Pskov area by rail over the past few days, but it now looks as if these troops are retreating to the northeast, east, and southeast. Strong enemy forces nevertheless remain, as demonstrated by the destruction of 140 tanks in the vicinity of Ostrov by the 1st Panzer Division. Even so, the panzer group does not expect that the enemy will launch an offensive. The panzer group instead hopes for a rapid and successful thrust, provided the enemy has not distributed his forces in depth. If he has, then the advance might proceed more slowly. There do not appear to be any enemy movements far to the east and southeast of Opochka. If enemy forces were to turn up here, they would pose a serious threat to our ever-lengthening right flank.

Our progress has been held up not only by strong enemy resistance but also by particularly bad roads. This is especially the case on our right wing, in the area of the LVI Panzer Corps. The 3rd Motorised Infantry Division, which was on its way from Ludza to Opochka via Cibla, had to come to a halt. The road here is impassable, so the division will be shifted to the left wing of the LVI Panzer Corps so as to continue its advance via Ostrov. The route of advance of the 8th Panzer Division from Karsava through Krasnoi towards the northeast is in similarly bad condition. Nevertheless, the LVI Panzer Corps believes that the road can be repaired to such an extent within 48 hours that the vehicles of the division will be able to continue with the advance. The troops of the division have in the meantime been forced to dismount, but they still managed to take Krasnoi yesterday evening.

The SS-Totenkopf Division is still fighting east of Rosenovo with the intention of advancing via Sebezh towards Opochka. It is questionable whether it will be able to break through the enemy forces there. If so, it cannot be done quickly. The panzer group is considering the possibility of sending the division through Ostrov instead.

If this were to transpire, the Opochka area will not be taken by the panzer group. The panzer group would then focus on assembling in and advancing out of the Ostrov bridgehead. The 290th Infantry Division would follow the 8th Panzer Division via Krasnoi and would be responsible for the protection of the right flank.

The expansion of the Ostrov bridgehead is necessary if it is to be the location of the assembly area. According to today's assessment from the XXXXI Panzer Corps, the possibilities in this regard are favourable. The corps plans to expand the bridgehead eastwards as far as the Opochka–Pskov railway line and northwards beyond the railway station in Cherskaya-Gorbova. This is to be achieved with an attack by the 36th Motorised Infantry Division from the southwest. On the right, the LVI Panzer Corps would proceed with the 8th Panzer Division through Shanino in the direction of Porkhov. The 3rd Motorised Infantry Division would advance on the left wing of the corps. It is important at this time that close attention be paid to the development of the situation in the area of the LVI Panzer Corps before a final decision is made.

However, what is most important for the renewal of the advance of the panzer group in the direction of Leningrad is the assembly of the troops of the XXXXI Panzer Corps. This can be done by 8 July, so the panzer group will be able to begin its advance on 9 July. Steps shall be taken to ensure that the flow of supplies is secured right up until this date.

The XXXXI Panzer Corps shall proceed along and to the west, and initially also to the east, of the main road leading towards Leningrad. The LVI Panzer Corps will drive further east towards Porkhov and Yamtesovo in the direction of Novgorod.

So as to ensure that the full force of the panzer group can surge forward in one united effort, it is important that the panzer group not be burdened with the responsibility for the right flank on the southern side of Lake Ilmen. The commitment of mobile forces of the Sixteenth Army in this area would be most welcome. The forces of the panzer group are not particularly strong, so they must be gathered together if they are to carry out their task effectively.

The following is requested for the upcoming operations:

(a) Reinforcement of aerial reconnaissance units in the area of the panzer group.
(b) Reinforcement in armour-piercing weapons (infantry assault batteries and antitank battalions).
(c) Reinforcement in antiaircraft weaponry.
(d) Additional machine-gun battalions for flank protection activities.

Hoepner, Commander of Panzer Group 4
Witness: Major on the General Staff von Schön-Angerer

APPENDIX 7

Order of Army Group North on 8 July 1941 (excerpts)

High Command of Army Group North, Ia No. 1660/41 classified. Headquarters, 8 July 1941.

Army Group Order

(1) The attempt of the enemy to form a new defensive front along the old Russian frontier has failed. Our forces have broken through.

(2) Army Group North will advance further in the direction of Leningrad and will take the city.

(3) The Finnish Army shall strike in a southerly direction on either side of Lake Ladoga. The northernmost elements of Panzer Group 3 will advance on Velizh via Nevel.

(4) Panzer Group 4 shall be put on standby between Lake Ilmen and Pskov. The army group will give the order for the resumption of its advance on Leningrad.

(a) The panzer group is to encircle Leningrad between Lake Ladoga and the Gulf of Kronstadt as tightly as its forces can manage.

(b) The panzer group must guard its own rear against enemy forces east of Lake Ilmen until the arrival of the Sixteenth Army.

(c) The panzer group shall occupy the sector between Narva Bay and Lake Peipus so as to cut off the route of retreat of enemy forces in Estonia.

(d) Waterworks and power stations are to be seized in the territory occupied by the panzer group. The water and electricity supply to Leningrad is to be cut off.

(5) The Sixteenth Army is to advance further towards the northeast so as to cover the east flank and the rear of Panzer Group 4. It will aim to reach the area between Kholm and Porkhov and will then detach the I. Corps on the right for an attack on Velikiye Luki. Advance detachments are to drive forward in the direction of Kholm, Staraya Russa, and Novgorod.

(6) The Eighteenth Army will come to the aid of Panzer Group 4 near and to the south of Pskov to the degree that is necessary. It will otherwise, after reaching the area west of the Ostrov–Pskov road (the road itself is for Panzer Group 4), pivot to the north. Proceeding on the east side of Lake Peipus, the Eighteenth Army will then follow in the wake of the left wing of Panzer Group 4. It shall retain responsibility for mopping-up operations in Estonia and for taking Reval and Baltic Port.

(7) and (8) Border and aerial reconnaissance ….

(9) First Air Fleet is requested to interrupt communications between Leningrad and Moscow as soon as possible and to further support the advance of Panzer Group 4.

Leeb, Commander of Army Group North

APPENDIX 8

Recommendation of the commander of the XXXXI Panzer Corps to cross the lower Luga

Commander of the XXXXI Panzer Corps, Corps Headquarters, 12 July 1941. To Colonel-General Hoepner, commander of Panzer Group 4.

I delivered an oral report on the afternoon of 11 July on the further prospects of success for my corps and the obstacles that would stand in our way in the advance on Leningrad. I now summarise my appraisal of the situation in writing so that it can be referred to in the conference that will take place today with the army group.

The enemy forces that have been encountered thus far by the corps have been smashed to pieces. Despite the rather bad roads, these successes were able to be achieved due to the ability of the panzer troops to exploit the vast terrain and thus bring their mobility and great fighting power to bear. Enemy forces, some of them hastily thrown together and others new and well-trained, were hurled against the corps over and over again in an attempt to keep us back, for the enemy is fully aware of the danger posed to him and his second-largest city by the panzer group. He is fighting tenaciously and deviously and is making maximum use of the advantages of the terrain.

On the other hand, I have to say that the terrain through which the corps will now have to fight, almost all the way to Leningrad, is barely suitable for mobile troops. The roads ahead of us are in rather poor condition. I do not think anyone who has not seen our troops struggling forward through marsh and sand can possibly imagine all of the road problems our men will be required to overcome day and night. Even the so-called 'causeway' between Pskov and Leningrad is in bad shape. It is peppered with bomb craters and is increasingly so day by day. If the attack columns of the corps attempt to advance along secondary roads, they often get stuck and must be slowly and arduously diverted or even forced to turn back.

Adding to the difficulties we are bound to encounter are a number of watercourses and large boggy forests that will significantly ease the defensive efforts of the enemy. He has also withdrawn over and then destroyed several bridges.

It is thanks to the readiness of the troops for action that the corps has thus far succeeded in covering large distances on a day-to-day basis and in annihilating strong enemy forces. However, such great successes can hardly be expected from now on. Even with our superior application of weaponry, especially of tanks and artillery, the terrain has now made rapid movement and decisive breakthroughs impossible. The corps now has to fight laboriously through wave after wave of enemy resistance. The inevitable result is that the spearhead of the corps has to bear the brunt of the fighting along and immediately to either side of the road, whilst the bulk of the corps finds itself further behind on the narrow roads and in a state of relative inactivity. The bad roads and the marshy terrain prevent their effective development on the battlefield. Under such conditions, the danger of an air raid against our forces is ever greater, for the presence of a mass of vehicles in a small area would offer the enemy an attractive target.

Given all of these difficulties, I must draw the conclusion that the advance of the corps will inevitably slow down. The troops have so far been able to maximise the potential of their excellent weaponry and have thus covered at least 50 kilometres per day. Now, despite the fact that our troops are applying the same degree of effort, the difficulties that have to be overcome and the ever-increasing losses that are being suffered have resulted in a daily gain of 10 kilometres or less.

I am unable to assess whether the corps, under such circumstances, can be shifted to an area with better terrain. If it can, it might be able to reach the same objective, Leningrad, much more quickly. Specifically, I am thinking of an advance through Estonia and through the area of land between Narva and Lake Peipus. I must at the very least request that the corps, if it is to proceed between the Pskov–Leningrad road and Lake Peipus, be given the freedom to place the emphasis of its advance as far to the left as possible. The main road leads through terrible terrain and invites enemy attacks, but the land further west, according to our maps, offers fewer difficulties.

The troops of the corps have thus far achieved a number of successes, and I have no doubt whatsoever that they are striving to reach Leningrad, that they want to reach Leningrad, and that they will reach Leningrad no matter how slowly. It is nonetheless my duty to report that the continued advance in this sector will be costly in terms of men and materiel, so it is important that time be allowed to refresh and replenish our forces.

Reinhardt

APPENDIX 9

Telephone memo from 13 July 1941

Sunday 13 July 1941, Anisimovo.

Telephone conversation between Field-Marshal Ritter von Leeb and Colonel-General Hoepner

Leeb: Amazed by the further advance of the divisions. Army Group was of the view that we might have had to advance more slowly, but faster progress is pleasing.

Hoepner: Despite the good progress overall, it is inevitable that the advance will slow down. XXXXI Panzer Corps wants to swing its forces to the west so as to advance in open terrain. Advancing along the road is difficult, e.g. the enemy has new positions near Zapolye in the path of the 1st Infantry Division. He has established more defensive positions along the Luga River and has mined the area to the north of the town of Luga. We hope to cross the river further to the west.

Leeb: It is necessary to find and pierce through the enemy's weak point. The army group depends on the panzer group, so the latter must not become worn out.

Hoepner: It is important that the enemy not be allowed time to recover. We must keep him at sword-point! The panzer group has not been too severely weakened in the fighting. We nevertheless wish for support from the rear divisions, e.g. assault batteries.

Leeb: This will be difficult. The divisions of both armies are already engaged in combat. The army group has nothing more available.

Hoepner: The only concern is the right flank.

Leeb: Hope that the X Corps will move forward quickly. The I Corps is advancing gradually in the Ostrov–Pskov area. It is essential that our divisions make as much progress as possible.

Hoepner: The road of advance must remain free for our units. The SS-Totenkopf Division cannot move forward. It must be kept ready in reserve and must be prepared to be sent to the northwest or to the northeast. The 269th Infantry Division is on the road to Luga. It will be able to fight effectively there.

Leeb: Once more on the question of support from the army group. All of the divisions of the Sixteenth Army are in combat. The Eighteenth Army is already assisting in the fighting in which the panzer group is engaged. Handing over forces will be extremely difficult.

APPENDIX 10

Order of Army Group North from 15 July 1941 (excerpts)

Army Group North Headquarters, Ia No. 1700/41 classified. 15 July 1941.

Army Group Order

(1) The enemy appears to be putting up tough and united resistance before the front of the army group.

(2) The objective of the army group is the same as before.

(3) The task of Panzer Group 4 is to reach the Novgorod–Luga–Narva line, and from there it will drive towards and encircle Leningrad (with the bulk of its forces in the southeast). The right wing of the panzer group shall commence its thrust only after the arrival of the I Corps so that the latter can provide flank protection.

(4) The Sixteenth Army shall advance in conjunction with the northern wing of Panzer Group 3 (LVII Panzer Corps with the 19th Panzer Division and half of the 14th Motorised Infantry Division) so as to prevent the enemy from retreating through Nevel, Velikiye Luki, and later Kholm.

The northern wing of the army (X Corps) is to eliminate enemy forces in its path and is to drive towards a position to the east of Porkhov. The ultimate goal of the forces of the Sixteenth Army will remain the same.

(5) The Eighteenth Army shall first of all destroy enemy forces in Estonia, after which it will capture Reval and Baltic Port and then carry out Operation Beowulf.

The I Corps is to advance to the area northeast of Porkhov so that it can assume responsibility for the protection of the flank of the panzer group. The corps will be placed under the command of the panzer group whilst undertaking this movement.

The XXXVIII Corps shall head towards the Osmino–Kingisepp area, from where it will be able to free up some of the forces on the western wing of Panzer Group 4. Specifically, it will take over responsibility for the section of land between Narva and Lake Peipus and will prevent the retreat of enemy forces from Estonia.

von Leeb, Commander of Army Group North
Witness: Herrmann

APPENDIX II

The intentions of Panzer Group 4 for the continuation of operations on 22 July 1941

Headquarters of Panzer Group 4, Ia No. 1516/41 classified, 15 July 1941.
Panzer Group Command Post, Anisimovo, 22 July 1941.

Re: Headquarters of Army Group North
Ia No. 1750/41 classified
22 July 1941
To: Headquarters of Army Group North

Intentions of Panzer Group 4 for the continuation of operations

(1) The continuation of operations by the panzer group in the direction of Leningrad will go ahead after the enemy forces facing the I Corps and the LVI Panzer Corps have been annihilated and after the lower Mshaga sector has been reached. Appropriate measures shall be taken in this regard. A coordinated attack shall be carried out by both corps early on 23 July.

(2) In carrying out operations against Leningrad, it is planned that the I Corps will be employed on the right, that it will capture Novgorod, and that it will then advance further in the direction of Chudovo. Immediately to the left of the I Corps will be the LVI Panzer Corps, which will advance along and on either side of the road through Luga. The panzer corps is to seize Luga and head towards Krasnogvardeysk. Further to the west, the XXXXI Panzer Corps must break out of

the Luga bridgeheads in Sabsk and Porechye towards the north. It is to fight its way out of the forests and then swivel to the east towards the Krasnogvardeysk–Krasnoye Selo line.

The security of the left flank of the panzer group between the Luga Bay and Lake Peipus will be assigned to the XXXVIII Corps. The XXXXI Panzer Corps will send the 1st Infantry Division from the Porechye bridgehead towards the northwest to provide initial cover on this flank.

(3) Organisation of the corps:

I Corps – 11th and 21st Infantry Divisions

LVI Panzer Corps – 269th Infantry Division, 8th Panzer Division, 3rd Motorised Infantry Division

XXXXI Panzer Corps – 1st and 6th Panzer Divisions, 36th Motorised Infantry Division, 1st Infantry Division (minus one reinforced regiment, which is to go to the XXXVIII Corps)

XXXVIII Corps – 58th Infantry Division and one reinforced regiment of the 1st Infantry Division

(4) Panzer Group Reserve:

The panzer group shall reserve for itself the decision as to whether to position the SS-Totenkopf Division behind the right or the left flank. Also in panzer group reserve will be a heavy artillery regimental group.

(5) Planned schedule:

23/24 July – annihilation of the enemy forces facing the I Corps and the LVI Panzer Corps and arrival at the Mshaga sector

24/25 July – expansion of the starting positions of the LVI Panzer Corps for the attack on Luga

23/25 July – expansion of the Luga bridgeheads for the 1st and 6th Panzer Divisions with the help of the 1st Infantry Division

26 July – planned date for the continuation of the advance on Leningrad

(6) The X Corps is to be sent behind the I Corps after it has carried out its current task.

Hoepner, Commander of Panzer Group 4

APPENDIX 12

Telephone memo from 23 July 1941

5:45 pm

Telephone conversation between the chief of staff of Panzer Group 4 and the chief of staff of Army Group North

The chief of staff of Panzer Group 4 referred to the telex message of Army Group North with regard to the altered plans for the LVI Panzer Corps, i.e. that the corps would not only be committed to the Luga area, as had been foreseen, but that it would also be required to extend itself as far as Lyuban. The chief of staff of the panzer group raised the following objections:

(1) A glance at the map on a scale of 1:300,000 is enough to make one realise that the terrain is unsuitable for a panzer corps. Leading through this terrain is just the one road on which motorised vehicles would be able to move and on which any withdrawal would be virtually impossible. Our experiences ought to have taught us, though, that the spearhead of an attack by the panzer divisions will always be counterattacked on the flanks if the terrain on either side is not combed through.

(2) Making the corps wheel to the right in the aforementioned direction will result in the splitting up of the forces of the corps. Given the current enemy position, this could only be regarded as a setback.

The chief of staff of Army Group North responded with the following comments:

The idea of launching the assault on Leningrad with the point of main effort in the southeast is the brainchild of the commander in chief of the army. The commander of Army Group North had recommended that this plan be implemented by Panzer Group 4, all the more so as he had gained the impression that the commander of the panzer group had shown no aversion to it during their meeting and that the movement of the XXXXI Panzer Corps to the left, away from the road leading to Luga, had been the result of unfriendly terrain there.

The chief of staff of the panzer group explained that the shift of the XXXXI Panzer Corps to the left had taken place due to the fact that the terrain leading from east to west had been particularly favourable. But this ought not to lead to the conclusion that the terrain along the main road to Luga was unsuitable for tanks. It is still far better there than along the Novgorod–Lyuban road.

Regarding the beginning of the attack of the panzer group, especially that of the XXXXI Panzer Corps, the chief of staff of the army group said it was essential that the entire panzer group be in a position to launch an assault on Leningrad. Under no circumstances is the XXXXI Panzer Corps allowed to thrust towards the city on its own; otherwise, the success of the entire operation might be endangered.

Chales de Beaulieu

APPENDIX 13

Order of Army Group North from 27 July 1941

Army Group North Headquarters, Ia No. 1770/41 classified, 27 July 1941.

Army Group Order No. 2 for the Continuation of the Offensive

(1) The enemy forces before the Sixteenth Army have been destroyed. Any remaining elements are retreating eastwards on the southern side of Lake Ilmen.

Panzer Group 4 has been pushing back the enemy forces it has encountered further to the northeast.

The Eighteenth Army has defeated the tenacious Russian forces in the area north of Dorpat.

(2) The Army Group will advance further into the Leningrad area.

In order to prevent the escape of the enemy to the southeast as much as possible, it is intended that Panzer Group 3 will be placed under the command of the army group.

(3) Panzer Group 3 is to move against the eastern flank of the enemy in the lake-filled territory in the vicinity of Ostashkov and Valdai, provided that the situation has not changed by the time of its arrival.

(4) The Sixteenth Army, with the I Corps (11th and 21st Infantry Divisions), will take over the sector on the right wing of Panzer Group 4. The army is to make arrangements with Panzer Group 4 as to when precisely the handover will take place.

Boundary between the Sixteenth Army and Panzer Group 4: … Strong forces (three divisions) are to be committed on the western side of Lake Ilmen.

The Sixteenth Army is to give one of its divisions, if possible the 126th Infantry Division, to Panzer Group 4 for the XXVIII Corps.

It is important that control be gained not only of the Moscow–Leningrad railway line but also of the road leading from Chudovo to the southeast.

(5) Panzer Group 4 is to hand over the I Corps (11th and 21st Infantry Divisions) to the Sixteenth Army and will keep the XXVIII Corps with the 122nd Infantry Division and an infantry division of the Sixteenth Army.

See section 4 for the boundary with the Sixteenth Army.

The panzer group is to commit the XXVIII Corps to the right wing. A motorised division of the LVI Panzer Corps is to be assigned to the XXVIII Corps so that both corps possess a motorised division.

It is requested that the 8th Panzer Division be kept on standby to begin with, after which it will be sent to add momentum to where the attack is making the most progress. This could be anywhere in the zone of Panzer Group 4 or in the sector of the Sixteenth Army west of Lake Ilmen (I Corps).

The objective of Panzer Group 4 is the encirclement of the Leningrad area. Specifically, it will aim to reach the following line: the Neva from Shlisselburg to Ivanovskoye, then Maryino, north of Krasnogvardeysk, Taytsy, Vysotskoye, and finally Peterhof.

If the mobile forces gain a head start, they will assume responsibility for maintaining the line of encirclement until the arrival of the infantry.

(6) The entire attack between Lake Ilmen and Lake Peipus will therefore be a united effort the moment the XXVIII Corps is ready.

Preparations are to be made in the meantime to create the most advantageous jump-off position for the upcoming attack. This will be done by taking into account where we can amass our own forces and where the enemy is likely to put up the greatest resistance.

(7) The task of the Eighteenth Army remains unchanged. If the situation continues to unfold favourably in Estonia, the 93rd Infantry Division

will be sent to the XXXVIII Corps via Narva, after which the corps itself will be placed back under the command of the Eighteenth Army.

(8) A corps headquarters from the Sixteenth Army will be placed in army group reserve as soon as possible. The army will also send the 96th Infantry Division to Porkhov.

Panzer Group 4 is to place the Police Division in army group reserve. The division will be sent to Novoselye, which lies on the main road leading to Leningrad.

(9) The headquarters of the army group will be shifted to Pskov from 29 July.

Leeb, Commander of Army Group North

APPENDIX 14

Report on the visit of Field-Marshal von Leeb on the afternoon of 31 July 1941

The field-marshal clearly conveyed his intention to place the point of main effort on the right, near Lake Ilmen. This is in the area of the I and XXVIII Corps, i.e. on the left wing of the Sixteenth Army. That this sector of the front is where the point of main effort will be is underlined by the fact that the commander of the army group plans to commit the entire VIII Air Corps there.

The commander of the army group emphasised that the 8th Panzer Division was to be kept on standby so that it could possibly be used in the vicinity of Novgorod. He also regarded it as necessary that the SS-Totenkopf Division remain in this same vicinity.

The result of this is that strong German forces, including an unfortunate one-third of our mobile units, will be committed to an area that, although operationally significant, is tactically disadvantageous. The terrain there is particularly unfriendly, and the enemy presence in that direction is rather strong. The panzer group has thus far shed much blood and has gained extensive combat experience, but none of this is being taken into account. We will just have to take the bull by the horns once more. What has once failed is to be tried again. Hopefully, it will not be in vain! The terrain is reasonable up to and including Novgorod, but it is unfriendly beyond that point! Any possibility of a chance success can be ruled out. From the point of view of the panzer group, the commitment of mobile forces in this direction is regrettable.

The decision to hold back one-third of the mobile forces can only have a negative effect on the prospects of success for the panzer group.

The XXXXI Panzer Corps, with its three mobile divisions, is too weak to be able to launch a deep thrust against Leningrad on its own. Ever since the decision had been taken to commit the XXXXI Panzer Corps to the advance on the city, it had been our intention to reinforce the corps with one more mobile division at the very least. This has now been prevented. At the same time, the possibility of a rapid advance by the LVI Panzer Corps northwards through Luga so that it can work in conjunction with the XXXXI Panzer Corps has been thrown into question due to the lack of mobile forces at its disposal. It has therefore become doubtful whether the LVI and XXXXI Panzer Corps will be able to cooperate in the encirclement of enemy forces northwest of Luga, as is the plan of the commander of the panzer group.

The unfortunate conclusion to be drawn is that even a successful thrust by the XXXXI Panzer Corps can hardly be expected to leave a lasting impression. The forces of the corps are too weak, and it would only be putting itself in a more dangerous position. Yet the decision that has been made by the field-marshal means that the forces of the army group will become increasingly dispersed.

Chales de Beaulieu
31 July 1941, 6 pm
Witness: First Lieutenant Schauwecker

APPENDIX 15

The assessment of the situation by the panzer group on 12 August 1941

The Commander of Panzer Group 4
To: Army Group North

With respect to the telephone conversation I had with the commander of the army group this morning, allow me to once more to clarify, this time in writing, the situation and the intentions of the panzer group.

The opinion that I expressed to the commander in chief of the army at the headquarters of the army group on 2 August 1941 has been confirmed by the way in which the fighting has unfolded since 8 August.

The enemy has embedded himself behind the field fortifications in the Luga sector. This includes a number of modern defensive installations. The bridgehead established by the enemy south of the town of Luga is particularly strong and stands right in the path of the LVI Panzer Corps. Defending this bridgehead are the 177th, 111th, and 302nd Rifle Divisions. The attack of the LVI Panzer Corps must therefore be carried out with as much force as can be mustered, but it can only be expected to gain ground gradually. Even so, the attack cannot be allowed to come to a stop. Not only must the LVI Panzer Corps seize the road and the railway line leading to Leningrad; it must also tie down as many Russian forces as possible so that they cannot interfere with the advance of the XXXXI Panzer Corps.

The bridgeheads formed by the XXXXI Panzer Corps on the lower Luga have disrupted the Russian line of defence along the river and have at the same time provided access to terrain that can be advantageously exploited by mobile troops. The observation that all the Russians have committed here are the battered 90th Rifle Division, some Leningrad army officer cadets, and a people's militia division has strengthened me in my decision to place the emphasis of the further advance of the panzer group in this sector of the front. This seems all the more to be the best place for the point of main effort given the slow progress to be expected from the LVI Panzer Corps. Nevertheless, the enemy has had three weeks in which to reinforce his defensive installations. It is thus clear that the attack here will still be difficult and could very well be costly. The fighting in which the XXXXI Panzer Corps has been engaged since 8 August has confirmed this to be the case.

To give the breakthrough greater impetus and to make up for our significantly diminished striking power, I have decided to place my own reserve unit, the 8th Panzer Division, under the command of the XXXXI Panzer Corps. New forces will be needed for the XXXXI Panzer Corps to be able to thrust as far as Krasnogvardeysk. Aside from the arrival of at least one Russian division in the area of Kotly (picked up by our listening posts) and one tank division, with which the 1st Panzer Division has already clashed near Syrkovitsy, we can expect that additional Russian forces will appear in the region of Krasnogvardeysk (intelligence provided by aerial reconnaissance this morning and by army group reconnaissance near the Bologoye–Tosno railway line).

I request that the SS-Totenkopf Division soon be placed at our disposal. I regard its use by the XXXXI Panzer Corps to be necessary from 15 August. It will take the division three days to reach the corps. My plan of detaching the 3rd Motorised Infantry Division from the sector of the LVI Panzer Corps and of sending it to the point of main effort, the point of penetration, can only be put into action once the enemy bridgehead around the town of Luga has been crushed. This will take three days at the very least, which means that 16 August is the earliest the division will become available.

Hoepner

Witness: First Lieutenant Voigts

APPENDIX 16

Report on 16 August 1941 regarding the handing over of the LVI Panzer Corps

The army group order that we received last night hit us like a bombshell. The order requires that the LVI Panzer Corps and the 3rd Motorised Infantry Division be sent to and placed under the command of the Sixteenth Army. General staff officers from these units are to be handed over to the headquarters of the Sixteenth Army. This order has been issued due to the deep penetration of the enemy south of Staraya Russa.

So it is that, on the day on which the attack wing of the panzer group (the XXXXI Panzer Corps) has succeeded in its brave but also costly advance and on which the enemy has finally yielded ground, the last reserves that have been carefully made ready for the security and reinforcement of the attack are going to be taken away from the panzer group.

Two motorised divisions (the SS-Totenkopf Division and the 3rd Motorised Infantry Division) are thus to be withdrawn from the essential task we had in mind for them, i.e. the support of the attack on Leningrad. The security of our ever-lengthening flanks, especially on the right, will no longer be guaranteed. The commander of the panzer group is faced by the difficult decision of having to forego the exploitation of what is now a successful breakthrough. The 1st Panzer Division already reached Volosovo this morning, and even the remaining divisions have been able to resume their advance! Now the troops will have to stop their forward movement. With their fighting strength significantly reduced (approximately 50 per cent), the four mobile divisions will be unable to thrust as far as Krasnogvardeysk. It is because of this that Panzer Group Order

No. 25, issued this morning, stipulates that the XXXXI Panzer Corps is not to proceed beyond the Volosovo–Begunitsy line.

This is the second time that the army group has stopped the panzer group from achieving its objective. The first occasion was on 18 July when we wanted to strike northwards from the Luga bridgeheads; now it is when we want to fully exploit the breakthrough of the XXXXI Panzer Corps. The enemy currently has no forces opposing the XXXXI Panzer Corps, even though we continuously expect him to ruthlessly throw something at us from the Leningrad reservoir. Whether the severely worn-out divisions of the XXXXI Panzer Corps will be able to continue to push forward after giving the enemy time to regroup is by no means certain. The divisions have been on the battlefield for eight weeks, and the interruptions they have experienced are not yet behind them.

Chales de Beaulieu
16 August 1941, 12 noon
Witness: Captain Litterscheid

APPENDIX 17

Remarks on 29 August 1941 regarding the security of the northern flank of the panzer group by the Eighteenth Army (fighting between Kingisepp and Krasnogvardeysk)

The army group order of 15 August required that the panzer group hand over the LVI Panzer Corps and the 3rd Motorised Infantry Division for the defence against the enemy attack south of Staraya Russa. Not only was the panzer group thereby deprived of its pool of reserves; it also had to abandon its plan of exploiting the success of the XXXXI Panzer Corps. Half of the 3rd Motorised Infantry Division had already been withdrawn from the front, and the remaining half has been pulling out over the course of the last two days. The lack of mobile forces means that Leningrad cannot be encircled anytime soon. This is a regrettable consequence for the entire operation, but something that the army group believed was necessary due to the enemy penetration in the area of the Sixteenth Army. It was left up to the panzer group to decide to what extent the success of the XXXXI Panzer Corps could still be exploited with the forces now available. The Volosovo–Begunitsy line had to be set as a temporary objective, and we have had to bear in mind the ever-lengthening flanks, especially in the north. The army group, in the meantime, has not been in the position to supply us with additional forces.

The panzer group has now had to do without the LVI Panzer Corps, the 3rd Motorised Infantry Division, and the SS-Totenkopf Division. We have had to limit our objectives and have ordered the XXXXI Panzer

Corps that it is only to advance in small leaps. We cannot do more than the available forces allow. Yet we must still somehow avoid a situation in which the Russians can regroup and form a new front; otherwise, we would have to shed more blood in penetrating it all over again. By scraping together any security forces we could, especially the 285th Security Division, the panzer group has sought to bring relief to at least the right flank of the XXXXI Panzer Corps. But this will naturally take some time to become effective.

The situation might be improved by the arrival of the XXVI Corps from Estonia. This will free up the forces of the XXXVIII Corps, allowing them to head northeast and cover the left wing of the XXXXI Panzer Corps. The panzer corps will in turn be able to pull forces out from its northern front and commit them further to the east. The possibility might still exist that the XXXXI Panzer Corps will be able to reach Krasnogvardeysk. Elements of the panzer corps can then pivot to the south and head towards Luga so as to help the L Corps!

The XXXVIII Corps took Kingisepp towards 10 am on 17 August, thereby paving the way for the forces approaching from the west. In order to help the left wing of the XXXXI Panzer Corps as quickly as possible, the 1st Infantry Division is once more being placed under the command of the panzer corps (except for one infantry regiment and one police battalion, which are to remain in the Kingisepp area). We must make haste in sending as many forces as we can to the northeast; Volosovo has already been reached, and the XXXXI Panzer Corps believes itself capable of being able to push further eastwards. A hole has been punched in the enemy front! The confidence of the panzer corps has therefore been growing. Unfortunately, we lack the forces needed to exploit this hole. This is a sad observation to make given the heavy casualties we have suffered! We will nevertheless push forward to the extent we are able to. The risk of a deep and vulnerable flank shall be taken by the XXXXI Panzer Corps, for the enemy currently has nothing with which to oppose or attack us.

Army Group Order No. 4 was issued on the evening of 17 August. It ordered that the Eighteenth Army was to provide protection for the left flank of the panzer group, yet it also gave the Eighteenth Army the additional task of annihilating the Russian 8th Army and of seizing the coastal fortifications. The main disadvantage of these multiple tasks for the Eighteenth Army is that the flank protection so desperately needed by the panzer group might actually be illusory in nature. Most regrettable is the fact that the XXXVIII Corps is to remain subordinate to the Eighteenth Army. The speed of the advance of the corps could very well decrease under such circumstances, which means that the panzer group, in its attempt to push forward, might find itself deprived of a formation it had been counting on. The commander of the panzer group had expressed this fear the moment he had received the order. The XXXVIII Corps had already been directed to send the remaining infantry regiment of the 1st Infantry Division to the northeast of this same division as soon as possible. This regiment could no longer be sent westwards through Kingisepp. It was a coincidence that the panzer group had once more subordinated the 1st Infantry Division to the XXXXI Panzer Corps on 17 August, just before we had received the army group order via telephone. More of our forces might have otherwise been tied down or pulled back to the rear.

It is clear from the way in which events are unfolding that the Eighteenth Army is conducting its own war. A telex message of the army group on 19 August at 7:40 pm had ordered the Eighteenth Army to send forces northeastwards through Kingisepp as quickly as possible to protect the flank of the panzer group. Moreover, Army Group Order No. 5 from 21 August stated that 'the task of the Eighteenth Army is unchanged; it must most urgently provide flank protection for Panzer Group 4'. Nevertheless, by 29 August, there is still no relief for the northern flank of the XXXXI Panzer Corps. This flank now extends as far as the area southeast of Krasnogvardeysk. The 1st Infantry Division has in the meantime once more been placed under the command of the XXXVIII Corps, itself subordinate to the Eighteenth Army. Only on 29 August, *twelve days* after the army group order had assigned it the task of flank protection, did the Eighteenth Army, led by the 1st Infantry Division, appear on the left wing of the XXXXI Panzer Corps. Now the 36th Motorised Infantry Division has been released!

Orders and their *practical* effects!

It may certainly seem from the point of view of the army group that the panzer group is being petty in its constant demands for the relief of its northern flank so that it can push further towards the east and towards Luga. The thrust on Leningrad has always been the objective of the panzer group, and the army group has not at any stage altered this objective in writing, even though it has imposed a number of restrictions orally. The requests made by the panzer group have been understood, but this has not made any impression on the Eighteenth Army, for it has taken its time in advancing to the northeast. In fact, between 20 and 25 August, the panzer group was asked over and over how *it* could support the advance of the Eighteenth Army. The formation at the front was being asked to help the formation in the rear, quite the reverse of what ought to be the case! The panzer group has repeatedly emphasised its view that the forces of the Eighteenth Army must advance along the road to Krasnoye Selo via Kingisepp so that they can assist the panzer group in swiftly reaching the most important operational objectives and so that they can carry out a frontal assault on the Luga west of Kingisepp. The latter task is currently being undertaken by the XXVI Corps and the XXXVIII Corps and is a much better alternative to fighting through the woodlands north of Kingisepp. Both corps have been engaged in fierce fighting and have sustained heavy casualties. They have also lost a lot of time. This is the main disadvantage for the panzer group!

In conclusion, what must be strongly emphasised is that the panzer group had been given no opportunity to withdraw forces from its northern front until the arrival of parts of the Eighteenth Army on 29 August. The result is that the offensive against Leningrad and the assault from the north against Luga have been unable to be carried out to the extent desired or with the rapidity needed.

Chales de Beaulieu
29 August 1941
Witness: Captain Litterscheid

APPENDIX 18

Assessment of the situation by the panzer group on 27 August 1941 (excerpts)

OKH Liaison Officer at Panzer Group 4, Major of the General Staff Golling, 27 August 1941.

To: Operations Department I N

The commander of Army Group North visited the panzer group this morning. The content of the discussion was approximately as follows:

(1) The commander of the panzer group provided an overview of the current situation. He was particularly pleased with the success of the 269th Infantry Division in its establishment of a bridgehead over the Luga and in its capture of Tolmachyovo.[43] It would be the intention of the L Corps to send the bulk of the SS-Police Division, which was bound to encounter difficult terrain as well as fierce resistance from Russian infantry north of the Oredezh sector, to the north and to pivot small elements of the division westwards against the Luga–Krasnogvardeysk road. The commander of the panzer group expressed the hope that the enemy forces north of the Luga between the L Corps and the 8th Panzer Division would be shattered quickly and that both divisions of the L Corps would be able to thrust towards the north in four days so as to perhaps make contact with the XXXXI Panzer Corps. The commander of the army group emphasised the

[43] On the north bank of the Luga, south of Zheltsy (see Map 8).

importance of making such contact. For this to be achieved, control of the main road would first and foremost need to be gained. The arrival of the L Corps in the vicinity to the south of Krasnogvardeysk would not only bring relief to the XXXXI Panzer Corps; it would also strengthen the entire position in the Leningrad area, for the ring of encirclement around the city would be secured. The deep flanks of the 8th Panzer Division (east and west of the main road) need to be covered by relatively strong security forces. Partly as a result of the mopping-up operations of the 285th Security Division, there are a number of enemy soldiers and groups scattered throughout the forests and marshland west of the main road, and they are currently attempting to escape to the east and northeast. It is here that partisans are carrying out their murderous activities. The moment any part of the flank is left unguarded, the Russians will emerge from the forests and cross the road. A number of enemy raids will then ensue. The resulting disquiet and uncertainty will be rather troublesome and will tie down significant forces. The line of security to the east of the main road runs as follows: Divenskaya railway station, Spaskoye (near Lake Orlinskoye), Novosiverskaya, Kurovitsy, Voskresenskoye, and east of Pizhma. It is because of the deep flanks of the 8th Panzer Division that the XXXXI Panzer Corps is reluctant to thrust further to the south.

(2) The commander of the panzer group then described the condition of the town of Luga and of the main road. Many of the buildings in the town have been mined and have as a result not yet been fully secured (there has been no shortage of mishaps). The surrounding terrain has also been heavily mined, so we have been using the main road almost exclusively. A pioneer battalion has been given the task of clearing away the mines as quickly as possible. The Russians have laid a number of time bombs throughout the terrain, many of them of primitive construction (with an ordinary timer, for example). They have also destroyed the station and have removed a decent amount of materiel we could have used. The main road, as far as it is occupied by the 8th Panzer Division in its attack from the north, is in good condition (it is a tarred road surface). Work has already commenced on widening the road and on improving the load-bearing capacity

of the bridges. The road leading from the south to Luga is likewise able to be used. We will not know what the section of road in between looks like until the Russians there have retreated in despair. It is hoped that it will be in good condition so that German traffic can flow continuously, for the panzer group intends to change the route of supply to the XXXXI Panzer Corps such that it will go through Luga.

(3) Intentions of the army group for the further conduct of battle:
Intelligence on the enemy – Recent signs indicate that the Russians have resigned themselves to the loss of Leningrad, although the reported arrival of the 292nd Rifle Division somewhat disrupts this impression. It could just be the case that this was a movement the enemy had planned a long time ago. Along the entire front of the army group, the enemy only seems to be willing to fight defensively, and this has been confirmed by radio messages that we have picked up. He has made no reference whatsoever to any intention to launch an attack. After his defeat at Staraya Russa, the enemy is incapable of offensive action.

The Sixteenth Army is to keep its front facing to the east. The bulk of the army is to the south of Lake Ilmen, while the left wing (the 21st Infantry Division) is near Chudovo. The Sixteenth Army is to advance through the area south of Lake Ilmen 'to the vast lake-dotted region' (presumably near and to the south of Valday). A defensive position will be maintained near Volkhov, north of Lake Ilmen.

The moment that the main road is completely open, Panzer Group 4 will have the Schmidt Group placed under its command (the XXXIX Panzer Corps with the 12th Panzer Division, the 18th Motorised Infantry Division, and the 20th Motorised Infantry Division, as well as the XXVIII Corps with the 121st Infantry Division and two-thirds of the 96th Infantry Division). The LVI Panzer Corps is no longer in the picture.

The task to be carried out is the isolation of Volkhov (north of Chudovo) and the encirclement of Leningrad. The outer ring of encirclement will serve as a jump-off line from which to assault the city from the southeast, south, and west. The ring will then be drawn tighter and tighter. The inner ring of encirclement to be aimed for will run as follows: the Neva up to Ivanovskoye, south of Kolpino, north of Detskoe Selo, and Uritsk. The formations of the panzer group will be arranged from right to left as follows: the XXXIX Panzer Corps, the XXVIII Corps, the L Corps, and the XXXXI Panzer Corps. A motorised division of the XXXIX Panzer Corps is to assume responsibility for the Neva front and is to make an attempt to cross the river. The commander of the panzer group confirmed his agreement with this plan and reported that he had already ordered aerial reconnaissance of the area. The commander of the army group referred to the line reached by the Finns west of Lake Ladoga. They would lend a helping hand!

The Eighteenth Army is to pivot to the northeast and is to advance with three divisions across a broad front in the direction of Leningrad. The commander of the army group hopes that the relief of the northern flank of the XXXXI Panzer Corps will become perceptible by 28 or 29 August. The right wing (the 1st Infantry Division) will foreseeably remain to the north of the main road right up to Begunitsy, beyond which it will make use of the road up to Krasnoye Selo. The 93rd Infantry Division shall lunge along the Luga towards the northwest.

Subsequent objectives – Once the ring of encirclement around Leningrad has been tightened, the Eighteenth Army shall assume sole responsibility for ensuring it remains tight. The army will have at its disposal the infantry divisions in the area and perhaps also a mobile division. Panzer Group 4, with the bulk of the mobile divisions, will proceed further eastwards. After a short pause, it will thrust to the northeast towards the Svir so as to make contact with the Finns to the east of Lake Ladoga.

The secondary objective is to cover the southeast. Whether a new operation can then be launched will depend upon the weather.

Major of the General Staff Golling
Witness: Captain Litterscheid

APPENDIX 19

Directive of the panzer group on 27 August 1941 regarding the approach of the corps on Leningrad

Headquarters of Panzer Group 4, Ia No. 1802/41 classified, Panzer Group Command Post Usadishche, 27 August 1941.

Directive for the approach of the corps on Leningrad

After the Luga–Leningrad road is completely in our hands, both corps will need to be made ready as quickly as possible so that they can continue the attack and approach the planned line of encirclement around Leningrad. As soon as the L Corps and the 8th Panzer Division have made contact north of the Luga, the panzer division will immediately be sent northwards by the XXXXI Panzer Corps on the western side of the main road.

The L Corps will mop up the terrain on either side of the road and railway line and will proceed towards and to the east of Krasnogvardeysk. It will then stand ready between the Soltsy–Leningrad railway line and the Luga–Krasnogvardeysk road until relieved by elements of the XXXXI Panzer Corps for the continued attack, which is to be carried out with the point of main effort on the right.

The XXXXI Panzer Corps, assigned the sector between the Luga–Krasnogvardeysk and Kingisepp–Krasnoye Selo roads, is to push further towards the line of encirclement and is to conduct ground and aerial reconnaissance so as to seek out the best points for the assault. The panzer corps cannot be allowed to get involved in heavy combat. It has to wait until its two panzer divisions could be relieved by the arrival of the Eighteenth Army so that they can be positioned in the Gubanitsy–Volosovo–Nikolskoye area, west of the main road. The panzer corps is to transfer two pioneer battalions to the panzer group. One of these will be the 62nd Pioneer Battalion, although only after the 36th Motorised Infantry Division has been relieved by the Eighteenth Army. The panzer corps will report once the pioneer battalions are available.

The continued attack towards the intended line of encirclement around Leningrad shall be ordered by the panzer group. The arrival of the neighbouring units to the right and left will probably have to be awaited. It is then that the ring of encirclement can be tightened.

Once the road to Krasnogvardeysk has been made secure, the supply traffic of the panzer group, including that of the XXXXI Panzer Corps, shall flow along this road.

In addition, it is foreseen that panzer group headquarters will be relocated to Mezhno, which lies on this road.

Hoepner, Commander of the Panzer Group 4

Index